Professional
Wikis

Professional
Wikis

Mark Choate

BICENTENNIAL
1807
WILEY
2007
BICENTENNIAL

Wiley Publishing, Inc.

Professional Wikis

Published by
Wiley Publishing, Inc.
10475 Crosspoint Boulevard
Indianapolis, IN 46256

ISBN: 978-0-470-12690-5

Manufactured in the United States of America

10 9 8 7 6 5 4 3 2 1

Library of Congress Cataloging-in-Publication Data is available from the publisher.

For Christine, with love

About the Author

Mark S. Choate (Washington, D.C.) is co-founder and CEO of The Choate Group, LLC, a research and communications consulting firm serving organizations in the areas of knowledge management, research methodology, funding strategies, and grant writing. He was the lead developer of The Choate Group's Metawrite authoring tool, a cross-platform desktop wiki, and he consults with organizations seeking to implement weblog and wiki solutions. He is the former vice president of interactive media for *The News & Observer*. He lectures at Georgetown University's Communication, Culture and Technology (CCT) graduate program where he teaches The Technology of News, which evaluates the impact of Internet technology on news dissemination.

Credits

Acquisitions Editor
Jenny Watson

Development Editor
Adaobi Obi Tulton

Technical Editor
Emmett Dulaney

Production Editor
William A. Barton

Copy Editor
Luann Rouff

Editorial Manager
Mary Beth Wakefield

Production Manager
Tim Tate

Vice President and Executive Group Publisher
Richard Swadley

Vice President and Executive Publisher
Joseph B. Wikert

Project Coordinator, Cover
Lindsey Osborn

Proofreader
David Nocturne, Word One

Indexer
Robert Swanson

Anniversary Logo Design
Richard Pacifico

Acknowledgments

I would like to thank those who helped make this book possible. In particular, I'd like to thank the developers of MediaWiki and the participants on the MediaWiki mailing list who have shared their insights with others in the generous spirit so often found among those involved in open-source software. I would also like to thank Carole McClendon at Waterside Productions, Kit Kemper, Jenny Watson, Adaobi Obi Tulton at Wrox, and my technical editor Emmett Dulaney. Special thanks to Cindy Swain, my editor at the Cutter Consortium. An early version of much of the content in Chapter 1 first appeared in Cutter Consortium publications (visit `http://cutter.com/` to learn more).

I would also like to thank Christine, Connor, Sarah, Ian, Lucy, and Sheba for their patience and support, as well as my parents, Dennis and Judy, for all the different ways they have helped me.

Contents

Contents

Contents

Contents

Contents

Introduction

This book is a book about how to install, use, manage, and extend a wiki using MediaWiki, the wiki engine used to power one of the world's most famous wikis, Wikipedia.

Wikis are the sleeper hit of the Internet, with roots that extend far back into the old days — the very first wiki deployed by wiki inventor Ward Cunningham was released to the world on March 25, 1995. (It can still be found at `http://c2.com/cgi/wiki`, with an informative history of those early days at `http://c2.com/cgi/wiki?WikiHistory`.) After that release, wikis crept along with an enthusiastic but narrowly defined group of devotees, programmers working on project teams who used wikis for software documentation. Credit for the sudden turn-around in fame (if not fortune) for wikis is certainly due to Wikipedia, the online encyclopedia that nearly anyone can contribute to and edit.

According to Wikipedia, this wiki started on January 15, 2001. At the time of this writing, there are well over 1.5 million English language articles and over 3 million user accounts. You can find the latest statistics at `http://en.wikipedia.org/wiki/Special:Statistics`.

In late 2005, Wikipedia garnered a bit of negative publicity as the result of a few bad posts, but on December 14, 2005, the well-respected scientific journal Nature published a report that found that Wikipedia's accuracy was comparable to the accuracy of Encyclopedia Britannica. As one might expect, this generated some protestations from Encyclopedia Britannica. As far as I'm concerned, the jury is still out and I'm not inclined to get into the fray. What I do know for certain, however, is that Wikipedia is extremely useful — it's free, and, for the vast majority of topics, it is accurate.

You can read about the controversy at `www.nature.com/news/2005/051212/full/438900a.html`.

The success of Wikipedia has served as an eye-opening example of just how effective wikis can be for collaborative editing on a large scale — much larger than many people (including me) thought possible. It shows that wikis can be used effectively in environments beyond that of the IT workgroup. At the same time, wikis have not fully entered the mainstream. The looks my talented but non-technical friends and colleagues would give me when I told them I was working on a book about wikis provides at least some anecdotal evidence that wikis are not yet as famous as iPods or Britney Spears' C-section scar.

Nevertheless, because of the fame (or notoriety) of Wikipedia, the open-source software package called MediaWiki that runs Wikipedia is becoming an increasingly popular package for developing wikis. It is by no means the only wiki application on the open-source market, but it is a good one, and one would be hard-pressed to find another wiki engine as widely used.

Who Should Read This Book

Wikis can be a valuable addition for any organization that wants to increase productivity using Web-based collaboration tools. The ideal reader of this book is a programmer or technical professional planning to implement a MediaWiki-powered wiki. The difference between a programmer and an author or a designer isn't as clearly defined as it used to be. The audience is not a particular profession. Web developers, information architects, designers, and content authors can all benefit from reading this book.

The brilliance of wikis is their simplicity. You can install and operate a very useful wiki without any detailed technical knowledge of the underlying system. That being said, the reader of this book does need to have certain technical skills to make the most of it. Familiarity with the World Wide Web, and solid knowledge of HTML, XML and CSS are essential. MediaWiki is written in PHP, and uses MySQL or PostgreSQL databases on the back-end. While much benefit can still be derived without PHP or SQL skills, basic programming knowledge is a necessity.

This is a book about MediaWiki — it's not a book about HTML, XML, CSS, PHP, MySQL, PostgreSQL, or anything else. Therefore, I will assume knowledge in all of these areas. If you are not familiar with these technologies, I can recommend the following books:

❑ *Web Standards Programmer's Reference: HTML, CSS, JavaScript, Perl, Python, and PHP*, by Steven M. Schafer (Wrox, 2005)

❑ *Beginning PHP5, Apache, and MySQL Web Development*, by Elizabeth Naramore, Jason Gerner, Yann Le Scouarnec, Jeremy Stolz, and Michael K. Glass (Wrox, 2005)

MediaWiki runs on Macintosh, Windows, or Linux platforms. The examples used in this book were written using MediaWiki 1.9.3, Apache 1.3.33, MySQL 4.1.10, and PHP 5.2, as well as the environment provided by the PHP Development Tool (PDT) plug-in for Eclipse 3.2 from Zend. Minimum requirements to run MediaWiki 1.9 are MySQL 4.0 or later and PHP 5.0 or later, although the developers recommend PHP 5.1.

How This Book Is Organized

This book has been organized in a natural way so that each chapter builds on previous chapters. The book is designed so that it moves from simpler tasks to those of increasing complexity.

Chapter 1: Wikis at Work

The most common question I get about wikis in my consulting practice is the question of when to use wikis, rather than a more formal content management system. The answer to this question depends on what you need to accomplish. This chapter introduces and defines wikis, and discusses how wikis are different from other content management systems. You will learn about how wikis are being used by different organizations and when the use of a wiki is your best strategy, or when you should look at other alternatives.

If you've already determined that you need (or want) a wiki, the next step is to decide how to implement your wiki. As a consequence of their simplicity and utility, many varieties of open-source wiki engines have sprouted all over the Web. There is also a growing number of commercial wiki applications billing themselves as enterprise wikis. You will learn about common wiki features and which questions to ask yourself when evaluating wiki engines, including what to look for in order to avoid any unexpected pitfalls.

Chapter 2: Installing MediaWiki

In this chapter, installation of MediaWiki is covered in detail. I cover the most common installation methods, using Apache, PHP, and MySQL. I also explain the basic configuration requirements when first installing your wiki.

Chapter 3: Getting Started with MediaWiki

Chapter 3 introduces a guided tour of MediaWiki, including wiki terminology, and reveals the basic steps required to get up and running as a new user. You will learn about creating user accounts, creating new pages, understanding wiki links, and how to find your way around the wiki.

Chapter 4: Writing and Editing Content

The beating heart of a wiki is user-generated content. Chapter 4 documents the details of wikitext, the shorthand markup used by MediaWiki that enables authors to edit content from any Web browser, apply formatting, and easily create links to other wiki pages.

Chapter 5: Images and Files

In addition to writing wikitext, users can upload images and files. In this chapter, you will learn how to configure MediaWiki to support image and file uploads, as well as how to refer to them using wikitext.

Chapter 6: Page Actions and Version Control

A user can do more than just edit a page. He or she can comment on pages, move them, track changes, use trackbacks to comment on them in their blog, and syndicate their wiki page with RSS. Some pages can also be protected from other users. There is also a class of pages called Special Pages that provide users with interesting information about the wiki itself, and that can be used to manage the site.

Chapter 7: Information Architecture: Organizing Your Wiki

The architecture of a site defines how a user finds the information he or she is looking for by following links or performing searches. Wikis take a different approach to information architecture than most websites — they have a flat hierarchy, and rely on a folksonomic form of categorization. This chapter focuses on navigation and search, and includes expanded coverage on categories, subpages, customizing namespaces, disambiguation, and using external search facilities.

Chapter 8: Magic Words, Templates, and Skins

The look and feel of a wiki is defined by what Wikipedia calls a *skin*, which is a combination of HTML, CSS, and PHP classes. In this chapter you will learn how to modify the default MediaWiki skin, as well as how to create a new one. In addition to learning how to modify the design of a site, you will also learn how to insert additional content on pages using *magic words*, a general term used by MediaWiki to cover a few different kinds of template elements.

Chapter 9: Extensions

Chapter 9 covers more advanced topics, including extending MediaWiki by creating new tags, parser functions, as well as extending or modifying the basic functionality of MediaWiki using hooks.

Chapter 10: The MediaWiki API

Bots are applications that can interact with MediaWiki wikis. In Chapter 10, the use of one such bot, called pywikipediabot, is introduced. External applications and systems can also interact with MediaWiki using a ReST style API. This chapter covers the functionality that can be accessed through the API and provides examples of how that functionality can be leveraged for your benefit.

Chapter 11: Wiki Performance

MediaWiki uses a many-layered approach to cacheing, an understanding of which is essential for running a wiki with acceptable performance characteristics. Chapter 11 explains MediaWiki's cacheing strategy.

Where to Find More Information

Programmers use wikis to document programming projects. Because MediaWiki is a programming project, it should come as no surprise that MediaWiki uses a wiki to document itself. The information available on the site varies with respect to timeliness — some of the information is out of date, but enough of it is current to make it useful. MediaWiki is also a dynamic project, always evolving, so there will likely be many new additions to the application in the future, and this is a good place to start.

Most documentation can be found on the MediaWiki website at `www.mediawiki.org`. You can also learn more about the Wikipedia family of sites and find information relevant to all users of MediaWiki software on `http://meta.wikipedia.org`. I also regularly write about wikis and blogs on my own blog at `http://choate.info/`.

You can also find plenty of friendly folks willing to answer your questions. Look on the #mediawiki IRC channel hosted on `Freenode.net`, or you can subscribe to the MediaWiki mailing list at `http://lists.wikimedia.org/mailman/listinfo/mediawiki-l`.

Conventions

To help you get the most from the text and keep track of what's happening, we've used a number of conventions throughout the book.

> *Tips, hints, tricks, and asides to the current discussion are offset and placed in italics like this.*

> *As for styles in the text:*

❑ *We highlight new terms and important words when we introduce them.*

❑ *We show keyboard strokes like this: Ctrl + A.*

❑ *We show filenames, URLs, and code within the text like so:* `persistence.properties`.

❑ *We present code in two different ways:*

> In code examples we highlight new and important code with a gray background.

> The gray highlighting is not used for code that's less important in the present context, or has been shown before.

Source Code

As you work through the examples in this book, you may choose either to type in all the code manually or to use the source code files that accompany the book. All of the source code used in this book is available for download at `www.wrox.com`. Once at the site, simply locate the book's title (either by using the Search box or by using one of the title lists) and click the Download Code link on the book's detail page to obtain all the source code for the book.

> *Because many books have similar titles, you may find it easiest to search by ISBN; this book's ISBN is 978-0-470-12690-5.*

Once you download the code, just decompress it with your favorite compression tool. Alternately, you can go to the main Wrox code download page at `www.wrox.com/dynamic/books/download.aspx` to see the code available for this book and all other Wrox books.

Errata

We make every effort to ensure that there are no errors in the text or in the code. However, no one is perfect, and mistakes do occur. If you find an error in one of our books, such as a spelling mistake or faulty piece of code, we would be very grateful for your feedback. By sending in errata you may save another reader hours of frustration, and at the same time you will be helping us provide even higher quality information.

To find the errata page for this book, go to `www.wrox.com` and locate the title using the Search box or one of the title lists. Then, on the book's details page, click the Book Errata link. On this page you can view all errata that has been submitted for this book and posted by Wrox editors. A complete book list, including links to each book's errata, is also available at `www.wrox.com/misc-pages/booklist.shtml`.

If you don't spot "your" error on the Book Errata page, go to `www.wrox.com/contact/techsupport.shtml` and complete the form there to send us the error you have found. We'll check the information and, if appropriate, post a message to the book's errata page and fix the problem in subsequent editions of the book.

p2p.wrox.com

For author and peer discussion, join the P2P forums at `p2p.wrox.com`. The forums are a Web-based system for you to post messages relating to Wrox books and related technologies and to interact with other readers and technology users. The forums offer a subscription feature to e-mail you topics of interest of your choosing when new posts are made to the forums. Wrox authors, editors, other industry experts, and your fellow readers are present on these forums.

At http://p2p.wrox.com you will find a number of different forums that will help you not only as you read this book, but also as you develop your own applications. To join the forums, just follow these steps:

1. Go to p2p.wrox.com and click the Register link.
2. Read the terms of use and click Agree.
3. Complete the required information to join as well as any optional information you wish to provide and click Submit.
4. You will receive an e-mail with information describing how to verify your account and complete the joining process.

You can read messages in the forums without joining P2P but to post your own messages, you must join.

Once you join, you can post new messages and respond to messages other users post. You can read messages at any time on the Web. If you would like to have new messages from a particular forum e-mailed to you, click the Subscribe to this Forum icon by the forum name in the forum listing.

For more information about how to use the Wrox P2P, be sure to read the P2P FAQs for answers to questions about how the forum software works as well as many common questions specific to P2P and Wrox books. To read the FAQs, click the FAQ link on any P2P page.

1

Wikis at Work

Wikis are websites that are collaboratively written by their readers. The software that makes wikis possible is called a *wiki engine*. This chapter introduces the wiki concept, and what you read here will apply to almost any wiki engine. The rest of the book, however, is devoted to one wiki engine in particular called MediaWiki, the wiki engine that runs what is arguably the world's most famous wiki, Wikipedia.

The idea that wikis are websites collaboratively written by their readers is simple enough, but the simplicity of the idea belies the profound impact a wiki can have on the flow of information among individuals. A wiki is to a typical website what a dialogue is to a monologue. On the surface, a conversation shares a lot in common with a lecture — in both cases, someone is talking and someone is listening, but the experience of a conversation is qualitatively different from the experience of either lecturing or being lectured, and the outcome of a conversation is qualitatively different from the outcome of a lecture as well.

In other words, authors are readers and readers are authors; there is no approval process required to post information on a wiki and there is no pre-ordained structure imposed on the content that is presented there. If you think of a regular website as a farm, with all the content organized into neat little rows of corn or beans, then a wiki is a meadow, teaming with grasses and wild flowers. A meadow isn't chaotic, however; there is order there, but it is a different kind of order. It's an emergent kind of order, one that evolves and is discovered, rather than imposed.

As with all definitions, this definition is only partly true. As time has passed, the principle of openness has been reshaped as a consequence of the hard realities of the world, and many wikis now restrict editing to certain users. Wikis have now become so popular that there are quite a few content management systems claiming wiki status with a completely different set of features than those conceived by the father of wikis, Ward Cunningham. He launched the first wiki (something he called a WikiWikiWeb back then) on March 25, 1995. A host of content management systems label themselves as wikis, even though they bear only a minor resemblance to the original wiki concept. This can make getting started with wikis a confusing affair.

The Wiki Way is the name of a book by Ward Cunningham, and it is also a phrase used in reference to what was originally called Wiki Design Principles, which can be found on Ward's wiki at `http://c2.com/cgi/wiki?WikiDesignPrinciples`.

The most common question I am asked in my consulting practice goes something like this: "We have a content management system in place, but we'd like to have a wiki, too. How can my wiki integrate with the content management system?" This is like someone walking up to me and saying, "I have a pair of red shoes and a pair of black shoes and I'd like to integrate them into the same outfit." I might suggest they wear both shoes — one red and one black. That might actually work if the only difference between the red shoes and the black shoes were the color. But what if the red shoes were running shoes and the black shoes were stiletto pumps? It would be very hard to get where you want to go.

The problem is this: A wiki is a content management system, not an alternative to a content management system. A website is a collection of related HTML pages that is accessible through the World Wide Web at a particular domain name (usually), and these pages are organized and linked to each other in a systematic way to make it easy for readers to find the information they seek. A content management system is a software application that provides tools to help people create and deploy websites. A wiki is a kind of content management system with a very special set of features that make it easy for people to use them to collaborate.

There are many different kinds of content management systems, each one suited to a different purpose, so the first question that really needs to be answered is "What are you trying to accomplish?"

There is a time and a season for everything. There is a time to wiki and a time not to wiki. This chapter aims to shed some light on when it makes sense to use a wiki, and when it may make sense to try a different approach. I start by exploring the history of wikis and why wikis have become such an item of interest in organizations. This is followed by a more detailed look at how wikis work and what kind of functionality is important when selecting a particular wiki engine. The chapter concludes with a discussion of best practices for running a successful wiki.

Once you know where you are going, it's a lot easier to figure out what kind of shoes you need to wear in order to get there.

Wiki History

Ward's original wiki is called the PortlandPatternRepository, and it can be found at `http://c2.com/`. The "WikiWikiWeb" name for the technology was inspired by the "Wiki Wiki" Chance RT-52 shuttle bus that runs between airport terminals in the Honolulu International Airport. *Wiki* is the Hawaiian word for quick, and that seemed to be an appropriate name for what Ward wanted to accomplish. His goal was to use the World Wide Web to develop a way for programmers to more readily share ideas about design patterns. In order for such a system to work, it needed to be something that was quick and easy to use.

In May of 1995, he invited a few of his colleagues to participate in his new site. It wasn't long before the idea began to slowly catch on, and over the last decade a lot has changed.

Despite the success of PortlandPatternRepository, wikis did not start out as mainstream tools. It was the open-source software movement that first embraced the idea of wikis as an opportunity for widely distributed, decentralized teams of people to collaborate to produce software.

The use of wikis by the open-source community is fitting, because wikis work on a principle similar to that which makes open-source software development so effective. The *Linus Principle*, named after Linus Torvalds, the original creator of Linux, is this: "Given enough eyeballs, all bugs are shallow." The benefit of sharing the source code with your application is that you have more people who can look at the code and find problems. Wikis provide the same logic to content development: The more people who can both read and edit a document, the more likely it is that errors will be caught and fixed.

The technology behind a wiki is relatively simple: Ward's contribution to humanity was not the code used to produce the first wiki (although I am sure it is fine code indeed), but getting the technology out of the way so that people can communicate and collaborate. In every organization on the globe, both large and small, there is information about the organization floating around inside people's heads that needs to be documented in some way. Practitioners of knowledge management call this kind of knowledge, which is informal and learned largely from experience, *tacit knowledge*. What they call *explicit knowledge* is formalized and documented knowledge. The goal of knowledge management is to transform tacit knowledge into explicit knowledge: In other words, the goal is to get all that information floating around inside people's heads written down. Much to everyone's surprise, wikis have proven to be remarkably effective in this regard.

When I first learned about wikis in the nineties, I was skeptical because I immediately imagined the fun that malcontents would have defacing whatever site you tried to manage this way. It wasn't until the success of Wikipedia that wikis caught my attention, along with the rest of the world. A relatively small team of technically savvy developers is one thing. A global pool of experts collaborating on an encyclopedia is another thing altogether. What is remarkable about Wikipedia is its scale and ambition. What is most surprising is that it works so effectively. This is what has gotten knowledge management experts so excited about wikis.

Wikipedia was an offshoot of the online encyclopedia Nupedia.com, founded by Jimmy Wales and funded by Bomis (something Wale's has reportedly called "a guy-oriented search-engine"). Nupedia was founded in March of 2000 and established as a peer-reviewed encyclopedia with a seven-step editing process. This seven-step process proved to be rather cumbersome and not enough articles were being generated.

As a solution to this problem, Editor in Chief Larry Sanger proposed a "feeder" site to Nupedia based on wiki technology on January 10, 2001. The idea was that people could post articles on the wiki and after those articles had been properly vetted, they could be moved onto Nupedia. The use of a wiki would make it easier for users to contribute and, it was hoped, speed up the process. There was never any expectation at the time that Wikipedia would replace Nupedia, although that is what quickly happened.

Five days later, Wikipedia was formally launched, and within its first year it generated over 18,000 articles. By the time Nupedia closed up shop in September of 2003, Wikipedia boasted over 160,000 articles, written by volunteers. In three and a half years, Nupedia's peer-reviewed process produced 24 articles, compared with 160,000 articles produced in the first year alone of Wikipedia's existence. It is a remarkable example of the impact that moving from a centralized, formalized decision-making process to a more decentralized, informal process can have. More important, the quality of the content generated on Wikipedia was high, and the user base found it to be a very helpful research resource, so the traffic grew quickly.

Web 2.0 and Social Media

While wikis are a distinct kind of website, they are often discussed along with other technologies under the label of *Web 2.0* or *social media*.

At one time, I considered "Web 2.0" to be a phrase in search of a meaning. My first reaction to the idea of Web 2.0 was a quick roll of the eyes. I fell into the camp shared by Tim Berners-Lee, inventor of what we can presumably call Web 1.0, who remarked that "Web 2.0 is, of course, a piece of jargon, nobody even knows what it means." (IBM DeveloperWorks Interview, www.ibm.com/developerworks/podcast/dwi/cm-int082206txt.html).

Despite my dismissiveness, the Web 2.0 meme has proven its resilience and is alive and well, having evolved into a number of variant phrases, such as Andrew McAfee's Enterprise 2.0, which he defines as "the emerging use of Web 2.0 technologies like blogs and wikis (both perfect examples of network IT) within the Intranet." (Andrew McAfee, http://blog.hbs.edu/faculty/amcafee/index.php/faculty_amcafee_v3/the_three_trends_underlying_enterprise_20/).

J. Bonasia, writing for *Investor's Business Daily* in June, 2007, said that users "are just getting familiar with the concept of Web 2.0, through which they can collaborate and share Internet content." (*Investor's Business Daily*, www.investors.com/editorial/IBDArticles.asp?artsec=16&artnum=3&issue=20070601).

According to Tim O'Reilly, Web 2.0 represents the movement to the "Internet as platform, and an attempt to understand the rules for success on that new platform" (O'Reilly.com, www.oreillynet.com/pub/a/oreilly/tim/news/2005/09/30/what-is-web-20.html). The term was coined in an effort to capture what was different about companies that survived the Internet bust of early 2000, and those that did not. As such, Web 2.0 is not a set of Web technologies per se; rather, it is a set of attributes shared by successful Internet companies.

The list of technologies commonly associated with Web 2.0 are wikis and weblogs, RSS, AJAX, Web services (SOAP, XML-RPC, ReST) and so on. Some of these are standards, some are concepts, some are architectures, and many of them have been around since the mid to late nineties. Unfortunately, the 2.0 designation implies new technology, although I do not think O'Reilly necessarily intended that.

While the definitions of Web 2.0 and social media are somewhat squishy, some common themes arise when pundits try to define them. Wikis and related tools all share four common attributes:

- ❏ Participatory
- ❏ Decentralized
- ❏ Linked
- ❏ Emergent

Wikis are clearly participatory. Unlike traditional content management systems, in which users have distinct roles and the set of content creators is entirely distinct from the set of content consumers (or, readers, as we once quaintly referred to them), all are equal (or mostly equal) in the public square of wikidom.

Likewise, wikis are decentralized in the sense that participants can be geographically disbursed. Wikipedia boasts authors from across the globe. They are also decentralized in the sense that wiki content isn't organized into a hierarchy and is not as structured as typical content managed by a content management system.

This decentralized content is structured by way of links, which can be old-fashioned hypertext links from one document to another document, or it can be a conceptual link made manifest by the sharing of a common tag (another word for what is essentially a keyword that represents the subject matter of a given page).

This participatory, decentralized, and linked collection of ideas is not organized in a top-down manner because there is no top or bottom. Rather, any order that arises is an emergent order. A system arises out of the interactions of many individual agents, each operating under its own set of rules, much like weather patterns emerge from billions of atoms acting the way that atoms do, completely unaware of the larger system in which they are unwitting participants.

New Business Models

In almost every case, these technologies, practices, and design patterns are continuations of the fundamental idea that has been central to the Web's success and pattern of development. Tim Berners-Lee did not invent hypertext. In his book *Weaving the Web* (HarperBusiness, 2000), he shares his experiences contacting commercial providers of hypertext systems in his efforts to convince them to open their platform. All the companies whose names remain obscure and unfamiliar refused to open their platforms. In the absence of cooperation from commercial vendors, Tim Berners-Lee developed the World Wide Web himself as an open standard.

Proprietary versus Open Standards

Prior to the Web, most businesses based their strategy on the creation of proprietary technology or platforms that provided them with a sustainable competitive advantage over any potential competitors. Whether you were a software developer or a content publisher, you differentiated yourself by being unique and maintaining strict control of intellectual property. The reason why commercial hypertext vendors resisted opening up their systems was because they feared that if they did, then they would not make any money from those systems.

They were right, of course, but they missed the point. While creating a hypertext system based on open standards may have made it impossible to make money selling that hypertext system, it also happened to create a platform through which money could be made (or efficiencies gained) that proved to be far more powerful than anyone could have predicted. The free and open nature of the platform made it ubiquitous and instantly relevant.

Network Effects

Network effects refers to the idea that networks become more valuable as the size of the network increases. Network effects tend to have a "winner take all" effect, with one platform emerging as the dominant platform. The World Wide Web itself is the perfect example. The more websites that were available on the Web, the more valuable the network became.

One way to differentiate social media from old media is to look at how network effects work in the old, proprietary environment and to contrast that with how they work now. I would argue that social media are harvesting network effects in a fundamentally new way.

The best example of the old network effect is that of Microsoft Word. The reason I have a copy of Microsoft Word on my computer is because so many other people have a copy of Microsoft Word on their computer. The more people who use Microsoft Word, the more it makes sense for me to use Microsoft Word because it is simpler to read documents they send to me, and simpler for me to send them documents I've written, and so on. The only connection between Word documents is the fact that they share a common platform and that the readers of those documents need certain software applications in order to create or read them.

In the pre-Web days, the platform was a proprietary software application. Because Microsoft owned the platform, Microsoft made a lot of money selling licenses to use that platform. This is an example of a network effect in a proprietary environment, which happens to be a very favorable environment for the owner of the proprietary system who is able to succeed in this environment.

But what happens when you create an environment based on open standards, without any proprietary technology, such as the one created by Tim Berners-Lee? How does one company compete more effectively than another company and, most important, how is value captured?

The search engine Google is often mentioned as an example of a Web 2.0 company. None of the technologies mentioned earlier explain why Google is a Web 2.0 company. It has nothing to do with AJAX, blogs, wikis, or Web services. What Google has done is successfully capture network effects in an open environment.

Google's PageRank algorithm (which is how the search results are prioritized) is based in part upon how many other sites link to a given page. If you have two separate pages, both with similar content (as ascertained by word count and position), favor is given to the page to which more sites link than the other. Google infers that a page with more links to it must be better than a page with fewer links to it. Every day Google learns more about the content that is distributed on the Internet. By doing this, Google leverages the wisdom of the crowd, using the aggregate wisdom of Web participants to make more effective guesses about what specific content is most relevant to the searcher. As a result, Google's site makes it easier for me to find the information I am looking for.

Google is not the only company doing something like this. Flickr does the same for photos. Flickr takes a simpler and more direct approach by having visitors tag photos — it simply enables users to assign a keyword of choice to any photo they come across. This ad hoc system of keywords is called a *folksonomy*, a term used to differentiate this approach from a taxonomy because it is a decentralized approach to organizing content, as opposed to a *taxonomy* (such as the Dewey decimal system, or the Yahoo! directory) in which content is placed in taxonomic classifications by experts or specialists. Again, Flickr is leveraging the wisdom of the masses. The knowledge is a consequence of the steady aggregation of knowledge in the form of links created by human beings.

Flickr is better every time a user adds a tag. The value of Flickr isn't the repository of photos; there are plenty of sites for hosting photos, and the technology required to host photos verges on the trivial. However, as time passes, the database of knowledge about the photos increases, and the connections between photos that can be made by the folksonomic tagging of information means that Flickr increases in value every day and as a consequence derives true competitive advantage.

Google is continuing to build on this by offering new services. One such service enables Google users to create their own search engines. This is a wonderful service and I have used it to aggregate content on a variety of sites of interest to me. Moreover, when you are aggregating content, you are leaving behind a trail of knowledge and human judgment that Google will be able to use to make their site's search results even more effective. Google harvests human knowledge in creative ways, by interpreting the results.

By enabling users to create and edit articles, Wikipedia, too, is leveraging the collective wisdom of Wikipedia users. Much like Flickr does, Wikipedia (and all wikis run on MediaWiki software) enables users to add arbitrary tags (called *categories* in MediaWiki) that describe the content of the page. Wikipedia, too, is a better product every time a category is added to a page.

New Publishing Model

Content-oriented websites have moved in a clear progression from a proprietary model to something completely different, a path that is mirrored by the path from Nupedia to Wikipedia. This is a path that emerged from a scenario in which content creation is centralized and controlled and a clear distinction is made between author and audience.

When a new technology emerges, it is always thought of in terms of the technology it replaces. Wireless telegraphs, horseless carriages, and the computer desktop are all examples of understanding a new technology using the terminology of the past. Eventually, wireless telegraphs were called radios and horseless carriages were called cars.

This is the purpose of metaphor — to use one idea in place of another because it makes it easier to understand, or evokes a sense that would otherwise be difficult to understand using more accurate, yet abstract language. Hence the desktop metaphor. There aren't really documents sitting in folders on your computer, but it certainly helps to think of your files that way.

We use metaphors because they can help us understand complex ideas, and it provides a frame of reference so that we know how to think about something new in familiar terms. The problem with metaphors, however, is that they can be limiting. Thinking about content in terms of folders and documents has narrowed our view of what they actually represent and what can be done with them.

The old way of thinking about documents emphasized the resemblance of computer files to paper documents — that is, tangible, discrete, and permanent things that can be filed away in folders. If the desktop metaphor is the old metaphor, then what is the new metaphor? How are we to understand communication in the post-Internet world?

The first websites used an old publishing model. Before the Web democratized publishing, the publisher owned the platform (the printing press or the content management system) and the content, all of which was highly controlled by a select few. Now, sites like Wikipedia have turned this publishing model upside down, eliminating the difference between author and reader. On Wikipedia and similar social media sites, authors are readers and readers are authors.

Wikis, Blogs, and Meme Trackers

Word documents are based on the metaphor of the typewritten page. Early websites were modeled after traditional print publications, and e-mail was delivered just like its printed, enveloped, and stamped counterpart. These tools are now officially out of fashion.

When a business adopts social media tools such as wikis and blogs within the organization, they are using the tools as a replacement to older forms of communication, such as e-mail. In doing so, they are abandoning the transitional tools based on older technology, and embracing new tools that leverage the power of the new technology.

Chapter 1: Wikis at Work

The one thing that social media sites, wikis, blogs, and meme trackers share in common is an understanding of the fundamentally dynamic nature of information. Content evolves. It is shared, modified, and shared again. It changes over time, it appears in different forms.

In the old way of thinking, if something has been "documented," the implication is that the information contained therein is correct, complete, authoritative, and permanent. No such assumptions are made with blogs and wikis. In the wiki application MediaWiki (the software that runs Wikipedia), an article is defined as a collection of revisions. There are no definitive or authoritative articles on MediaWiki; there's only the most recent revision.

Time plays a pivotal role in both. Blogs are organized according to when they were posted and, secondarily, by category or topic. A blogger doesn't revise earlier posts; if a correction needs to be made or if new information surfaces, then a new post is all that is required. Much like on a wiki, everything on a blog is provisional.

It is the very public and transparent nature of wikis and blogs that creates their value. E-mail is fundamentally a private form of communication. The content goes from one mailbox to the next and the pieces of information in them remain separate from each other, discrete little bits of data hidden away in folders, much like the paper documents that serve as the underlying metaphor. Communicating and collaborating with wikis and blogs opens up that process and creates opportunities to discover new things, to make connections between things that we might not have thought of or understood before.

The network effect isn't driven by the format because the format is open; the network effect is driven by the participants themselves and their aggregate wisdom. Web 1.0 is the linking of one HTML page to another. Web 2.0 is ferreting meaning and creating value through emergent properties associated with aggregating human judgment. Organizations that do a better job of making information available in useful formats will succeed, whereas those that attempt to control their information with proprietary constraints will whither.

In the post-proprietary world, the nodes of the network are not connected simply by sharing a common platform. In the post-proprietary world, the nodes of the network are points of data, information and ideas that are linked and aggregated and universally available.

Tim Berners-Lee and others originally envisioned the Web as a global repository of human knowledge, but the Web is not a library or a warehouse. As it turns out, the Web is emerging as a source of discovery, a phenomenon that, like other phenomena, can be analyzed and studied empirically and from which inferences can be drawn with a scope and a scale unknown before.

The Web does not simply store knowledge; it creates it.

Now, organizations both large and small are adopting wiki technology for a variety of purposes. Teams of developers still use wikis for documentation and project management. Some companies use wikis as the engine that powers their intranet — it's free to install and easy to learn, so no other content management system offers a better cost/benefit ratio. MediaWiki is the software that runs Wikipedia. Because of Wikipedia's success, MediaWiki is one of the most commonly used wiki engines available. It's open source and free and runs on PHP and MySQL, making it easy for many organizations to adopt it. MediaWiki is not your only option, however, so in the next section I will go into greater detail about MediaWiki's features and how they compare with more traditional content management systems.

Web Content Management Systems

Content management systems are software applications used to facilitate the creation, storage, and distribution of digital content, and a wiki is a kind of content management system, with a twist. There are three areas where wiki engines really differentiate themselves from other run-of-the-mill content management systems: *access control*, *content authoring*, and *site organization*. In the following sections, I'll look at each one individually and discuss the features in depth.

Content Management Life Cycle

A Web content management system is a software application that provides tools to support the various activities required to maintain a website. As content flows through a content management system, it flows through four distinct phases, and all content management systems provide tools for each of these phases.

Content Acquisition

All content management systems receive their content from somewhere, a process I refer to as *acquisition*. The content may come from a legacy system or from another website in the form of syndicated content, or the content can be generated and edited directly in the content management system itself. Content management systems usually provide some kind of interface that enables users to create content, often through a Web browser. They also provide a system for managing workflow, which tracks content through various stages — from authoring to editing and ultimately to being published on the site.

Content Organization

Content management systems organize content so that readers can more easily discover the information they are looking for. This organization is called *information architecture*. Users find information on a website in two ways: they browse the site, navigating from page to page looking for the information, or they search for the information using a search engine.

Typically, content management systems provide a means for organizing content into a hierarchy, which is reflected in the system of navigation through which a user browses a site by following links. They also provide some form of search based on keywords, or some more elaborate scheme.

Content Storage

Content management systems also provide storage for content. How this is done varies from system to system. In some cases, the content is stored in a relational database; in others it is stored as XML on the file system. Many early wikis stored content simply as wikitext in plain text files. MediaWiki, too, stores content as raw wikitext, but it stores it in a database. It also happens to store all the previous versions of every page, which is a useful feature for websites that anybody can edit. From time to time, you'll find the need to roll back to earlier versions of a page.

Content Distribution

Finally, content management systems provide a means of distributing the content, which in the case of Web content management means providing a system of dynamically generating pages, and a set of tools that enable the publisher to schedule when content is viewable and by whom it is viewable.

Wikis are unique in how they shepherd content through these stages. In the following sections, you will learn more specifics about the wiki approach to workflow, content authoring, and site organization, and the specific features offered by MediaWiki to support these processes.

Workflow and User Management

Because wikis are websites that are collaboratively written by their readers, the most unique characteristics of a wiki can be found in the systems that support user access control and workflow.

User Access Control

There are three stages to access control:

1. **Authentication:** This is the stage during which the system becomes reasonably assured that the person accessing the site is who they say they are. Most content management systems, including MediaWiki, do this with passwords.

2. **Authorization:** The authorization aspect of user access control works by assigning users roles. The role to which a user is assigned determines to which content objects that user has access. This can limit what a user sees on the site, as well as what a user can do.

3. **Activity tracking:** The final step is activity tracking, which means that the system generates an audit trail so that you can determine who did what to your site.

You will see this access control system at work with Wikipedia. If you have not registered on the site you have the role of an anonymous user, which means that you can view articles, but you cannot create them. In order to create articles, you need to be a registered user. Once you have registered for the site, you can customize certain features, such as the skin being used; you can create your own user page; and you can both create your own articles and edit articles that already exist.

Workflow Policies

Whereas access control systems control who can perform what task on a given content item, workflow takes this a step further and enforces a set of policies based on the state of the document. Workflow represents what tasks are to be performed, in what order they should be performed, and who should perform them in any given stage. From a content management perspective, workflow is the approval process as content moves from the authoring phases to the publishing phase of its life cycle.

In a typical workflow system, a user who is assigned an "author" role can create an article and submit it for approval by someone in an "editor" role. Once the editor approves the content, it will be published. In the world of wikis, there is no distinction between the two. Any changes made to an article are immediately published.

Control over the content is exerted by the fact that changes to articles are tracked, so that one can easily find out who made a particular change. From the access control perspective, most of the management comes from the ability to track what was done, rather than to use authorization to limit what one can do. This is why logging plays such an important role in wiki management.

Change Monitoring

As one might expect, one layer of defense is to simply monitor changes that have been made to the wiki. In addition to monitoring changes, you want to be able to do something about fixing, or editing, unwanted changes, such as rolling them back to a previous version. Therefore, the "change monitoring" approach requires two basic features: the ability to monitor recent changes, plus some kind of version control.

Recent changes can be monitored as follows:

❑ Most wikis have a Recent Changes page that lists all the pages that have been changed and who made each change.

❑ E-mail notification of changes is just an e-mail version of the Recent Changes page, but with the convenience of notification.

❑ A variant of e-mail notification is support for RSS syndication, which means you can monitor a wiki for recent changes using your favorite RSS reader.

❑ MediaWiki allows you to differentiate trivial changes from more substantive ones. For example, you may not want to be notified by e-mail every time someone fixes a spelling error.

❑ If more than one person has been tasked with monitoring changes, another useful feature tracks whether a recently changed page has been checked yet, reducing the possibility of duplicating work. On MediaWiki, this is called marking a page as *patrolled*.

Version Control

I once encountered a philosophical debate about whether wikis should have version control. The idealist in the conversation argued that version control was against the "wiki way" and somehow lacked philosophical purity. The realist argued that people make mistakes and sometimes deliberately do bad things, so the ability to roll back changes was indeed a good thing and a feature that all wikis should have. I'm pleased to report that the realist won the argument in the broader marketplace of ideas, and many (if not most) versions of wiki software have version control.

Features include the following:

❑ The ability to roll back changes to the previous version

❑ The ability to compare different versions side-by-side

❑ The use of diffs between versions so that specific differences between them can be easily identified

Spam Prevention

Another approach is to monitor the content of changes programmatically, and this is sometimes referred to as spam prevention. This differs from user access control in the sense that it monitors wiki edits based on the content of the edit or the patterns of user behavior. Systems can block access to IP addresses and URLs, or they can block the posting of individual changes based on the following:

❑ Maintaining a spam blacklist, restricting access from certain domains

❑ Restricting the use of certain words or phrases, using word lists or regular expressions

❑ Blocking access based on excessive activity

- ❏ Blocking by IP address or name
- ❏ Blocking content by type (or size)

Content Authoring

When we read a Microsoft Word document on our computer, we think nothing of the fact that not only can we view the document, but we can edit it as well. When dealing with online content, the fact that we can directly edit the content we are viewing is something of a novelty because in most cases, the content we encounter is read-only. There is, in fact, an effort to separate the creation of content from the design of content in the underlying technology (think HTML and CSS), and many websites have a publication mentality that draws a clear distinction between the readers and writers (hence the term *read/write web* that is used to refer to tools like wikis).

The wiki approach to authoring shortens the distance between editing and publishing a page in two ways. First, you edit the page using the same application used to view the page — a Web browser. Second, edits are posted immediately. There is no staging of draft versions, and no workflow requirements.

- ❏ Wiki pages are editable through a Web interface so that no special software is needed, other than a Web browser.
- ❏ Users with access to the site can edit pages directly, and the changes are published immediately.
- ❏ Wikis use a special markup sometimes called *wikitext* to specify formatting on the text of the page, or to automatically create links to other pages (see Chapter 4 for more information about wikitext). Many wikis now boast a WYSIWYG (what you see is what you get) interface because many users are more comfortable writing pages this way. Most of these interfaces are embedded into Web pages, but many require the use of a specific browser, such as Firefox or Internet Explorer. Ideally, a wiki should make editing available anywhere, on any browser, which is why some form of wikitext is required.

Organization

Ultimately, the goal of a content management system is to organize content in such a way that people can find it when they need it. The way in which content is organized depends on the goals of the site and the nature of the content itself.

All content management systems serve as a repository for content, but these systems are more than just a repository for the same reason that a library is more than just a repository for books. Documents in a content management system are organized in the same way that books in a library are organized. In a library, books are grouped together by a classification system so that like subjects are located in one place. For example, biographies are in one section, fiction is in another, and so on. There is also an index, which shows the exact location of any book within the library.

When you go to the library, you might decide to browse the books, rather than go straight to the index. In this case, you could walk to the section you are interested in and begin looking at the spines of the books to see if you can find something you like. Conversely, you might go to the library with a different goal in mind. That is, if you want to find a specific book, then you will go to the index. (When I was a child, this index was a physical card catalog, long rows of wooden boxes containing 3×5 index cards. This has since been converted to a digital index in those libraries that can afford it.) These two activities, browsing and searching, are also possible with content management systems. In fact, you can think of a library as a content management system, but one that deals with physical content, rather than digital.

Taxonomy

Most sites organize their pages by grouping similar pages together, the way the library groups similar books together. This classification is called a *taxonomy*, and on most sites it manifests itself as a hierarchical taxonomy, with a home page, sections, and subsections. For example, a typical newspaper website might have the hierarchical organization shown in Figure 1-1.

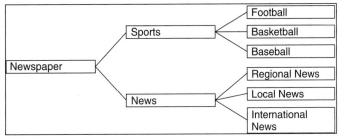

Figure 1-1: Typical hierarchy

The content of the site is first classified as either news or sports. Then, each of these classifications is subclassified, so that news is broken down into local news, international news, and regional news, and sports is broken down into football, basketball, and baseball.

As you navigate through the hierarchy from the home page, to sports, to baseball, you are arriving at more narrowly defined categories. The purpose of this kind of hierarchy is primarily to assist the user when navigating the site.

In a well-designed site, the taxonomy ultimately translates into site navigation and there should be a correlation between the taxonomy and the URL. In the example shown in Figure 1-1, the URL for basketball could be `http://choate.info/Sports/Basketball`.

One of the advantages to organizing sites in this way is that it makes it easier for users to guess the URLs for different areas of the site. After seeing the `http://choate.info/Sports/Basketball` URL, it would not be such a big leap to suppose that if you wanted to read something about baseball, you could go to `http://choate.info/Sports/Baseball`. Likewise, if you just wanted to see what kind of sports you could find more information about, you could navigate to `http://choate.info/Sports`. Having an intuitive URL namespace greatly improves the quality of a site.

These hierarchical structures can be topic-based, like the example I just used, but content can be grouped according to a variety of different criteria. Weblogs organize content in reverse chronological order, rather than by topic (some weblogs support categorization of content, but the basic structure of the weblog is chronological, as it is modeled after a journal or diary).

Wikis are organized using a flat hierarchical structure. One consequence of this is that URLs are simple. For example, the following URLs link to Wikipedia's articles about football, basketball, and sports in general. All article URLs are this simple:

```
http://en.wikipedia.org/wiki/Football
http://en.wikipedia.org/wiki/Sport
http://en.wikipedia.org/wiki/Basketball
```

Folksonomy

Imagine if the library let you put the books back anywhere you wanted — that would lead to chaos, right? This means that if you put the book back into a different section, then other people wouldn't know where to find it because it wasn't put away according to the system. That would be bad in a library, but not in a wiki. Wikis employ a system of organization that lets you "put the book" wherever you please.

The reason is very simple. Wikis don't like hierarchies. They employ what is called a *folksonomy*. In terms of the URL space of a wiki, the hierarchy is flat. There are no sections and subsections. All pages maintain simple, non-nested URLs. Additional layers of organization evolve as tag-based folksonomies.

The excessively rural-sounding folksonomy is not the study of senior citizens; nor is it a measure of how much money grandpa has — it's just a clever way to refer to taxonomies that are created by a site's users in a decentralized, ad hoc manner. It is accomplished by allowing each user to assign tags to pages. Tags are really nothing more than searchable keywords that users decide to apply to a page.

In the case of MediaWiki, users can set categories for pages. There is no predetermined list of categories, and the terms used are entirely up to the user. This is in stark contrast to a taxonomy, which uses controlled vocabularies and rigidly defined structures into which individual units of content must be organized.

A list of categories on Wikipedia can be found at `http://en.wikipedia.org/wiki/Wikipedia:Browse`.

When to Wiki

I've seen business people and educators throw wikis at many problems (as the latest cure-all), only to see them splat against a wall and slowly slide down into a puddle of ooze. Wikis are wonderful things, but only when used correctly. The successful operation of a wiki requires both the right kind of technology and the right kind of governance. You cannot load up MediaWiki, flip a switch, and expect a wiki to perform wonders for you. You need to apply a wiki to the right problem, and you need to manage it properly in order to derive the greatest benefit. In this section, you will learn about the key management elements that contribute to successful wiki implementations.

There are two ways in which organizations begin to use a wiki. The first is by way of a top-down decision that takes place when someone in senior management decides that a wiki is the solution for some particular problem and thus mandates its use. The second way is by way of a grass-roots movement whereby individuals or workgroups begin to use wikis because they help them get their jobs done.

The very open and decentralized nature of wikis makes the grass-roots path the most common way that wikis find their way into an organization. Providing an environment in which wikis are allowed to emerge in a grass-roots fashion has some definite advantages. In the following sections, you will learn how best to foster the successful use of wikis within your organization. It is something of a contradiction to mandate the use of wikis. A better approach is to persuade through success. First, provide a fertile field in which the wiki seed can take root and thrive.

Running a Successful Wiki

Despite declarations of "Web 2.0" and the read-write Web and other trendy nomenclatures, the rules for a successful wiki are very similar to the rules that one should apply to any community site (that's what we used to call them before we started to call them social media sites). One could argue that a wiki is a modified forum, as it retains many forum features.

The advice contained in this section is based in large part on my years of experience managing community-oriented sites for which the users are the main contributors of content, much like wikis. I also owe a large debt to Christian Wagner and Ann Majchrzak, whose paper "Enabling Customer-Centricity Using Wikis and the Wiki Way," provided me with some particularly useful insights (see the *Journal of Management Information Systems*, Winter 2006–2007, Vol. 23, No. 3, pp. 17–43).

Their research focused on enhancing constructive customer engagement in a wiki, which is not necessarily how most companies will use one. However, the principles they suggest are good ones that, in my experience, do in fact foster a sense of community and collaboration.

In their review, they compared wikis operated by the *Los Angeles Times* (thinly veiled with the name "Boomtown Times"), Novell, and, of course, Wikipedia. *The Los Angeles Times* wiki was a dismal failure, the Novell wiki was a moderate success, and the Wikipedia wiki was, and is, of course, a smashing success.

Wagner and Majchrzak offer six propositions based on their research, but I have taken the liberty of condensing them into four rules of thumb, based upon my own experience with managing collaborative websites.

Alignment of Goals

Wikis got their start by being used by programmers to document software projects. This is an ideal use for a wiki because there is a strong incentive on the part of the programmer to participate. A social contract is at work: The software needs to be documented and all participants must be kept in the loop, so each programmer keeps his or her documentation updated with the understanding that the other programmers will do the same, in a mutual back-scratching arrangement.

This apparent no-brainer is, apparently, not a no-brainer. At least, it is not a no-brainer to the editors of the *Los Angeles Times*, which decided that it would be good to have a "wikitorial" — an editorial composed and edited by the masses. The *Los Angeles Times* started by posting their editorial, and then provided a wiki for the public to respond. As Wikipedia has learned, there is no alignment of goals among political types, and the partisans reigned supreme during the very brief life of the wikitorial. In the organic, evolving world of wikis, consider the wikitorial an evolutionary dead end.

At first, the users made a good faith effort to collaborate on an editorial, but they soon concluded that producing a single editorial that was acceptable to everyone was not going to happen, and there had already been attempts to delete the entire editorial, so by the second day, they forked the editorial so that it would be possible to represent different points of view. Once news of the wikitorial experiment showed up on Slashdot, a technology-related news website (http://slashdot.org), it attracted a lot of attention and was soon followed by pornographic posts, and so on. On the third day, the wikitorial was shut down.

The kind of vandalism encountered by the *Los Angeles Times* represents the nightmare scenario that is almost always raised as an objection to using a wiki. In fact, the first time I saw a wiki I thought it was a lousy idea for this very reason. As it turns out, this kind of defacement is not as common as one might think; and when a wiki is set up and managed properly, that kind of mischief can largely be avoided.

In the late nineties, I was responsible for what we called *community publishing* sites. It wasn't a wiki per se, but it had many of the features of a wiki, the most important one being that we (the newspaper) used the Internet to let the community participate in the publishing process. The site was called NCHome-team.com, and it represented a partnership between *The News & Observer* and WRAL-TV5 in Raleigh, North Carolina. It was a statewide high school sports site. Coaches and interested parents were recruited statewide to update the rosters each season, and then to update scores after the games on Friday night (which often finished too late to make it into the paper and/or there was not enough space).

Following were the main concerns we had when launching the site:

❑   Would the sites be as credible as the newspaper itself given the fact that the content was published without being vetted by an editor?

❑   Would the coaches reliably post their scores?

❑   Would the coaches post inaccurate results?

❑   What kind of liability would the newspaper have as a publisher? If acting as a publisher (as it does when things are printed), then the newspaper is responsible for all the content that is published. That means if someone is libeled in the newspaper, then the newspaper is responsible. (The first reaction was to avoid any activity that would make the newspaper look like a publisher — in other words, it didn't monitor posts.)

We quickly learned that the coaches were enthusiastic participants, and they were just as committed as we were to making sure that the information was timely and accurate.

In retrospect, it's easy to see why fears about false sports scores being posted were unfounded. While coaches did have an incentive to win, they had no incentive to cheat and post false scores because with so many other people at the game, they would easily get caught. The transparency of the process meant that it was in everybody's interest to post factual data. In other words, the goals of the entire community were aligned.

The reason why the *Los Angeles Times* wikitorial failed is because an editorial is a point of view about a controversial subject. The goals of the individuals on either side of the debate are to discredit those who disagree with them and to establish their worldview as pre-eminent. In other words, the goals of the left and the right are not aligned. Therefore, I recommend no bipartisan wikis. Ever. There is no such thing.

This does not mean that everyone who participates in a wiki has the same goals, or that they involve themselves in the same activities. Goal alignment only means that their goals are not in conflict; they all head in basically the same direction.

A Culture of Collaboration

In practice, the most common problem encountered by new wikis is that it can be difficult to get people to participate. Several psychological and organizational barriers need to be overcome. Most important, in addition to needing the technical apparatus to operate a wiki, you also need an organization with a culture that fosters collaboration. If you don't, your wiki is unlikely to thrive.

For example, a certain government agency has decided to launch a wiki that will capture all of the undocumented but highly useful information that floats around in people's heads. They are facing two sources of internal resistance.

First, they have a hierarchical culture whereby every communication is approved by proper channels. Being propositioned by some young twenty-something about brain-dumping your wisdom into a wiki after having every utterance scrutinized by your superiors for your entire career is like suddenly being told by your wife of twenty years that she thinks you should loosen up a little and get a girlfriend.

The second source of resistance is the fact (or perception) that once your brain is dumped, it becomes communal property; and while you may be fairly certain that you will continue to get your paycheck, you are not so certain that you will continue to get credit for your faithful fidelity and the cultured wisdom you have nurtured for so many years. Owning information is a source of power; that's why it can be so hard to get people to share it.

In one case, a department was more than willing to post content in a content management system, but they were unwilling to do the same work if it was with a wiki. The reason? They feared a lack of control. It can represent a loss of ownership for people. When people are rewarded for individual output, they are going to be less inclined to participate in a project with collective output. While they may not say this aloud, they are worried about whether they will still get credit for their good ideas and hard work.

Universities are also experimenting with wikis. If you were a professor, you might reason that because Wikipedia is such a wild success, it would be fantastic to set up a wiki for the class. Then, instead of requiring students to write papers for an audience of one (which is you), they can write them for their peers, their fellow students; and for posterity, all the students that will follow. In that case, a classroom becomes a source or repository of knowledge. You even dreamily fantasize about students correcting and expanding upon the postings of other students in a communal editing effort whereby everyone is both student and professor.

The only problem is that students have no interest in correcting (or updating or expanding) another student's work. What's in it for them? They annoy a potential date and don't really have much to show for their work. There are two reasons to go to college: to learn and to acquire documentation that you have learned in the form of a transcript or diploma. I've used papers that I have written in graduate school as part of my portfolio. What kind of portfolio do I have if all the work was done in a wiki?

Most of your school life is spent being told to do your own work and keep your eyes on your own paper, while being forced to read wordy honor codes and the like. Traditionally, schools have not fostered a collaborative environment, so students aren't quite sure how wikis fit in with the culture of the school. In fact, wikis are an excellent tool for the classroom, but you need to be prepared to help the students unlearn some of what they have learned about what is appropriate behavior in school, just like employees of the government agency have to relearn what's appropriate for them.

The one common theme that runs through all of these examples is that the goals of the participants were not aligned. In some cases, their respective goals were in direct opposition to each other, while in other cases there was a belief that participating in the wiki would not provide enough individual benefit. If you want to derive a benefit from collaboration, you need to ensure that everybody in the organization also benefits from collaboration.

Community Custodianship

I have already mentioned that when I first worked on community publishing sites for a newspaper, we conscientiously avoided creating the appearance that we were the "editors" of the content. In this case, we were doing so in order to avoid liability for what was posted on the community sites. This meant that we didn't actively monitor user posts and that we wouldn't remove posts unless a member of the community raised a concern with us.

What we had done inadvertently was to shift the monitoring responsibility to the community itself. Again, this was not for any altruistic reason, such as a belief in decentralized decision-making. As it turns out, however, letting community sites be managed, in effect, by the community is an important component of successful sites.

Despite the open nature of wikis, an effective wiki is not an egalitarian free-for-all. Just as the members of the community share reading and authoring privileges, they must also share custodianship of the community. The community rules the community. In this custodial role, the community of users needs to establish rules of conduct for contributors to the site, and they need to monitor user activity, to ensure that it is in conformance. The custodial role means that users are not only responsible for identifying suspect content, but they also serve on the decision-making bodies that establish guidelines regarding when such content is deleted, or when users should be banned.

Clearly Defined Rules for Posting Content

Successful custodianship means that in order to get your users to participate fully, your wiki needs to have clearly defined rules and processes. These rules include a clear description of the kind of content that should be contributed to the wiki as well as rules for handling disputes. For example, Wikipedia has "five pillars" that define the character of Wikipedia. The following is a sampling of a few of the rules:

"Wikipedia is an encyclopedia incorporating elements of general encyclopedias, specialized encyclopedias, and almanacs. All articles must follow our no original research policy and strive for accuracy; Wikipedia is not the place to insert personal opinions, experiences, or arguments. Furthermore, Wikipedia is not an indiscriminate collection of information. Wikipedia is not a trivia collection, a soapbox, a vanity publisher, an experiment in anarchy or democracy, or a web directory. Nor is Wikipedia a dictionary, a newspaper, or a collection of source documents; these kinds of content should be contributed to sister projects, here, Wiktionary, Wikinews, and Wikisource, respectively."

"Wikipedia has a neutral point of view, which means we strive for articles that advocate no single point of view. Sometimes this requires representing multiple points of view; presenting each point of view accurately; providing context for any given point of view, so that readers understand whose view the point represents; and presenting no one point of view as "the truth" or "the best view." It means citing verifiable, authoritative sources whenever possible, especially on controversial topics. When a conflict arises as to which version is the most neutral, declare a cool-down period and tag the article as disputed; hammer out details on the talk page and follow dispute resolution."

The rules are very explicit and leave little room for ambiguity. The preceding rules and others can be found at the following locations:

- ❏   `http://en.wikipedia.org/wiki/Wikipedia:List_of_policies_and_guidelines`
- ❏   `http://en.wikipedia.org/wiki/Wikipedia:Five_pillars`

In addition to establishing rules, you need to seed your wiki with content when it is first launched. The presence of content will facilitate the creation of even more content. One of the advantages of seeding the wiki prior to opening it up to a larger group is that the pages that you create serve as a kind of template for the new users to refer to when creating their own pages. In other words, they serve as an example of the kind of content you want to see on the site; and, it is hoped, having seen an example, people will be more comfortable producing their own content for the site.

Monitoring User Behavior

When Ronald Reagan talked about nuclear arms reduction treaties with the former Soviet Union, he espoused the following philosophy: "Trust, but verify." Running a wiki requires trust on the part of management in the capacity of their employees, their customers, and the community at large to behave reasonably well, most of the time. Because it is not realistic to believe that they will behave reasonably well all of the time, then you must switch to "verification" mode and monitor behavior.

Despite the part of the definition declaring that wikis are sites that anybody can edit, the truth of the matter is that if you let just anybody edit it and do not, at the same time, provide a mechanism for proper oversight, your wiki will not work.

The ability to monitor user behavior creates transparency, and transparency is good. The very fact that behavior can be monitored will keep most of the behavior that needs to be monitored from ever happening. In fact, while the most common objection managers have to using wikis is fear of vandalism, the biggest problem they end up having is just the opposite: no activity at all.

The monitoring requirement varies according to how widely available the wiki is. In other words, a workgroup wiki behind the corporate firewall needs less monitoring than a customer-accessible wiki that the public can see.

It is also important that monitoring and policing the wiki remain the responsibility of the community. As I said earlier, community custodianship is one of those factors that creates well-run wikis, and one of the roles the community plays while acting in the capacity of custodians is the role of monitor. Not only should the community itself be the monitor, it should also be the body that helps to determine what the rules are in the first place.

Monitoring behavior can be more than simply a policing role. As mentioned earlier, one of the reasons employees can be reluctant to participate is a fear of losing credit. If anybody can edit a document, how am I going to get credit for writing this one? Most wikis can now track changes (MediaWiki can), and you can monitor activity on the wiki as a means of identifying good uses of wikis. This is especially true in educational settings where students might be graded on their activity.

Wikis in the Enterprise

There are a lot of wikis on the market, both open source and commercial. If you want to learn more about the others, Wikipedia is a good place to start:

- ❑   `http://en.wikipedia.org/wiki/Comparison_of_wiki_farms`
- ❑   `http://en.wikipedia.org/wiki/Comparison_of_wiki_software`

Summary

In this chapter, you learned what wikis are, you learned about the role of a wiki within an organization relative to other content management systems, and you discovered some rules of thumb for managing a successful wiki. In the next chapter, the discussion moves away from a general discussion about wikis to a more specific discussion about MediaWiki. In Chapter 2, you will learn how to install and run MediaWiki software, including system requirements, options, and alternatives.

2

Installing MediaWiki

In order to run MediaWiki, you need a Web server, support for PHP, and a database, either MySQL or Postgres. The simplest way to install MediaWiki is to install it on a computer running Linux or a Unix-like operating system, with the Apache Web server and mod_php installed. The PHP installation should be version 5.0 or later (don't use 5.1 with 64-bit computers, as there are reportedly some bugs), and the database should be either MySQL 4.0 or later, or Postgres 8.0 or later. This is the basic configuration that Wikipedia's servers run and the configuration on which the developers of MediaWiki focus their efforts. It is also possible, although a little more difficult, to install and run MediaWiki on Windows servers.

Apache is not the only Web server you can use, but it is the best of the options, for a few reasons. First, because of the success of Wikipedia, we know that MediaWiki has been installed on a high-traffic website that uses Apache servers, and we know that this configuration works reliably and can scale to accommodate whatever optimistic growth expectations we have about our own wiki endeavors. Second, the Apache/PHP combination is pervasive and readily available. PHP can be loaded as a dynamic shared object (DSO) in Apache, which makes installation and configuration a much simpler task in most cases. While the core PHP libraries are supposed to be threadsafe, not all of the many extensions available for it are, so experts often recommend that you do not run PHP on Web servers that are threaded — this includes Internet Information Server (IIS). If you are running Apache 2, then you need to use the pre-forked version.

In all other cases, the most stable approach is to use FastCGI to run PHP. FastCGI is a speedier alternative to regular old CGI, as it allows CGI applications to stay in memory between requests, something that CGI does not do and that leads to a lot of overhead as the program is reloaded into memory every time it is executed. Note that not all of the features or options available to MediaWiki when running under Apache with mod_php work when running in CGI mode, with or without FastCGI.

Development Environment

All testing for this book was done using MediaWiki 1.9.3. This version is a moving target — the application is actively maintained and is on a schedule of continuous integration with quarterly snapshot releases.

All of the testing was done on a Macintosh MacBook Pro, running Tiger (10.4) version of OS X, Windows Vista, and SuSE Linux 9.2, with MediaWiki installed and running on all three operating systems. Two different configurations are running on OS X: one that uses MySQL 4.1.22 and another that uses PostgreSQL 8.2.3.

The examples used in this book were developed using Eclipse PHP Development Tools, available at www.zend.com/pdt. While other PHP IDEs are available, this one works well for the purposes of this book and provides very powerful debugging tools, which would normally only be available in a commercial IDE.

There are many administrative tasks for which no Web interface is provided by MediaWiki. This means that you will often have to update the underlying SQL tables in order to accomplish what you want. While this can be done from the command line, it is much simpler using a Web-based front end such as phpMyAdmin for MySQL, or phpPgAdmin for Postgres, which is what was used for this book.

This book focuses on getting MediaWiki up and running using the Apache Web server, but if that does not meet your needs, you can find a lot of information online that is worth checking. The MediaWiki wiki (http://MediaWiki.org) is a good starting point, and the mailing list is a good source of information; you can ask specific questions about different installation issues.

Installing the Prerequisites

If you are running Linux, then you'll have the easiest time of all, and there is a good chance you can install MediaWiki as is. If you are running Macintosh OS X, then you will have to make a few tweaks in order to get it configured properly. If you are running Windows, your best bet is to download a preconfigured package of Apache, PHP, and MySQL.

Once we step through the typical Linux Apache MySQL PHP (LAMP) installation of MediaWiki, we'll review a few installation variants too, such as using Postgres instead of MySQL.

Before getting started, we need to address a few issues. If you are unfamiliar with these concepts, then you should get help from somebody more familiar with Apache, PHP, or MySQL, depending on the source of your confusion. Entire books have been written about each of these software packages individually, and there is not space (or time) available to delve too deeply into them here, so you should have at least a moderate level of experience in all three. If you run into trouble, don't forget to check the MediaWiki mailing lists, as well as look into documentation or books specifically related to Web servers, PHP, and databases.

1. Do you have root privileges on your server (or administrator privileges on Windows)? If you do not, then you will not be able to install the necessary software. If you do not have the required software already installed, then you will need to get a systems administrator to set things up for you.

2. Do you have Apache installed? If you do, which version is it? If you have Apache 2 or later, then you need to know which multi-processing module (MPM) is being run. While it may be

possible to run MediaWiki with other MPMs, it is advisable to run it only with the pre-fork multi-processing module because of potential threading conflicts between some third-party PHP libraries and threaded Apache modules. If you do not have Apache installed, or it's the wrong module, then read the section "Installing Apache."

3. If Apache is already installed, do you have access to the Apache configuration file, `httpd.conf`? You will if you have root privileges on your server. If not, you may have to rely on `.htaccess` files for some configuration options. You also need to determine whether you have the `mod_rewrite` and `mod_alias` modules enabled, as well as `mod_php`. If they are not enabled, then you need to enable them. If you do have access to `httpd.conf`, then you can check and update the configuration file yourself. You can read about how to do that in the section "Configuring Apache and mod_php." If you do not have access to `httpd.conf`, then you need to have a systems administrator update the configuration for you.

4. Is the installed version of PHP 5.0 or later, and is the PHP command-line interface (CLI) installed, as well as the dynamic shared object (DSO) module for Apache? MediaWiki includes several PHP maintenance scripts that must be run from the command line, which is why the CLI version should be installed. See the section "Installing PHP" in this chapter for instructions on how to install PHP. Again, if you don't have root privileges and cannot install software, you need to find someone to help you.

5. Is MySQL installed? If so, do you have superuser privileges on MySQL? This means you can create new databases and new users. If you do not have superuser privileges, are you at least able to create your own databases? If you are not able to create your own databases, has a database already been created that you can use? You will need to have privileges to CREATE tables, and to do SELECT, INSERT, UPDATE, DELETE and LOCK operations on tables in the database. If you do not have these privileges, then you will not be able to run MySQL; otherwise, read the section "Installing MySQL."

Installing Apache

On most Linux distributions, Apache and PHP are already installed. If for some reason you do not have them installed, or you have the wrong versions installed, the simplest way to install them is using the package manager for your distribution, such as yum, which is just about as easy as it gets. Throughout the book, when demonstrating commands that you enter on the shell in Linux or Macintosh OS X, $ represents the shell prompt — you do not need to type in the shell prompt, only the characters that follow it:

```
$ sudo yum install httpd
```

You can also download the source code for Apache at `http://apache.org`. Once downloaded, you must unpack the distribution:

```
$ tar xvfz httpd-2.2.4.tar.gz
```

Change directories and open the Apache directory that was created when you unpacked the distribution, and do the usual installation procedure. You will need to log in as root, or use sudo when installing it:

```
$ ./configure --prefix=/apache2 --enable-module=so --enable-rewrite
$ sudo make
$ sudo make install
```

Apache can now be started and stopped by typing the following command:

```
$ /apache2/bin/apachectl start
$ /apache2/bin/apachectl stop
```

This is only a cursory description of how to install Apache. If you will be running Apache in a production environment, then you need to be aware of numerous security concerns and configuration options, so be sure to take the appropriate precautions and consult with experts or more detailed documentation about Apache.

If you are interested in running a test server and want to get up and running as quickly as possible, you can also download a pre-packaged bundle of Apache, PHP, and MySQL called XAMPP from the Apache Friends website: `www.apachefriends.org/en/xampp-linux.html`. Other such packages are available, but XAMPP works well because it maintains distributions for Linux, Windows, and Macintosh OS X. They are designed to be used for test environments, so they are not configured for security out of the box. They also tend to have a "kitchen sink" mentality, meaning that every possible Apache module and PHP extension is installed. This is good for getting started and not an issue on a test server, but is probably not ideal on a high-traffic website.

The download instructions are simply and clearly articulated on the website, so there is no need to repeat them here. Once you have downloaded the bundle, you can skip to the "Installing MediaWiki" section.

Macintosh OS X

Macintosh OS X comes with Apache 1.3 installed, which is sufficient for our purposes, but it also has PHP 4.4.4 installed, which will not work with MediaWiki. There are two ways to get the right version of PHP installed. The simplest is to download the PHP distribution maintained by Marc Liyanage at `www.entropy.ch/software/macosx/php`. He only maintains a distribution for the current version of OS X, which is 10.4. The advantage of using Marc's distribution is that it comes with an installer that configures the default Apache installation to use PHP 5. Follow the download instructions and you will have a working Apache/PHP 5 installation on your Macintosh.

Another alternative for Macintosh OS X is to use Fink, available from `http://fink.sourceforge.net`. Fink is a package manager for OS X, like yum for Linux. You need to have the Apple developer tools installed in order to use Fink, but they are freely available at the Apple developer website at `http://developer.apple.com`.

The XAMPP option is available for OS X as well, and it can be downloaded from `www.apachefriends.org/en/xampp-macosx.html`. The same caveat about Linux applies to OS X — that this is good for a test server, and not a production environment.

You may run into a slight permissions problem when installing it on OS X. The Apache server runs as user *nobody*, and when first installed, there were permissions errors when accessing the sample PHP files. Once you make the offending files readable by Apache, everything should work fine. Because OS X already has Apache installed, you need to turn off the other Apache, which you can do by turning off Personal Web Sharing in the System Preferences pane.

Windows

The simplest route to getting MediaWiki up and running on Windows is to use a pre-packaged installation of Apache, PHP, and MySQL. Several such packages are available, including XAMPP, which was used for this book and is available at www.apachefriends.org/en/xampp.html. Others have had equal success with WAMP, which is available at www.wampserver.com/en/. Note that WAMP only works on Windows, and not on Linux and OS X.

If you are going to use Internet Information Server (IIS), then it is best to use MediaWiki with FastCGI, rather than regular CGI, or ISAPI. PHP is not as stable under ISAPI on IIS because some PHP extensions are not threadsafe, whereas IIS is a threaded server. At the time of this writing, there is a preview release of a FastCGI component for IIS 7.0; it can be downloaded from http://blogs.msdn.com/hsshin/archive/2007/01/17/fastcgi-for-iis.aspx.

Installing PHP

The first step is to check whether you have PHP and if so, which version it is. If the path where PHP resides is in your path, you can just enter **php –v** on the command line to determine which version is running; otherwise, you need to use the full path. The following example will query the default PHP implementation on Macintosh OS X. The results return the version number, followed by the API of this particular implementation of PHP. In this example, the version is 4.4.4 of the command-line interface version:

```
$ /usr/bin/php -v
PHP 4.4.4 (cli) (built: Nov  1 2006 18:10:56)
Copyright (c) 1997-2006 The PHP Group
Zend Engine v1.3.0, Copyright (c) 1998-2004 Zend Technologies
```

You need the CLI, but the version number is too low; and after checking the other version you have downloaded, you can see that you are running version 5.2.1 and that it is the cgi-fcgi version, which is the same thing as CLI, except that FastCGI support was enabled when it was compiled:

```
$ /usr/local/bin/php -v
PHP 5.2.1 (cgi-fcgi) (built: Mar 17 2007 20:28:34)
Copyright (c) 1997-2007 The PHP Group
Zend Engine v2.2.0, Copyright (c) 1998-2007 Zend Technologies
```

If you are running Linux or Macintosh OS X and you do not want to download a pre-packaged version of PHP, you may want to download and compile it yourself. The pre-packaged installations are frequently packed with a lot of libraries, many of which you do not necessarily need, so in the interests of economy you might compile a slimmer version.

You can download pre-compiled binaries for Windows, and source code for Linux and OS X, at http://php.net.

Compiling PHP

In order to compile PHP, you need to have GNU make. Go into the source directory and first execute the configure script. At a minimum, you need to enable Apache — in the following example, I am building PHP to be used for Apache 2 with the option -with-apxs2=/apache2/bin/apxs (you will change the path to match your Apache installation).

You also need the GD graphics library installed, which varies according to libJPEG and libPNG. The -with-zlib option enables PHP to compress pages in order to save bandwidth.

Finally, you need to enable multi-byte strings (mbstring) and iconv, which allows you to convert easily between encodings. The following code shows a minimal PHP configuration for use with MediaWiki:

```
$ sudo ./configure '--prefix=/apache2/php' '--with-mysql=/usr/local/mysql' '--with-
   apxs2=/apache2/bin/apxs' '--with-zlib' '--with-gd' '--with-jpeg-dir=/sw' '--with-
   png-dir=/sw' '--with-iconv-dir' '--enable-mbstring'
```

Once configured, run make and make install, as described in the Apache installation instructions.

In addition to the required libraries, a handful of optional libraries are of value. One group of options includes libraries or tools to increase PHP performance through different kinds of caching. Several different libraries support opcode caching, which means that your PHP code doesn't have to be recompiled with every request. These libraries are Turk MMcache, eAccelerator, and Alternative PHP Cache (APC). You also have the option of page caching using memcached, which is a distributed object store suitable for high-volume sites. In order to enable this option, you need to have memcached installed; then you can compile PHP with the -enable-sockets option. This chapter does not go into detail about caching, but it is covered in depth in Chapter 11.

Another option is to enable Tidy with the --with-tidy[=/path/to/tidy] option enabled. MediaWiki uses Tidy to fix the sometimes malformed HTML submitted by users when they are editing pages. The code directly generated by MediaWiki is well formed, but there is no way to ensure that users on the site will use wikitext correctly, so tidy is used as the last line of defense.

Configuring Apache and mod_php

Once PHP is installed, you need to configure Apache to work with PHP. The following is an example configuration from Apache 1.3 on OS X. These changes need to be made in the httpd.conf configuration file, or in .htaccess:

```
LoadModule php5_module          /usr/local/php5/libphp5.so

<IfDefine APACHE1>
AddModule mod_php5.c
</IfDefine>

<IfModule mod_php5.c>

    AddType application/x-httpd-php .php
    AddType application/x-httpd-php-source .phps

    <IfModule mod_dir.c>
        DirectoryIndex index.html index.php
    </IfModule>
</IfModule>
```

When configuring Apache for PHP, make sure that PHP 5 is mapped to the .php extension. On some installations, if you have both PHP 4 and PHP 5 installed, the administrator may have PHP 5 mapped to the extension .php5. Of course, MediaWiki requires PHP 5.x, but all of its files end in .php.

Installing MySQL

You can download MySQL binaries for Windows, Macintosh OS X, and a variety of Linux implementations directly from the MySQL website at http://dev.mysql.com/downloads/mysql/5.0.html. You can download PHPMyAdmin, the Web front-end for MySQL, at www.phpmyadmin.net.

Of the two database options, MySQL is definitely the more mature implementation. Postgres was only added relatively recently. Some people make their selection based on the different open-source licenses used. MySQL is licensed under the GNU General Public License, and Postgres is licensed under the BSD open-source license. This means that Postgres can be used and distributed in commercial applications. Of course, MediaWiki is GPL'd too, so this may not be a compelling reason to use Postgres in this particular instance.

The general rule of thumb in terms of performance is as follows: On the one hand, MySQL is fast, especially on sites containing a lot of SELECTs and not as many INSERTs and UPDATEs. Postgres, on the other hand, scales better, especially with large transactions and a lot of INSERTs and UPDATEs. If you are not familiar with databases, or you do not have a compelling reason to use Postgres, it's definitely simpler to stick with MySQL in this instance.

The out-of-the-box MediaWiki uses MySQL's full-text indexing for the site search, or it can use Postgres' tsearch2. The actual Wikipedia website uses Apache Lucene for its full-text indexing, so you will notice a difference in the output of search results if you compare Wikipedia's search results with your own.

If you have a superuser account on MySQL, the installation script will handle creating the database and users for you, but in the interest of providing complete information, the steps needed to create the necessary database and user are outlined here.

The first step is to create a database, which by default is named wikidb (but does not need to be), using the following command:

```
$ mysqladmin -u root -p create wikidb
```

Next, you need to grant appropriate privileges to wikiuser, the username that MediaWiki uses to access MySQL. In order to do this, log into mysql as root, and then enter the following GRANT statement:

```
$ mysql -u root
mysql> grant create, select, insert, update, delete, lock tables on wikidb.* to
    'wikiuser'@'localhost' identified by 'password';
flush privileges;
```

Once the user is created, you can then start the MySQL server. The following command launches MySQL on OS X or Linux (the actual path will vary depending on your installation):

```
$ /usr/local/mysql/bin/safe_mysqld &.
```

Installing Postgres

PostgreSQL does not offer as many options at their site for downloads, but you can download Linux and Windows binaries at www.postgresql.org/download. Fortunately, Marc Liyanage has prepared binaries for Mac 10.4, which can be downloaded at www.entropy.ch/software/macosx/postgresql.

You can download the Web front end to Postgres at http://phppgadmin.sourceforge.net.

In order to use PostgreSQL, you need to have plpsql and tsearch2 installed. Depending on your distribution, it may or may not have it installed. As a consequence, it is probably a good idea to manually create the users and database in Postgres, rather than rely on the automated process. When Postgres is first installed, the superuser is postgres, and it has no password. You are also provided with a number of administrative programs that make it easy to create users and databases.

The first step is to create wikiuser, using the following command:

```
$ createuser -D -P -E wikiuser
```

After you enter this line, you will be prompted for the new user's password, two consecutive times. Then you'll be asked whether this user should be allowed to create new users. The answer should be no.

```
Shall the new user be allowed to create more new users? (y/n) n
CREATE USER
```

Once this is done, you can create the new database and assign ownership of it to wikiuser:

```
$ createdb -O wikiuser wikidb
```

In order for Postgres to work with MediaWiki, plpgsql (PL/pgSQL), a procedural language used to write functions, needs to be installed as well. This can be done with the following command, which tells Postgres to enable plpgsql with the wikidb database:

```
$ createlang plpgsql wikidb
```

The other addition to Postgres is tsearch2, which enables full-text searching. If you have downloaded the Postgres source code, then you will find the tsearch2 directory inside the pgsql/share/contrib directory.

tsearch2 is actually a SQL program, and you run it against a database that you want to have full-text indexing capability. Postgres has a default table called Template1, which is used as a template to create new databases, so you can install tsearch2 there if you want every database produced by Postgres to use it. For the purposes of this example, install tsearch2 directly into your wikidb database.

In order to do this, access the tsearch2 directory and run the following commands:

```
$ make
$ make install
```

After you've run make, you can then apply tsearch2 to the wikidb database that you just created:

```
$ psql wikidb < tsearch2.sql -U postgres
```

After you've installed `tsearch2.sql`, you need to provide the right privileges to wikiuser. To do this, log in to the interactive prompt as the postgres user and issue the following series of grant statements. After the permissions have been granted, you need to update the locale in the pg_ts_cfg table, which defaults to the "C" locale. In order for full-text indexing to work, you need to have the right locale set up:

```
$ psql wikidb -U postgres
wikidb=# grant select on pg_ts_cfg to wikiuser;
wikidb=# grant select on pg_ts_cfgmap to wikiuser;
wikidb=# grant select on pg_ts_dict to wikiuser;
wikidb=# grant select on pg_ts_parser to wikiuser;
wikidb=# update pg_ts_cfg set locale =
    current_setting('lc_collate') where ts_name = 'default';
```

Now you have the wikidb database created, you have both `plpgsql` and `tsearch2` installed on wikidb, and you have created the wikiuser user and granted this user the appropriate privileges to interact with the database on behalf of MediaWiki.

Installing MediaWiki

You can now turn to the task of actually installing MediaWiki. In most respects, the installation process will be exactly the same whether you are using MySQL or Postgres, with a couple of exceptions, which you will see as you follow along with this example.

Step One: Download MediaWiki

You can download the most current official releases from SourceForge, at `http://sourceforge.net/projects/wikipedia`, or from the wikimedia.org site at `http://download.wikimedia.org/mediawiki`. Once you have downloaded the source, unpack it using the following command:

```
$ tar xvzf mediawiki-1.9.3.tar.gz
```

If you are using Windows, then you need to have software to unpack the code, such as 7-Zip, an opensource application available from SourceForge at `http://sourceforge.net/projects/sevenzip` that knows how to manage tarred and gzipped files.

Once unpacked, you will find a folder called `mediawiki-1.9.3`.

If you prefer, you can check out the latest release from the MediaWiki Subversion repository by entering the following command:

```
$ svn checkout http://svn.wikimedia.org/svnroot/mediawiki/branches/REL1_9/phase3
```

If you like to live dangerously, then you can check out the developer version here:

```
$ svn checkout http://svn.wikimedia.org/svnroot/mediawiki/trunk/phase3
```

Step Two: Copy to Web Server

Once MediaWiki is unpacked, it needs to be copied into the document root of the Apache Web server. On Macintosh OS X, that would be /Library/WebServer/Documents/; on Windows with XAMPP, it is C:\Program Files\XAMPP\htdocs; and on Linux, it can be any number of places, depending on where the Web server has been installed, such as /srv/www/htdocs/.

It is important that you put the MediaWiki folder in the document root folder and change the name from mediawiki-1.9.3 to something simple like w (this is because it will make it easier to configure Apache to support shorter URLs, which are demonstrated later in the chapter). With this done, the path to the MediaWiki installation on OS X would be /Library/WebServer/Documents/w/, and so on.

Directory Structure

At this point, it is instructive to look inside the MediaWiki folder to see how the code is organized. Following are the list directories and PHP files inside the mediawiki-1.9.3 directory:

```
-rw-r--r--     1 mchoate   admin     825 Feb 20 21:20 AdminSettings.sample
-rw-r--r--     1 mchoate   admin     605 Feb 20 21:20 StartProfiler.php
-rw-r--r--     1 mchoate   admin    1316 Feb 20 21:20 api.php
drwxr-xr-x     4 mchoate   admin     136 Feb 20 21:20 bin
drwxrwxrwx     3 mchoate   admin     102 Feb 20 21:20 config
drwxr-xr-x    22 mchoate   admin     748 Feb 20 21:20 docs
drwxr-xr-x     3 mchoate   admin     102 Feb 20 21:20 extensions
drwxr-xr-x     3 mchoate   admin     102 Feb 20 21:20 images
-rw-r--r--     1 mchoate   admin    1978 Feb 20 21:20 img_auth.php
drwxr-xr-x   187 mchoate   admin    6358 Feb 20 21:20 includes
-rw-r--r--     1 mchoate   admin    1756 Feb 20 21:20 index.php
-rw-r--r--     1 mchoate   admin    3899 Feb 20 21:20 install-utils.inc
drwxr-xr-x     8 mchoate   admin     272 Feb 20 21:20 languages
drwxr-xr-x     3 mchoate   admin     102 Feb 20 21:20 locale
drwxr-xr-x   138 mchoate   admin    4692 Feb 20 21:20 maintenance
drwxr-xr-x    23 mchoate   admin     782 Feb 20 21:20 math
-rw-r--r--     1 mchoate   admin    1532 Feb 20 21:20 opensearch_desc.php
-rw-r--r--     1 mchoate   admin    6173 Feb 20 21:20 profileinfo.php
-rw-r--r--     1 mchoate   admin     319 Feb 20 21:20 redirect.php
-rw-r--r--     1 mchoate   admin      91 Feb 20 21:20 redirect.phtml
drwxr-xr-x     7 mchoate   admin     238 Feb 20 21:20 serialized
drwxr-xr-x    22 mchoate   admin     748 Feb 20 21:20 skins
drwxr-xr-x    18 mchoate   admin     612 Feb 20 21:20 tests
-rw-r--r--     1 mchoate   admin    2408 Feb 20 21:20 thumb.php
-rw-r--r--     1 mchoate   admin    1384 Feb 20 21:20 trackback.php
-rw-r--r--     1 mchoate   admin      88 Feb 20 21:20 wiki.phtml
```

In order to complete the installation, you need to access MediaWiki through your Web browser, but before you can do that you need to make MediaWiki's config directory writeable by the Apache server prior to running the Web-based installation. In this case, you can make the directory world writeable by typing the following:

```
$ chmod 777 config
```

Installing Through the Web

In order to load the installation script, you need to make sure your Apache server is running, as well as MySQL (or Postgres). If both are working, then you will see the page shown in Figure 2-1 when you type in the address of http://localhost/w/ (remember that we renamed the MediaWiki directory from mediawiki-1.9.3 to w).

Figure 2-1: The start page of MediaWiki's installation script

If all goes well when you do this, you will be redirected to http://localhost/w/config/index.php. If something goes wrong, it's probably because you forgot to make the config directory writeable by the Web server. MediaWiki will cordially inform you of your error and ask that you fix it and try again. The reason why config needs to be writeable is that during the installation, a file called LocalSettings.php will be created inside the config directory. Once the installation is complete, you need to copy LocalSettings.php from the config directory into the main MediaWiki directory. At that point, you can delete the config directory, or change permissions so that it is no longer world writeable.

Ideally, after the installation is complete you will change ownership of LocalSettings.php to the user who runs the Web server (oftentimes, it's nobody). Then enter **chmod 600 LocalSettings.php** in the command line, so that prying eyes can't see it.

If you get partway through the installation process and decide to start over again, you need to ensure that LocalSettings.php has been deleted from the config directory. As long as MediaWiki sees it, MediaWiki assumes that the installation has been completed.

If all goes well (and it usually does), then you will see the installation page, shown in Figure 2-2.

The top of the page outlines what it has found out about your system and whether you are able to finish the install:

```
apache 2 installation results:
PHP 5.2.1 installed
Found database drivers for: MySQL PostgreSQL
PHP server API is apache2handler; ok, using pretty URLs (index.php/Page_Title)
Have XML / Latin1-UTF-8 conversion support.
PHP's memory_limit is 128M. If this is too low, installation may fail!
Have zlib support; enabling output compression.
Couldn't find Turck MMCache, eAccelerator or APC. Object caching functions
    cannot be used.
Found GNU diff3: /usr/bin/diff3.
```

```
Found GD graphics library built-in, image thumbnailing will be enabled if you
    enable uploads.
Installation directory: /apache2/htdocs
Script URI path:
Environment checked. You can install MediaWiki.
```

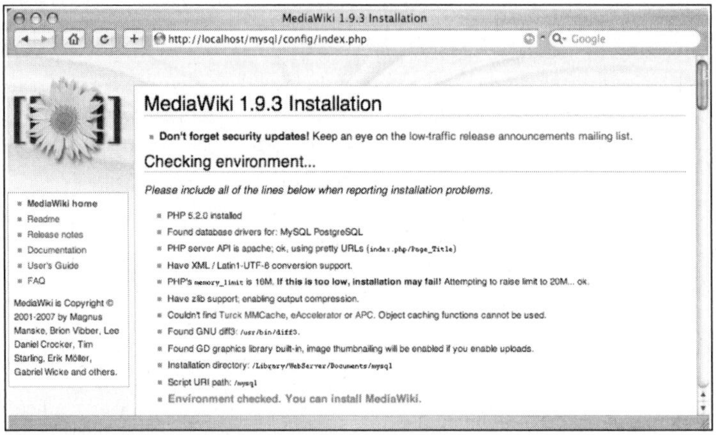

Figure 2-2: The results of executing MediaWiki's installation script

Farther down on the page, it is divided into a few different sections where you are prompted for some basic configuration information.

Site Configuration

The site configuration section of the installation script is shown in Figure 2-3.

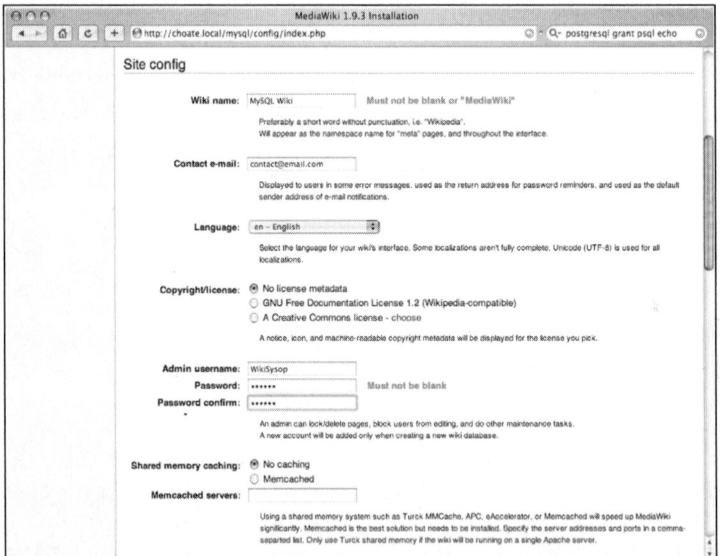

Figure 2-3: The configuration section of MediaWiki's installation script

In this section, you need to enter the name of your wiki (this example is called "MySQL Wiki" because it is a test installation that will run using the MySQL database). Then, you enter a contact e-mail address. This is the e-mail address that is used in error messages, and as the sender of password reminders and other e-mail notifications. You should create an e-mail address to be used exclusively for this purpose. Next, you select the language to use in the wiki. In this case, it is English (en – English).

The next option deserves some consideration. MediaWiki gives you the opportunity to select a license for your content. (You can read more about licensing options for your content in the "Page Metadata" section of Chapter 6.) You are also given the option of including no license metadata, which means that the license defaults to traditional copyright regulations. Due to the nature of wikis and the fact that many people post to them and more than one person can be responsible for an article, selecting one of the other two alternatives is a good idea (if you are a public-facing website, at least). The GNU Free Documentation License 1.2 is used by Wikipedia.

This excerpt from the GNU Free Documentation License, posted at `www.gnu.org/licenses/fdl.txt`, provides a good summary:

> *"The purpose of this License is to make a manual, textbook, or other functional and useful document 'free' in the sense of freedom: to assure everyone the effective freedom to copy and redistribute it, with or without modifying it, either commercially or noncommercially. Secondarily, this License preserves for the author and publisher a way to get credit for their work, while not being considered responsible for modifications made by others.*
>
> *This License is a kind of 'copyleft', which means that derivative works of the document must themselves be free in the same sense. It complements the GNU General Public License, which is a copyleft license designed for free software."*

Choosing a Creative Commons license gives you more flexibility over the rights you keep and give away. You can fill out a questionnaire at `http://creativecommons.org/license` to help you decide which license you would like to offer.

Next, you need to select the name and password of the site's administrator. You can choose whatever password you want for the wikisysop, but be sure to keep a copy of the password!

The next section is for configuring shared memory caching. For now, leave this option off. While caching is very useful on production sites, it can be a hassle when you are developing a new site, but changes that you make aren't automatically reflected in the site. Caching is discussed in more detail in Chapter 11, and you will learn how to set it up at that time.

E-mail Notification and Authentication Setup

The notification and authentication setup section, shown in Figure 2-4, gathers information about how e-mail should be used. The selections are self-explanatory, but pay attention to e-mail address authentication, which means that when new users sign up, they have to provide their e-mail address. The system then e-mails the users at the e-mail addresses they gave when they signed up, and they are asked to confirm their registration. Only after confirming their registration are users allowed to edit pages. (More information about setting access permissions for users can be found in Chapter 6.) If you use a public-facing wiki on which people "off the street" can sign up, it's a very good idea to keep this enabled.

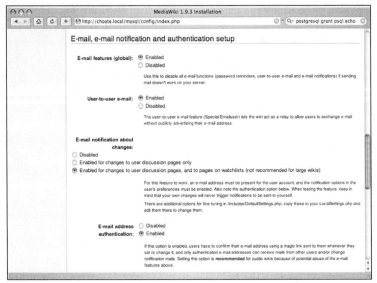

Figure 2-4: E-mail notification and authentication configuration

Selecting a Database

If you have access to the MySQL superuser (root, by default), then the MediaWiki installation script can create the necessary database and users for you. In the Database Config section on the same page, you are given the option to select MySQL or Postgres for your wiki's database. Select the MySQL radio button, as shown in Figure 2-5.

Next, you are asked to enter the database host. If the database is being hosted on the same server as MediaWiki itself, then you can enter `localhost`. If MySQL is being hosted on a different database, which will likely be the case if you run a very active wiki, then you would enter the appropriate host in that field.

The form will have wikidb pre-filled for the database name, and wikiuser for the database user's name that will be used to access the wikidb database. These names can be changed if you'd like. After the name are two blank fields for you to enter the password twice (just in case). Further down is a checkbox that you should select if you have access to the superuser account on MySQL. The example that follows indicates that you do have access to it, so you can select it and enter the superuser name (there's no password on the default installation — this should be changed in a production setting). You can, of course, have a different superuser name and password if MySQL has been configured that way.

There are a few other items to configure and then you'll be able to complete the installation. First, you are asked to provide a prefix for the database tables. This is a good idea because it will enable you to run more than one wiki out of the same database. In this example, the tables are prefixed with mw_. Then, when asked what charset to use, choose the default, utf-8.

If you do not have access to the MySQL superuser (if you are using a hosting service, for example), then you need to have a username and password already created. If that's the case, then enter your username and password in place of "wikiuser." If you do not have privileges to create a database, then you will need to use the database you already have, so enter that information into the database field.

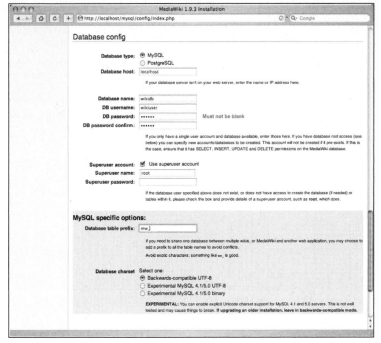

Figure 2-5: Database configuration for MediaWiki

The important things to remember at this stage are as follows:

❑   You can choose any name you would like for the database, even though the default is wikidb. If you have a pre-existing database that you want to use, then you can enter the name of that database into the name field.

❑   The database user, wikiuser, can be named anything you'd like. If you have already created a user in the database that you intend to use, then you should enter that user's name and password instead of wikiuser.

❑   The only time you need to select the superuser checkbox is when you do not already have a database and user already created and you know the username and password of a superuser. On the default MySQL installation, a superuser called "root" is installed; and, by default, there is no password for this user, so the Password field is left blank. This is a pretty big security hole, so you should assign a password to the user as soon as you can. If there is a password, then you obviously need to enter the password into the Password field.

If you have decided to use Postgres, then you need to check the Postgres radio button, and then fill out the fields according to the database and username you created earlier. Do not select the superuser checkbox, even if you know the superuser name and password — you do not need to use it because you have already created everything you need.

Once the configuration process is completed, a file called LocalSettings.php is created in the config directory. This file needs to be moved into the base directory for the installation, and the permissions need to be set so that only the Web server can read it (chmod 400 for Unix-like systems). The config directory can then be deleted and the site accessed from the primary URL. Figure 2-6 shows the front page of a freshly installed wiki.

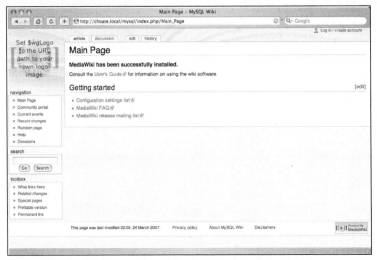

Figure 2-6: The front page of a wiki after a successful installation

Configuring Short URLs

You need to make quite a few customizations once MediaWiki is installed. Most of those are discussed in subsequent chapters, but there is one such customization that most people want to change immediately, which is configuring Apache to use shorter URLs.

When using Apache, the URL for the main page (aptly called Main_Page) is `http://mysite.tld/mediawiki/index.php/Main_Page`. If you happen to run under CGI or FastCGI, then the URL is even longer, `http://mysite.tld/mediawiki/index.php?title=Main_Page`. There is also a chance that the URL will look like this when you are running Apache. If it does, that's because the `AcceptPathInfo` directive is set to "off." It is normally set to "on" by default, so it is unlikely that you will encounter this, but if you do, then enter the following in `httpd.conf` or in an .htaccess file:

```
AcceptPathInfo On
```

Many people want to get rid of the `index.php` in the middle of the URL because it's not really useful and makes the URL longer than it needs to be. There is a lot of confusion about how this should work, but it's fairly straightforward once you understand the relationship between the variables in the `LocalSettings.php` file and the directives used by Apache.

Using the `Alias` directive in Apache is the easiest way to dispense with the "index.php." In the following example, the /wiki path is mapped to /Library/WebServer/Documents/pg/index.php, which is where one of my WikiMedia installations is located. Pay special attention to the absence of "/" at the end of /wiki. That's a requirement. A second path, /index.php, is also mapped to the same index.php file:

```
Alias /wiki /Library/WebServer/Documents/pg/index.php
Alias /index.php /Library/WebServer/Documents/pg/index.php
```

In order for this to work, you need to have the `$wgArticlePath` variable defined in `LocalSettings.php`:

```
## This variable determines who MediaWiki builds links to
## articles from other articles. This pattern must correspond
## with the RewriteRule.
$wgArticlePath          = ''/wiki/$1'';
```

This tells MediaWiki to use the path `/wiki/Article_Name` when generating links to articles within MediaWiki. Then, if one of these links is clicked, Apache handles the request and substitutes `/Library /WebServer/Documents/pg/index.php` for `/wiki` (using the full path from the system, rather than just the request path).

The problem with using `Alias` is that you cannot use it in a `.htaccess` file, and many users do not have access to `httpd.conf`. Another approach is to use Apache's `Mod_Rewrite`, which uses regular expressions to map URLs to items in the underlying file system. It's similar to `Alias` but much more flexible, and, as a consequence, much more complicated. In the end, though, it's the better route to take.

One reason for using `Mod_Rewrite` is that it can be used in .htaccess files. However, unless you truly need to use .htaccess files, you shouldn't, because they slow things down considerably. If you have access to `httpd.conf`, then you can use `Mod_Rewrite` there.

If you are using virtual hosting in Apache, then you can put the `RewriteRule` directive in `<Virtual>`; otherwise, you can put it anywhere in the configuration file.

You need to change the `LocalSettings.php` file, in either the `httpd.conf` file for Apache, or create a .htaccess file in the doc root of your Apache installation:

```
RewriteEngine on
RewriteRule ^/wiki/?(.*)$ /w/index.php?title=$1 [L,QSA]
```

`LocalSettings.php` should be configured in this way:

```
$wgSitename             = ''MySQL Wiki'';

## The URL base path to the directory containing the wiki;
## defaults for all runtime URL paths are based off of this.
$wgScriptPath           = ''/w'';
$wgScript               = ''$wgScriptPath/index.php'';
$wgRedirectScript       = ''$wgScriptPath/redirect.php'';

## This variable determines who MediaWiki builds links to
## articles from other articles. This pattern must correspond
## with the RewriteRule.
$wgArticlePath          = ''/wiki/$1'';
```

The `RewriteRule` directive takes the path as defined in `$wgArticlePath` and maps it internally to the actual URL, making the URL `http://mysite.tld/wiki/Main&uscore;Page` effectively the same as if you had called `http://mysite.tld/pg/index.php?title=Main_Page`.

You can put the `RewriteRule` into a .htaccess file, but when you do, it needs to be in the top-level directory or the doc root of your Apache implementation.

Summary

This chapter covered how to install MediaWiki. By this time, you should be able to get MediaWiki up and running with an Apache Web server. Now, with MediaWiki installed, it's time to take a look at the ins and outs of using MediaWiki software. In the next chapter, you'll learn MediaWiki terminology and find a user's guide to MediaWiki, detailing information about user accounts, how to create and edit pages, and more.

3

Getting Started with MediaWiki

In the previous chapter, you learned how to set up the Web servers and PHP implementations necessary to run MediaWiki. In this chapter, you will learn about the basic configuration options for MediaWiki, and get a general overview of how the software works "out of the box." Many of the topics touched on lightly in this chapter are handled in much greater depth in subsequent chapters. When appropriate, cross-references are provided directing you to the chapter of the book that covers a given topic so that you can jump directly to it if you are particularly eager to learn more.

The authors of MediaWiki are unabashed in their commitment to develop MediaWiki primarily for Wikipedia. The fact that others can also make use of it is an added bonus, and certainly a "nice-to-have," but at the end of the day it's not their primary goal. Despite this, the developers have been generous by making MediaWiki highly configurable. You can customize a great deal of your wiki without doing any kind of programming other than changing the values of a few variables.

Much of this chapter serves as an introduction to how MediaWiki is organized. In addition to covering the basic features of the software, it also describes how to customize those features when appropriate. You should have a fresh, virgin wiki at your disposal to experiment with. In some instances, it may be most useful to look at an actively maintained wiki to see how a certain feature works; and in those instances you'll see examples in Wikipedia. In other cases, examples are based on the newly minted wiki installed in the previous chapter, in case you want to follow along and perform the tasks yourself.

The MediaWiki Application

Before you get too far along, you'll first get a brief outline of how the code is organized. Wiki features will be accompanied by examples of actual wikis to show you how the features work from the users' perspective, and you will learn where you can find the source code, too, if you'd like to go ahead and take a look at that. You will also become familiar with some of the basic debugging configuration options you have, which are turned off by default. This way, you can log your activity as you go and more easily see what's happened in the code.

Code Organization

The primary script that is executed with each request is index.php, which can be found in the root directory of your installation. Alongside index.php are some additional directories that house the code used to run and support MediaWiki.

The following directories are inside the installation directory and contain scripts or data that support the application:

- ❑ bin/: This folder contains a couple of shell scripts that are executed by MediaWiki. There's no reason to modify these; but for the curious, they are executed by the global function wfShellExec (see "Global Functions," the next section).

- ❑ docs/: Some incomplete documentation is available in this directory. If you have doxygen installed, then you can generate MediaWiki code documentation (the same documentation is available online at MediaWiki).

- ❑ extensions/: Code written for MediaWiki but not part of the core MediaWiki distribution is stored here.

- ❑ images/: This directory is intended for user image uploads, if you have enabled that feature in MediaWiki. All images related to the user interface are in the skins/commons/ images directory.

- ❑ includes/: The bulk of the code that runs MediaWiki is in the includes folder.

- ❑ languages/: Inside the languages folder is Language.php, which contains the PHP code for the Language class. The Language class manages the translation of all the text produced by MediaWiki into the appropriate language. There are two subfolders: classes and messages. The classes folder contains a subclass of Language for each language supported by MediaWiki. In the messages folder are the system messages for each language. $wgLang is a global instance of the Language class.

- ❑ maintenance/: The maintenance folder contains a host of PHP scripts that are executed from the command line and that support miscellaneous maintenance and testing functions needed to run a wiki. More details about maintenance scripts can be found in Chapter 11.

- ❑ math/: Information about handling math can be found in Chapter 4, "Writing and Editing Content."

- ❑ skins/: Skins contain all the files responsible for expressing the MediaWiki look and feel, and include PHP files, cascading stylesheets (CSS), images, and JavaScript. All the glorious details are covered in Chapter 8, "Magic Words, Templates, and Skins."

Global Functions

GlobalFunctions.php can be found inside the includes/ folder. This PHP document contains a number of global functions that can be helpful for development and debugging. MediaWiki uses a naming convention to help identify global functions in code. In almost every case, the name of a global function begins with the letters `wf`. For example, the two debugging functions discussed later in this chapter are called `wfDebug` and `wfDebugLog`.

Global Variables

MediaWiki supplies a number of global variables as well. They are defined in a few different locations and are discussed in more detail in the "Settings" section later in this chapter. MediaWiki uses a naming convention for global variables as well. Each variable starts with `$wg`. The variable that represents the user object is `$wgUser`, and the variable that represents a title is `$wgTitle`.

Architecture

The architecture of MediaWiki is driven in large part by the idiosyncrasies of PHP. When MediaWiki was first developed, it used PHP 4.x, which lacked much in the way of object-oriented programming features. As of July 7, 2006, MediaWiki 1.7 was released, and it was the first version to require PHP 5.0 or better. With the adoption of PHP 5.x, and its much more robust and complete object-oriented approach, the developers have begun to migrate the core code into an object-oriented paradigm. At this time, the move is not complete. As a consequence, you need to use a lot of global variables and functions. This transitional state of affairs can sometimes make some of the code a little baffling at first, but the learning curve isn't especially steep compared with other frameworks you may have worked with.

MediaWiki is highly customizable through a variety of mechanisms, including numerous global variables (over 300 of them, I understand, although I haven't actually counted them myself) that can be tweaked to modify this or that behavior, and you can also extend MediaWiki's functionality through extensions and hooks. In addition, it includes a robust templating system that you can extend as well. All of these features are discussed at length in subsequent chapters.

Customizing the Installation

When MediaWiki is first installed, you are prompted to make a few configuration decisions to get you started. These are only a few of the literally hundreds of configuration variables that can be modified in some form or other. While some items can be configured through a Web form, the vast majority of configuration is done in the PHP code itself. At this point, no strong coding skills are necessary, but it is helpful if you have a basic understanding of how programming works. The configuration items are stored in global variables, and the task of customizing the configuration involves changing the values that are assigned to those variables.

With each request, the `index.php` script is accessed. One of the first things this script does is include the `WebStart.php` script, which is found at `includes/WebStart.php`. When this script is executed (scripts are executed when loaded), it in turn loads `includes/Defines.php` and `LocalSettings.php`. `LocalSettings.php` is the file that is generated when MediaWiki is first installed, and it contains the basic configuration items that were selected during the installation process.

Settings

In practice, configuration settings are scattered throughout the code, but the following files are primarily responsible for managing the configuration of MediaWiki.

All of your custom settings should be used in the `LocalSettings.php` file. You can look in `DefaultSettings.php` to see what is available and read the documentation that's there, but then copy them into `LocalSettings.php` before you change them. When you upgrade to the next version of MediaWiki, you will not lose your customizations this way, as the upgrade process won't overwrite the `LocalSettings.php` file.

- ❑ `Defines.php`: All of the MediaWiki constants are defined in this file.

- ❑ `LocalSettings.php`: This is the file that was created when you configured MediaWiki through the Web browser.

- ❑ `DefaultSettings.php`: All of the configurable variables are located here. If you want to change the values of an item listed here, add it to the `LocalSettings.php` file and make your change there. You should never edit `DefaultSettings.php` because it will be overwritten when you install an upgrade.

- ❑ `Setup.php`: This script is responsible for defining the global variables based upon what is defined in `LocalSettings.php`, and, if not defined there, then in `DefaultSettings.php`.

The file `DefaultSettings.php` contains the default values for MediaWiki. Some values are defined in `Setup.php`. When `Setup.php` executes, it checks to see whether the values of these variables are false. If they are not, then it assumes that new values have been set and uses them. Otherwise, it uses the hard-coded values in the code itself. I really don't understand why the developers didn't just put the default values in `DefaultSettings.php` instead of using this false check. It's as if they went out of their way to preserve hard-coded default values.

LocalSettings.php

It is worthwhile at this point to examine the `LocalSettings.php` file to see how the configuration choices made during the installation are manifest in the code. Once you've reviewed that, you will learn how to make specific customizations by turning on debugging and profiling for MediaWiki.

The following code listing is a sample of the contents of the `LocalSettings.php` file that was automatically generated during the installation process. If you are not familiar with PHP programming, the primary thing to pay attention to is the global variables. In PHP, all variables start with $; and by convention, all MediaWiki global variables are prefixed with `wg`. As a consequence, the global variable that represents the site's name is `$wgSitename`, and so on.

In addition to the comments that are already in the document, additional comments are inserted in the code to offer further explanation about what is going on. One important thing to note is that `LocalSettings.php` includes `DefaultSettings.php` prior to making modifications to any global variable. This is because the global variables are defined in `DefaultSettings.php`, along with their default value, so the assignment that takes place in `LocalSettings.php` needs to take place after the assignment in `DefaultSettings.php`, because the last assignment made will be the official assignment used by the application. Here is the automatically generated file:

```php
<?php

# This file was automatically generated by the MediaWiki installer.
# If you make manual changes, please keep track in case you need to
# recreate them later.
#
# See includes/DefaultSettings.php for all configurable settings
```

```
# and their default values, but don't forget to make changes in _this_
# file, not there.

# If you customize your file layout, set $IP to the directory that contains
# the other MediaWiki files. It will be used as a base to locate files.
if( defined( 'MW_INSTALL_PATH' ) ) {
 $IP = MW_INSTALL_PATH;
} else {
 $IP = dirname( __FILE__ );
}

$path = array( $IP, "$IP/includes", "$IP/languages" );
set_include_path( implode( PATH_SEPARATOR, $path ) .
   PATH_SEPARATOR . get_include_path() );
```

The `DefaultSettings.php` script contains the default values for the site settings. It is loaded first, so any global variables that are assigned in this document overwrite the values defined in `DefaultSettings.php`:

```
require_once( "includes/DefaultSettings.php" );
```

Normally, the following line is enabled, but I have disabled it because compressing the output was causing errors in Safari and Firefox on Macintosh OS X when trying to use the `profileinfo.php` file. See the section "Profiling" later in this chapter for more details.

```
# If PHP's memory limit is very low, some operations may fail.
ini_set( 'memory_limit', '20M' );

if ( $wgCommandLineMode ) {
 if ( isset( $_SERVER ) && array_key_exists( 'REQUEST_METHOD', $_SERVER ) ) {
        die( "This script must be run from the command line\n" );
 }
} elseif ( empty( $wgNoOutputBuffer ) ) {
 ## Compress output if the browser supports it


#if( !ini_get( 'zlib.output_compression' ) ) @ob_start( 'ob_gzhandler' );
}


$wgSitename = "ProfWikis - MySQL";

## The URL base path to the directory containing the wiki;
## defaults for all runtime URL paths are based off of this.
```

During the installation process in this example, MediaWiki was installed in a directory called w. Obviously, this value will vary depending on where you decided to install MediaWiki. Note that this path is relative to the document root of your Web server installation. For this example, the full file path would be `/Library/WebServer/Documents/w`:

```
$wgScriptPath     = "/w";

## For more information on customizing the URLs please see:
## http://www.mediawiki.org/wiki/Manual:Short_URL
```

When MediaWiki was originally installed for this example, no emergency contact e-mail address was assigned, nor was an address provided to use as the sender when password reminders are e-mailed:

```
$wgEnableEmail      = true;
$wgEnableUserEmail  = true;

$wgEmergencyContact = "[no address given]";
$wgPasswordSender   = "[no address given]";
```

These values can now be manually changed to whatever you choose. For example, the emergency contact variable could be set as follows:

```
$wgEmergencyContact = "fakeaddress@choate.info"
```

The next values determine how and when the user receives e-mail notification. The details of this process are discussed in more detail later in this chapter in the "Preferences" section.

```
## For a detailed description of the following switches see
## http://meta.wikimedia.org/Enotif and http://meta.wikimedia.org/Eauthent
## There are many more options for fine tuning available see
## /includes/DefaultSettings.php
## UPO means: this is also a user preference option

$wgEnotifUserTalk = true; # UPO
$wgEnotifWatchlist = true; # UPO
$wgEmailAuthentication = true;

$wgDBtype           = "mysql";
$wgDBserver         = "localhost";
$wgDBname           = "wikidb";
$wgDBuser           = "wikiuser";
$wgDBpassword       = "password";
$wgDBport           = "5432";
$wgDBprefix         = "profwiki_";

# Schemas for Postgres
# These are only meaningful if you are running
# Postgres for your database.
$wgDBmwschema       = "mediawiki";
$wgDBts2schema      = "public";

# Experimental charset support for MySQL 4.1/5.0.
$wgDBmysql5 = false;
```

```
## Shared memory settings
```

> **Chapter 11 contains more information about caching issues.**

Initially, you should probably not have memcached *installed because caching can make it more difficult to see changes that you've made in your site right away (because the page is cached). When the wiki is ready to go live, caching is usually a good idea.*

```
$wgMainCacheType = CACHE_NONE;
$wgMemCachedServers = array();

## To enable image uploads, make sure the 'images' directory
## is writable, then set this to true:
```

Information about uploaded images is available in Chapter 6, "Page Actions and Version Control." For now, it is disabled.

```
$wgEnableUploads      = false;
$wgUseImageResize     = true;
```

During the initial installation process, the ImageMagick libraries were not installed and ImageMagick is not being used for image processing. However, if it were installed, you could use ImageMagick, rather than PHP's GD graphics library, for creating thumbnails. Some users think the quality of ImageMagick is better. If you change your mind, you can simply uncomment the following lines, making sure you have updated the path to reflect where the convert application was actually installed:

```
# $wgUseImageMagick = true;
# $wgImageMagickConvertCommand = "/sw/bin/convert";

## If you want to use image uploads under safe mode,
## create the directories images/archive, images/thumb and
## images/temp, and make them all writable. Then uncomment
## this, if it's not already uncommented:
# $wgHashedUploadDirectory = false;

## If you have the appropriate support software installed
## you can enable inline LaTeX equations:
$wgUseTeX = false;

$wgLocalInterwiki = $wgSitename;

$wgLanguageCode = "en";

$wgProxyKey = "40a245133b5843c54ca98e48659914c8811aedaf72548699843e8e9e2f90ba24";

## Default skin: you can change the default skin. Use the internal symbolic
## names, ie 'standard', 'nostalgia', 'cologneblue', 'monobook':
$wgDefaultSkin = 'monobook';
```

For more information on copyright issues, see Chapter 6, "Page Actions and Version Control."

The next passage in the LocalSettings.php file documents the licensing information you selected when installing MediaWiki. In the basic installation, I did not specify any rights. You will learn how to change this configuration in Chapter 6.

```
## For attaching licensing metadata to pages, and displaying an
## appropriate copyright notice / icon. GNU Free Documentation
## License and Creative Commons licenses are supported so far.

# $wgEnableCreativeCommonsRdf = true;
```

```
$wgRightsPage = ""; # Set to the title of a wiki page that
    describes your license/copyright
$wgRightsUrl = "";
$wgRightsText = "";
$wgRightsIcon = "";
# $wgRightsCode = ""; # Not yet used
```

The next section shows the configuration of $wgDiff3. This variable represents the application that is used to identify the differences between different versions of a file. For Unix-like systems, the default is diff3, which is typically installed in /usr/bin/diff3. You can use a different diff application if you choose.

```
$wgDiff3 = "/usr/bin/diff3";
```

Finally, you can configure LocalSettings.php so that whenever it is changed, cached pages will be purged, so the changes will be reflected immediately in the site:

```
# When you make changes to this configuration file, this will make
# sure that cached pages are cleared.
$configdate = gmdate( 'YmdHis', @filemtime( __FILE__ ) );
$wgCacheEpoch = max( $wgCacheEpoch, $configdate );
```

Debugging

MediaWiki provides debugging tools to help you develop customized extensions. They can also be helpful when learning how to use and program for MediaWiki.

The variables and comments in LocalSettings.php came from DefaultSettings.php, with additional comments for clarification.

The log file needs to be in a place that is accessible by PHP, which means it needs to be in the Web server's document root. In order to protect it, you should either password-protect the directory or configure Apache (or your Web server of choice) so that it will not return files that end in .log (or whatever you decided to call it):

```
## The debug log file should be not be publicly accessible if it is used, as
## it may contain private data.
$wgDebugLogFile     = '/Library/WebServer/Documents/mediawiki.log';
```

Redirects are files that point to other files so that when you request a page, you are automatically redirected (or switched) to a different page. This is often used to map synonyms to a common page. When the following value is set to true, then the redirect is interrupted and you will encounter a page that shows where the redirect is pointing:

```
$wgDebugRedirects     = true;
```

For example, with this value set, you get the following notification when you go to http://127.0.0.1/wiki:

```
Location: http://choate.local/wiki/index.php/Main_Page
```

This indicates that you are being redirected to the Main Page of my wiki.

When $wgDebugRawPage is set to true, MediaWiki will track debugging information for raw pages as well:

```
$wgDebugRawPage        = true;
```

Raw pages are generated by using the following URL:

```
http://127.0.0.1/wiki/index.php/Main_Page?action=raw
```

This is an example of an *action*, which is discussed later in this chapter. A raw page contains the wikitext content for a page and none of the HTML, including navigation elements.

Several globals can be set to log various SQL-related issues:

```
/**
 * Write SQL queries to the debug log
 */
$wgDebugDumpSql        = true;
$wgLogQueries          = true;
```

The next SQL-related variable determines whether SQL errors are displayed in the Web browser when they occur. This can be helpful in debugging, but is probably not such a good idea on a live site:

```
$wgShowSQLErrors       = true;
```

You can also tell MediaWiki how much information to send to the log. The following variable can be set to send the complete stack trace to output whenever an uncaught exception occurs:

```
## If set to true, uncaught exceptions will print a complete stack trace
## to output. This should only be used for debugging, as it may reveal
## private information in function parameters due to PHP's backtrace
## formatting.

$wgShowExceptionDetails = true;
```

When the following variable is set to true, the debugging data will be displayed as a comment inside the HTML output of the page. Normally, you would set this value to true and the $wgDebugFile to false or vice versa. If the wiki is in a publicly available location, it is unwise to include debugging information inside the page.

```
$wgDebugComments       = true;
```

The following code listing is an example of the commented debugging output that is included in the page when $wgDebugComments is set to true. Note that this debugging log also includes SQL queries, as defined in the previous listing. The following sample debugging output is abbreviated in the interests of saving space, but it should give you an idea about the kind of information that is available:

```
<!-- Debug output:
Fully initialised
Unstubbing $wgContLang on call of $wgContLang-&gt;checkTitleEncoding from
  WebRequest::getGPCVal
```

```
Unstubbing $wgUser on call of $wgUser->isAllowed from Title::userCanRead
Cache miss for user 3
Unstubbing $wgLoadBalancer on call of $wgLoadBalancer->getConnection from wfGetDB
SQL: BEGIN
SQL: SELECT /* User::loadFromDatabase */ * FROM 'profwiki_user' WHERE user_id = '3'
    LIMIT 1
SQL: SELECT /* User::loadFromDatabase */ ug_group FROM 'profwiki_user_groups'
    WHERE ug_user = '3'
Logged in from session
SQL: SELECT /* Article::pageData */
    page_id,page_namespace,page_title,page_restrictions,page
    _counter,page_is_redirect,page_is_new,page_random,page_touched,
    page_latest,page_len FROM 'profwiki_page' WHERE
    page_namespace = '0' AND page_title = 'Main_Page'    LIMIT 1
Unstubbing $wgLang on call of $wgLang->getCode from User::getPageRenderingHash
OutputPage::checkLastModified: -- client send If-Modified-Since: Tue, 10 Apr 2007
    21:34:36 GMT
Unstubbing $wgMessageCache on call of $wgMessageCache-
    &gt;getTransform from wfMsgGetKey
SQL: SELECT /* MediaWikiBagOStuff::_doquery */ value,exptime
    FROM 'profwiki_objectcache' WHERE keyname='wikidb-profwiki_:messages-hash'
SQL: SELECT /* MediaWikiBagOStuff::_doquery */ value,exptime
    FROM 'profwiki_objectcache' WHERE keyname='wikidb-profwiki_:messages'
MessageCache::load(): got from global cache
Language::loadLocalisation(): got localisation for en from source
Unstubbing $wgParser on call of $wgParser->firstCallInit
    from MessageCache::transform
<output deleted>
-->
```

You can add to the debugging information that MediaWiki logs by using two different functions. Both are defined in includes/GlobalFunctions.php. The first is wfDebug:

```
function wfDebug( $text, $logonly = false )
```

You call it by passing it the message you want sent to the log:

```
wfDebug('this is my debugging info')
```

If the optional $logonly parameter is set to true, then the debug messages are only sent to the log file, and not to HTML comments, if $wgDebugComments is also set to true.

The second function is wfDebugLog:

```
function wfDebugLog( $logGroup, $text, $public = true )
```

You can call this function if you have also configured the $wgDebugLogGroups global variable. In order to use it, you set it to an array of log group keys that will be used for filenames. When set, wfDebugLog output for that group will go to that file instead of the regular $wgDebugLogFile.

```
## Set to an array of log group keys to filenames.
## If set, wfDebugLog() output for that group will go to that file instead
```

```
## of the regular $wgDebugLogFile. Useful for enabling selective logging
## in production.

$wgDebugLogGroups    = array();
```

If the optional `$public` parameter is `true`, then the text in `$text` will also be sent to `wfDebug`. Otherwise, the debugging information only goes into the defined `$logGroup`.

Profiling

This section explains how to configure profiling, which adds to the information that is logged by the debugging functions. The profiler tells you how long it takes to execute a given function, measured in microseconds (which is 1/1,000,000th of a second). This will help you identify the slow spots in your application. The act of profiling itself can exert a burden on the application, so some variables are available that enable you to limit what is profiled.

`$wgProfileLimit` enables you to log only function profile data for functions that take more than a certain number of seconds to execute. In the following sample `LocalSettings.php` file, the limit is set to 0.0, meaning that all the profile data will be logged:

```
#
# Profiling / debugging
#
# You have to create a 'profiling' table in your database before using
# profiling see maintenance/archives/patch-profiling.sql .
#
# To enable profiling, edit StartProfiler.php

/** Only record profiling info for pages that took longer than this */
$wgProfileLimit = 0.0;
/** Don't put non-profiling info into log file */
$wgProfileOnly = false;
/** Log sums from profiling into "profiling" table in db. */
$wgProfileToDatabase = true;
/** If true, print a raw call tree instead of per-function report */
$wgProfileCallTree = false;
/** Should application server host be put into profiling table */
$wgProfilePerHost = true;

/** Detects non-matching wfProfileIn/wfProfileOut calls */
$wgDebugProfiling = true;
/** Output debug message on every wfProfileIn/wfProfileOut */
$wgDebugFunctionEntry = 0;
```

You also need to update `StartProfiler.php`, which is in the top-level directory of MediaWiki. When a request is first made and `WebStart.php` is executing, it loads the `StartProfiler.php` script. By default, `StartProfiler.php` loads a stub object that doesn't do any actual profiling. You need to modify it so that it loads a real profiler.

In the following example, the code was changed to use the profiler found in `includes/ProfilerSimple.php`. This gives you the flexibility to develop a customized profiler, suited to your needs.

```
<?php

/*require_once( dirname(__FILE__).'/includes/ProfilerStub.php' );*/

/**
 * To use a profiler, delete the line above and add something like this:
 **/
require_once( dirname(__FILE__).'/includes/ProfilerSimple.php' );
$wgProfiler = new Profiler;



?>
```

If you want to have profiling data stored in a database, then you need to take a few more steps before profiling is enabled on the wiki. If you enable $wgProfileToDatabase, you need to first create a new table in your wiki database.

The SQL code can be found inside the MediaWiki installation directory in maintenance/archives/patch-profiling.sql:

```
-- profiling table
-- This is optional

CREATE TABLE /*$wgDBprefix*/profiling (
   pf_count int NOT NULL default 0,
   pf_time float NOT NULL default 0,
   pf_name varchar(255) NOT NULL default ",
   pf_server varchar(30) NOT NULL default ",
   UNIQUE KEY pf_name_server (pf_name, pf_server)
) TYPE=HEAP;
```

This table will be accessed by the profileinfo.php script, so you need to ensure that the table you create matches the table that profileinfo expects to be there. Remove the /*$wgDBprefix*/ string from the SQL statement because the profileinfo.php script does not expect a prefix on the name of the profiling table.

However, if you have multiple wikis running out of one database, then you may need to use the prefix (if you recall, you configured a prefix for the database when running the install script). If you do, then you need to manually update the SQL code in the profileinfo.php script, as well as the SQL. In the sample wiki set up for this book, the names of the tables use a prefix of profwikis_ (underscore). In the following snippet of code, you would need to change the line that reads FROM profiling to FROM profwikis_profiling:

```
$dbh = mysql_connect($wgDBserver, $wgDBadminuser, $wgDBadminpassword)
       or die("mysql server failed: " . mysql_error());
mysql_select_db($wgDBname, $dbh) or die(mysql_error($dbh));
$res = mysql_query("
      SELECT pf_count, pf_time, pf_name
      FROM profiling
      ORDER BY pf_name ASC
", $dbh) or die("query failed: " . mysql_error());
```

Finally, if you want to profile to the database, then you must also configure $wgProfileCallTree to false. Regardless of whether you are using the database, the profiling data is also written out to the debug log file, if that is configured.

The following listing is a snippet from the debugging log file, which includes profiling data. As you can see, it repeats the same information that's included in the HTML comments, but also includes the profiling data. $wgProfileCallTree is set to false (which is required to include this data in the database).

```
Profiling data
Name
    Calls         Total           Each              %
    Mem
-total
    1         459.062       459.062       100.000%    7329576
    (         459.062 -     459.062) [0]
MediaWiki::initialize
    1         239.825       239.825        52.242%    3493997
    (         239.825 -     239.825) [26]
Database::query
    6         232.231        38.705        50.588%       7296
    (           2.382 -     123.493) [8]
MediaWiki::finalCleanup
    1         152.069       152.069        33.126%      76571
    (         152.069 -     152.069) [11]
<deleted output>...
SQL: COMMIT
Request ended normally
```

PHP output is compressed by default and is configured in the LocalSettings.php file. There's usually no reason to change this, but in some instances the use of compressed output can cause problems (it makes Safari throw an error, for example) on pages that take a long time to create. During testing of MediaWiki, you can disable compression by commenting out the following:

```
## Compress output if the browser supports it
    #if( !ini_get( 'zlib.output_compression' ) ) @ob_start( 'ob_gzhandler'
```

Both Firefox and Safari on Macintosh were not able to display the output from the profileinfo.php script. Once you eliminate compression, you will be able to view the pages just fine.

Fresh Wiki

The best place to start is to visit a live wiki, and Wikipedia seems appropriate. In this section, Wikipedia will be the example used to illustrate the basic features of the software. Bear in mind that even though MediaWiki is made for Wikipedia, Wikipedia also uses customizations (called *extensions*) that are not turned on by default. They also use the bleeding-edge version (at the time of this writing, it's 1.10), so you may see things there that are not available in 1.9.3, or whatever the current version happens to be wherever and whenever you are reading this.

Wiki Pages

A wiki is made up of pages. MediaWiki uses several different kinds of pages in different situations. The key to understanding wiki pages is to understand how MediaWiki takes a page title and turns it into a URL. This is what you learn about in the following sections.

Creating Pages

Links can be created automatically in a wiki, just by wrapping a title in double brackets, like so:

```
This is my new [[link]]
```

When MediaWiki processes this page and converts it into HTML, it creates a link to a page called Link, regardless of whether that page exists. If the page doesn't exist, then the link will show up colored red (this can be changed, too, in stylesheets); otherwise, it will show up colored blue. If the page doesn't exist, then you can simply click on the red link and you will be taken to the editing form for the new Link page. You will go through all of this in more detail in the next chapter, but it is mentioned now so that you can see that links are commonly used within the text of a page. Therefore, you need to create titles that can be used naturally in that setting. That means keeping them simple and descriptive.

There are two ways for you to link to pages within MediaWiki. The first is with a wiki link. In that case, MediaWiki eventually converts the wiki link into a URL. You can also enter in a URL to create a link. In fact, if you type in a raw URL while editing a page, MediaWiki will automatically convert that URL to a link. Because of the way URLs are handled by Web browsers, certain limitations are placed on how titles are created.

Wiki Titles and URLs

The starting point for all wiki pages is the title. In MediaWiki, there is a `Title` class that is defined in `includes/Title.php`. An instance of this class is defined in the global variable `$wgTitle`. Titles are used to create URLs in MediaWiki, which places limitations on how titles are formed.

Title Rules

1. MediaWiki uses the UTF-8 encoding for all text, including titles.

2. Titles must be unique. Every document in MediaWiki has to have a unique title.

3. ASCII control character codes from 0 to 31 (hex 00 to 1F) and the delete character code 127 (hex 7F) are not allowed.

4. Character codes 128 to 255 (hex 80 to FF) are used in Latin-1 (by Windows) and are officially not part of the UTF-8 specification, but MediaWiki allows them to be used in titles, for compatibility reasons.

5. Titles must be less than or equal to 256 bytes. Remember that MediaWiki defaults to using UTF-8, so that does not mean 256 characters (some characters in UTF-8 require multiple bytes to represent them).

6. The following characters are not allowed and will generate an error. The reason is that they conflict with codes used by wikitext and MediaWiki's templating system:

```
# < > [ ] | { }
```

7. A space is converted to an underscore (_) when used in a URL.

8. You cannot use the title . or . . or start a title with . / or . . / because these have special meaning when dealing with file paths.

Title Suggestions

Some allowed characters cause problems in certain instances. Depending on the nature of your wiki, you may or may not want to avoid them altogether.

For example, / is OK as long as you are in a namespace that does not support subpages (by default, the main space does not support them). The primary problem with using it otherwise is that it is interpreted as a subpage, so that a/b means page b is a subpage of page a, which may or may not be what you intend.

In addition, if you link to a page whose title starts with / and that page is in a different namespace (namespaces are covered in more detail in the next section), then you need to either replace the slash with the HTML entity &#43 or prepend a ":" to the title.

Question marks and plus signs are problematic because they have a special meaning when used in URLs. The question mark represents the start of the query string, and the plus sign is interpreted as a space character in URLs when they appear in a URL after a question mark:

```
http://127.0.0.1/wiki/Main_Page?action=my+fake+action
```

The best example is the article for the programming language C++. The manner in which the + characters are treated depends on how the URL is formed. For example, if you are using rewrite rules in Apache to have short URLs, then the following URL will work just fine:

```
http://en.wikipedia.org/wiki/C++
```

If you are not using short URLs, then the equivalent MediaWiki URL will be as follows:

```
http://en.wikipedia.org/w/index.php?title=C++
```

In this case, because the + signs show up after a ?, they are interpreted as spaces by Web browsers and are dropped. Therefore, following this link will take you to the article about the C programming language, rather than C++ as expected.

If you use a wiki link, like [[C++]], MediaWiki will create a link to the following URL, using the percent encoded (also called URL encoded) form of the % character:

```
http://en.wikipedia.org/wiki/C%2B%2B
```

If you create a link for which you need to type in the actual URL, then you need to replace the plus signs with %2B yourself.

The same is true for using a question mark in a title. You should encode it as %3F in URLs. If you embed them in a wiki link, MediaWiki will convert it for you. In addition, note the following guidelines:

❑ Percentages aren't allowed if they are followed by two characters from a valid pair of hexadecimal digits (0 through 9 and A through F) because these represent entities (characters).

❑ You are allowed to use percent encoding in wiki links, but if you do so you cannot use the percent character in titles.

- ❑ You can use three or more colons (in interwiki links) in a title; however, avoid two or more colons, or one colon when the word preceding the colon is the same as a namespace.

- ❑ Using superscripts and subscripts in titles can be problematic (although you can use in wikitext markup.

Title Customizations

You can change the rules that determine what characters are allowed in titles. MediaWiki uses a regular expression to validate titles, and this expression can be overridden by setting a new value to the global variable $wgLegalTitleChars:

```
$wgLegalTitleChars = " %!\"$&'()*,\\-.\\/0-9:;=?@A-Z\\\\^_'a-z~\\x80-\\xFF+";
```

You can also modify the $wgCapitalLinks variable. It is true by default, which is why the first letter of all titles is converted to a capital letter when transformed into a link. Under normal circumstances, namespace prefixes are not case sensitive, nor are titles, except for the first letter (this is because MediaWiki capitalizes it when $wgCapitalLinks is set to true. The following two URLs go to the same page:

```
http://127.0.0.1/wiki/HeLP:Main_Page
http://127.0.0.1/wiki/Help:Main_Page
```

The next two URLs go to separate pages:

```
http://127.0.0.1/wiki/Help:Main_Page
http://127.0.0.1/wiki/Help:Main_page
```

The impact that setting $wgCapitalLinks has is modest, but important nevertheless. If set to true, then the first letter of the title is case sensitive (MediaWiki no longer changes the first character to uppercase). When set to true, the following two wiki links now point to two different files:

```
This is my [[link]] now, and this is my new [[Link]]
```

In addition to the technical restrictions regarding how titles are written, Wikipedia has also established detailed guidelines regarding how editors should create titles in Wikipedia. Of course, you can set whatever policy you'd like on your wiki, but they are good rules to follow because of the unique way in which wikis manage links.

You can find the most recent version of their style guide at http://en.wikipedia.org/wiki/Wikipedia:Manual_of_Style.

Page Types

MediaWiki uses several different page types. In order to review their individual features, it's helpful to have an example for demonstration purposes. The following sections refer to pages from MediaWiki to serve as examples. Keep in mind that MediaWiki is always changing, so the actual pages may be different by the time you read this. The page serving as our example is the page for Belgian Shepherd Dogs. While it's possible to go directly to the page by typing in the URL (can you guess what it would be?), you can also use the search field that is displayed on every Wikipedia page.

Finding Pages (Search)

Go to the English version of Wikipedia at en.wikipedia.org and type in **Belgian Shepherd Dog** in the search form. There are two buttons for the search: one labeled Go and the other labeled Search. The Go button interprets the information entered into the field as the title of a page, and will take you directly to the page if it exists. If it doesn't exist, then the results page will notify you that it doesn't exist, and then return any results you would have received had you pressed the Search button. The Search button does a full-text search on Wikipedia, looking for the phrase typed into the field.

Press Go and Wikipedia takes you to a page about Belgian Shepherd Dogs, with the following URL (see Figure 3-1):

```
http://en.wikipedia.org/wiki/Belgian_Shepherd_Dog
```

Figure 3-1: The Belgian Shepherd Dog article from Wikipedia

Article Pages

Across the top of the Wikipedia page are four tabs (keep in mind that some of the details described here may have changed by the time you read this): Article, Discussion, Edit This Page, and History. You will also see, at the upper-right corner, the link Sign in/Create Account, also shown in Figure 3-1.

The selected tab, Article, represents the page being viewed. The Discussion tab takes you to a page on which people talk about the article. This is used to separate conversations, or input, about the status of the page — ideas about changes to the page that can be engaged in without muddying up the page itself. If you click the Discussion tab, your browser will jump to the following URL:

```
http://en.wikipedia.org/wiki/Talk:Belgian_Shepherd_Dog
```

The only thing that has changed in this URL is that the characters `Talk:` have been prepended to the document title. Recall that different kinds of pages in MediaWiki are used in different ways, or offer distinct functionality. Page types are identified by namespace, and this is an example of a page in the Talk namespace. Any URL that does not contain a namespace is considered to be in the content namespace. This is where articles are found in MediaWiki. The simplest definition of an article is simply a page in the default namespace with at least one internal link (excluding redirects, which are discussed later in this chapter).

One of the primary functions of namespaces is to be able to differentiate between Wikipedia's content and content about Wikipedia. The Talk namespace was created to provide a channel for discussions about articles that appear on Wikipedia so that disagreements could be moved out of the article itself, and discussed on a separate page where (it is hoped) consensus can be reached.

If you click back to the Article tab to return to the article, and then click the Edit This Page tab, you will be taken to a page whose URL looks like this:

```
http://en.wikipedia.org/w/index.php?title=Belgian_Shepherd_Dog&action=edit
```

Note a few things about the preceding URL. First, notice how the path now looks different from the other path. Instead of `/wiki/Belgian_Shepherd_Dog`, it is now `/w/index.php?title = Belgian_Sheperd_Dog &action = edit`. In the previous chapter, you learned how to shorten the URL using rewrite rules in Apache, and this is exactly what Wikipedia has done. On article pages, you get a short URL, but not on other references to the same page. These other references are called *actions*, and in this case, requesting the "edit" action enables you to edit the page.

Whenever you call an action on Wikipedia, you will see the full URL, rather than the short one. It is possible to update these pages with rewrite rules as well, but it is not done as often as it is on the primary article page. This is because search engines such as Google tend to avoid indexing dynamic pages, which are identified by the ? in the URL. The advantage of using short URLs on the main article page is that the pages can be indexed on search engines. It is less likely that you will want to index action pages.

Pages in the Special namespace (known as Special pages) are pages that are dynamically produced. While there are all sorts of different Special pages, these tend to be pages that handle forms for user data entry, generate reports, perform searches, generate tables of links, and so on. One way to customize MediaWiki is to write your own Special page. You will learn how to do this in Chapter 9, "Extensions."

The basic organization you see on Wikipedia is the basic organization you will see when you first install MediaWiki. MediaWiki organizes the site into different kinds of content. The primary content type is the article, which is an item in the encyclopedia.

MediaWiki also has different kinds of pages, one of which is an article. MediaWiki describes an article as "a page in the main namespace, or a content namespace (see `$wgContentNamespaces`) that is not a redirect and contains at least one internal link."

The definition of the Content namespace is important, because it helps MediaWiki determine how content should be indexed. It separates the article content — the heart and soul of a wiki — from all the other kind of content that is also part of the larger system, such as user discussions, help, and so on.

Redirect Pages

If you were to type in "Belgian Sheepdog" instead of "Belgian Shepherd Dog" in the search form, you'd end up in the same place (eventually), and that's because MediaWiki employs pages it calls *redirects*, which are used for just this purpose, as many of the things written about in Wikipedia can be referred to by more than one name. You can find information about creating redirect pages in Chapter 6.

Disambiguation Pages

A relative of the redirect page, a disambiguation page serves a similar purpose, except that instead of dealing with the issue of multiple words with the same meaning, it handles the problem that occurs when a single word has multiple meanings. Disambiguation pages are like normal Wiki article pages, except the content is organized for the express purpose of shepherding users to the appropriate page, utilizing a few different kinds of templates. For more details, see the following URL:

    http://en.wikipedia.org/wiki/Wikipedia:Disambiguation

Namespaces

Wikis are organized into a flat hierarchy; they don't have sections and subsections. The reason for this is that flat hierarchies on sites and publications like dictionaries and encyclopedias are much easier to navigate. All you need to know is the basic URL structure and you can more or less guess the name of all of the articles on Wikipedia. This is good for finding articles, but not every page on Wikipedia is an article. Numerous other kinds of pages are required, such as help pages, for example.

MediaWiki organizes pages with the use of namespaces. You've already seen an example of the Talk namespace, but MediaWiki defines 15 namespaces, all of which have slightly different uses.

The constants are defined in `includes/Defines.php`:

```
/**#@+
 * Virtual namespaces; don't appear in the page database
 */
define('NS_MEDIA', -2);
define('NS_SPECIAL', -1);
/**#@-*/

/**#@+
 * Real namespaces
 *
 * Number 100 and beyond are reserved for custom namespaces;
 * DO NOT assign standard namespaces at 100 or beyond.
 * DO NOT Change integer values as they are most probably hardcoded everywhere
 * see bug #696 which talked about that.
 */
define('NS_MAIN', 0);
```

```
define('NS_TALK', 1);
define('NS_USER', 2);
define('NS_USER_TALK', 3);
define('NS_PROJECT', 4);
define('NS_PROJECT_TALK', 5);
define('NS_IMAGE', 6);
define('NS_IMAGE_TALK', 7);
define('NS_MEDIAWIKI', 8);
define('NS_MEDIAWIKI_TALK', 9);
define('NS_TEMPLATE', 10);
define('NS_TEMPLATE_TALK', 11);
define('NS_HELP', 12);
define('NS_HELP_TALK', 13);
define('NS_CATEGORY', 14);
define('NS_CATEGORY_TALK', 15);
```

In `includes/Namespace.php`, the constants are associated with text.

```
NS_MEDIA             => 'Media',
NS_SPECIAL           => 'Special',
NS_TALK              => 'Talk',
NS_USER              => 'User',
NS_USER_TALK         => 'User_talk',
NS_PROJECT           => 'Project', (ProfWikis - MySQL)
NS_PROJECT_TALK      => 'Project_talk', (ProfWikis - MySQL talk
NS_IMAGE             => 'Image',
NS_IMAGE_TALK        => 'Image_talk',
NS_MEDIAWIKI         => 'MediaWiki',
NS_MEDIAWIKI_TALK    => 'MediaWiki_talk',
NS_TEMPLATE          => 'Template',
NS_TEMPLATE_TALK     => 'Template_talk',
NS_HELP              => 'Help',
NS_HELP_TALK         => 'Help_talk',
NS_CATEGORY          => 'Category',
NS_CATEGORY_TALK     => 'Category_talk',
```

Category Namespace

Any page generated by MediaWiki can be assigned to one or more categories. Categories work like tags do on Flickr and other such sites. It's an example of a folksonomy. In other words, readers can define categories for different pages independently, however they see fit. The pages can then be organized and grouped by category, and you can browse category pages using the category namespace. Note the following about categories in MediaWiki:

❑ You can assign a page to any category you choose.

❑ You can assign as many categories to a page as you like.

❑ Categories are not pre-defined for you; you can type in whatever you want. Much like a link, linking to a category creates it.

Figure 3-2 shows the categories at the bottom of the Belgian Shepherd Dog page.

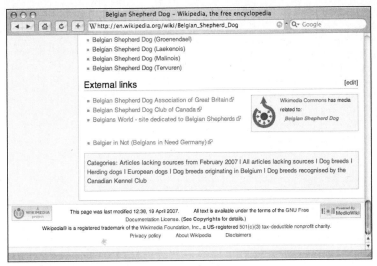

Figure 3-2: Belgian Shepherd Dog Categories

If you click the Edit tab and scroll down to the bottom of the page, you can see how the categories were assigned to this page:

```
[[Category:Dog breeds]]
[[Category:Herding dogs]]
[[Category:European dogs]]
[[Category:Dog breeds originating in Belgium]]
[[Category:Dog breeds recognised by the Canadian Kennel Club]]
```

As an example, the category "Dog breeds originating in Belgium" links to a page with the following URL:

```
http://en.wikipedia.org/wiki/Category:Dog_breeds_originating_in_Belgium
```

More information about categories and namespaces is available in Chapter 7.

Image Namespace

The Image namespace is used to refer to image pages (which is not the same as referring to a graphic file — see the Media namespace below for more of an explanation). The Belgian Shepherd Dog page contains photographs of different kinds of Belgians. For example, if you click on the image for Groenendael, you will be taken to a page in the image namespace:

```
http://en.wikipedia.org/wiki/Image:Belgian_Groenendael_600.jpg
```

User Namespace

The User namespace is used to create pages for MediaWiki users. If you are registered, then you can access your user space by using your registered username, such as the following:

```
http://en.Wikipedia.org/wiki/User:Mchoate
```

If you are not registered with the wiki, then your IP address is used to identify you. Note that because most ISPs and institutions use dynamic assignment of IP addresses, a single IP address does not necessarily represent a single individual. This means that you should take what you read on such a user page with a grain of salt. You can turn off the use of IP addresses by including the following namespaces in the LocalSettings.php page.

Talk Namespace

The Talk namespace is used for pages about articles in the Content namespace. All the other namespaces have a similar namespace as well — that is, composed of the namespace name, followed by _Talk. So, for example, in addition to the Image namespace, there is also an Image_Talk namespace; and in addition to the User namespace, there is a User_Talk namespace. If you click the Discussion link on the Belgian Shepherd Dog page, you will be taken to a page in the Talk namespace:

```
http://en.wikipedia.org/wiki/Talk:Belgian_Shepherd_Dog
```

On this particular page (as I write) are some comments about the disposition of Belgian Shepherd Dogs and how well the article portrays their true temperament.

Project Namespace

The Project namespace is used for pages that discuss the project itself. In practice, the Project namespace is the name of the wiki. In other words, if your project is called Professional Wikis, instead of using

```
http://127.0.0.1/wiki/Project:All_About_My_Project
```

you would use

```
http://127.0.0.1/wiki/Professional_Wikis:All_About_My_Project
```

On the Wikipedia site, the name used for the Project namespace is Meta, rather than Wikipedia, reflecting the underlying purpose of the Project namespace: that it reflects information about a project, rather than the project itself (just as metadata is data about a document, and not the content of the document).

Help Namespace

The Help namespace is self-explanatory. It contains pages that are intended to help users understand how to use your wiki. When you first launch a MediaWiki wiki, there are links in the template to Help pages, but there isn't any help in them. If you follow the link, you'll be taken to a page that asks you to edit it. You might expect the Help pages from Wikipedia to be there, but they are not. You can, however, upload the Help pages if you would like because all of the content on Wikipedia is available for downloading at `http://download.wikipedia.org/`. More details about how to upload pages into a wiki will be found in Chapter 11.

MediaWiki Namespace

The MediaWiki namespace is used by the MediaWiki application for the management of system messages. As I've already mentioned, MediaWiki supports the use of many different languages, and this affects the wiki manager in three distinct areas: the language of the content of the articles, the language of the user (which is set in user preferences) and the language of the MediaWiki user interface. The MediaWiki namespace enables you to localize the system messages that a user sees, which affects the user interface, error messages, and so on.

Template Namespace

The Template namespace is used in support of, you guessed it, templates. In MediaWiki, templates have a slightly different meaning than how the term is used in other content management systems. Typically, a template is an HTML page that contains some sort of identifier that is replaced by dynamic page content.

Templates in MediaWiki don't refer to the actual page itself, but to elements within the page that are inserted into the page in order to hold content. Templates and user interface customization are discussed in gory detail in Chapter 8, "Magic Words, Templates, and Skins."

Special Namespace

You have already been introduced to the Special namespace, but you haven't seen any examples of Special namespaces until now. There are actually quite a few Special pages that you will find quite helpful as you learn how to use MediaWiki, extend it, and administer it. The first one you'll be introduced to is the Specialpages Special page, which lists all the Special pages available to the logged in user:

```
http://en.wikipedia.org/wiki/Special:Specialpages
```

One of those Special pages that is of interest is the following, which lets you know which version of MediaWiki the wiki is running. This can be helpful when you are looking at other wikis and see a feature that you've never seen before or you want to know how to implement a feature:

```
http://127.0.0.1/wiki/index.php/Special:Version
```

From the Belgian Shepherd Dog article, you will find a Special Pages link in the left-hand column. You can click it to find out the configuration of MediaWiki:

```
MediaWiki: 1.10alpha (r21377)
PHP: 5.1.2 (apache)
MySQL: 4.0.26-standard-log
```

A particularly useful Special page is Special:Version. This provides you with information about which version of MediaWiki is being run, as well as which version of PHP, MySQL (or Postgres), and so on. If you go to `http://en.Wikipedia.org/wiki/index.php/Special:Version` on Wikipedia, you will see the current version of MediaWiki that is running, plus a list of extensions that they use as well. This can be especially helpful if you see a feature on Wikipedia that you would like to replicate in your own wiki.

Another Special page of interest to wiki managers is Special:Statistics, which will tell you everything you want to know about how often your site is being accessed.

```
http://127.0.0.1/wiki/index.php/Special:Statistics
```

The most useless Special page is Special:Random. For those of you who are longing for serendipity, follow a link to this page, or type the URL into your browser, and you'll be taken to a random page that may or may not be interesting or meaningful to you (or anybody else, for that matter).

Media Namespace

When files are uploaded, a description page is created for them, which is accessible through the Images namespace, as discussed previously. Sometimes, however, it is convenient to refer to the actual image file itself, and you use the Media namespace to do that.

User Actions

Two user groups are created at first: bureaucrats and sysops. There are two implicit groups as well: one for anonymous users and another for registered users.

When you first configured MediaWiki, you created a sysop, which by default was called WikiSysop. The WikiSysop user is a member of the bureaucrat and sysop groups. By default, anonymous users of MediaWiki can create their own accounts, read pages, edit pages, create pages, and create talk pages. A registered user can also move pages, upload and reupload files, and identify edits as minor edits (these are edits that are not tracked as a different version).

Users and Roles

A user's role determines the kind of actions he or she can perform on a given page. It also determines the options that are displayed on a given page.

Anonymous Users

When you first visit your newly installed wiki, prior to registering or logging in as a sysop, you will see the main page, and right above the title are four tabs:

❑ Article

❑ Discussion

❑ Edit

❑ History

The Article tab is selected, and it represents the article's Main Page. If you click the Discussion tab, you will be taken to a page in the Talk namespace: Talk:Main_Page.

If you click Edit, you will be taken to the following URL:

```
http://127.0.0.1/wiki/Main_Page?action=edit
```

This is an example of an action. Actions do things to pages, and a user's role determines which actions he or she can perform. In the preceding example, it's the edit action, and by default any user can edit any page. Later in this section, you'll learn how to change which actions are available for particular users. Also provided is a more complete list of available actions. In the meantime, click the History tab to see another action:

```
http://127.0.0.1/wiki/Main_Page?action=history
```

This action takes you to a page where you can review earlier versions of a page, and compare different versions with each other.

At the very top of the page, to the right, you will see links similar to this:

- ❑ 127.0.0.1
- ❑ Talk for this IP
- ❑ Log in/create account

Recall that anonymous users are identified by their IP address. This isn't particularly useful, as most ISPs and employers use dynamically assigned IP addresses, which means a user's IP address doesn't necessarily stay the same between visits. Nevertheless, the anonymous user is tracked that way and has all the accoutrements of a registered user: a User page for that IP address as well as a User Talk page, and so on.

The anonymous user does have slightly fewer privileges than the default registered user. The registered user can move and watch pages in addition to joining in the discussion about them and viewing their history.

User Registration

The final option is Log in/create account. By default, anonymous users are allowed to create their own accounts, but this is a configuration item that can be changed (see "Changing Permissions," later in this chapter). If you are following along on your own wiki, go ahead and click this link and create an account. You'll first be taken to the Login page, but if you have not already registered, you will need to click the Create an Account link.

Creating an account is straightforward, and you can configure a few parameters. Again, the default values can be found in DefaultSettings.php. In order to override the default value, copy the variable into LocalSettings.php and modify it there.

Using Real Names

The first option determines whether you allow the use of real name fields (which you will see on the Registration page by default). Set this value to false if, for some reason, you don't want to know a user's real name.

```
/** Whether or not to allow and use real name fields. Defaults to true. */
$wgAllowRealName = true;
```

Password Length

The second configurable variable establishes the allowable minimum length of a password. By default, the minimum is 0, meaning that empty passwords are allowed. Of course, even a minimal level of security would suggest that passwords be at least six to eight characters long:

```
/**
 * Specifies the minimal length of a user password. If set to
 * 0, empty passwords are allowed.
 */
$wgMinimalPasswordLength = 0;
```

Registered Users

Once you have registered, you will be afforded some additional privileges. If you return to the main page of the wiki after logging in as a registered user, you will see that in addition to the tabs that were available for the anonymous user, you have now been granted two new tabs:

- ❏ Move (Special:Movepage)
- ❏ Watch (logged in s mchoate) (action = watch)

You also have many new options at the top of the page:

- ❏ Username (whatever username you are using)
- ❏ My talk
- ❏ My preferences
- ❏ My watchlist
- ❏ My contributions
- ❏ Log out

Moving a page in MediaWiki is really just renaming a page. If you are in a namespace that allows subpages, you can move it to a subpage, which is what is often done in order to archive talk pages when they get too long.

If you click the Move tab from the main page, it will take you to the following URL:

```
http://127.0.0.1/wiki/index.php/Special:Movepage/Main_Page
```

There, you will be prompted for the new name of the page.

Clicking the Watch tab toggles the tab to Unwatch. By clicking it when it says Watch, you are requesting that the current page be tracked and displayed in your watchlist, which you visit by clicking the My Watchlist link at the top of the page. More details about watchlists are available in the section "My Watchlist," later in this chapter.

Preferences

The Preferences pages enable users to update their own preferences. The items are self-explanatory, except for one item in the miscellaneous section labeled "Threshold for Stub Display." You can change the Threshold for Stub Display to 50. This tells MediaWiki that entries with fewer than 50 characters will be considered stubs, rather than full articles. Links to those stubs will appear as brown links, rather than traditional blue. Disable page caching.

My Talk

My Talk links to the same page that the Discussion tab links (I don't know why one is called "discussion" and the other is called "talk").

My Watchlist

Active participants in your wiki (or management) may want to keep a closer eye on certain pages so they can be notified when they are changed. The My Watchlist page is a Special page, Special:Watchlist.

In user preferences, you can define how many days an item should be in your watchlist, whether to hide your own edits, whether to hide the edits of bots (mass edits handled by scripts), and which namespaces to pay attention to, as well as whether to bother watching minor edits.

My Contributions

My contributions enables you to track your contributions to the wiki.

Autoconfirmed

The next user group is considered an *implicit* group. You become a member of the Autoconfirmed group after you have been a user for a certain amount of time, which is configured in the usual way. By default, you are automatically in the Autoconfirmed group, because the $wgAutoConfirmAge value is set to 0 by default. The purpose of this is to stop spammers from automatically signing up and posting nonsense. It also allows sysops to monitor new users more closely, which is a much better use of their time than monitoring long-time participants who are well behaved.

```
/**
 * Number of seconds an account is required to age before
 * it's given the implicit 'autoconfirm' group membership.
 * This can be used to limit privileges of new accounts.
 *
 * Accounts created by earlier versions of the software
 * may not have a recorded creation date, and will always
 * be considered to pass the age test.
 *
 * When left at 0, all registered accounts will pass.
 */
$wgAutoConfirmAge = 0;
//$wgAutoConfirmAge = 600;     // ten minutes
//$wgAutoConfirmAge = 3600*24; // one day
```

Emailconfirmed

The Emailconfirmed group adds another layer of security. It requires that the e-mail address of a registered user be confirmed prior to being granted the editing privilege. When this value is set to true, an e-mail message is sent to the e-mail address provided by the user when he or she registered. The user must then respond to that message, proving that the recipient of the e-mail message is in fact the person who has registered. Having a confirmed e-mail address also makes e-mail notification possible.

The default value is `false`:

```
/**
 * Should editors be required to have a validated e-mail
 * address before being allowed to edit?
 */
$wgEmailConfirmToEdit=false;
```

Bots

Bots refer to scripts that are run in order to process numerous pages at one time. Only certain users are allowed to use bots; and because of the automated nature of bots, the configuration variables pertaining to bots focus on keeping bot activities out of the logs (see "Changing Permissions").

Sysops and Bureaucrats

When you first created your wiki, you were prompted for a password for a user named "WikiSysop." The user who was created in that instance is a member of both the Sysop and the Bureaucrat groups. The only thing a bureaucrat can do is modify user permissions. All other powers are delegated to the sysop. The actual permissions are outlined below, in the code pulled from `DefaultSettings.php` that defines the default permissions.

Much of what a sysop does represents more advanced features of MediaWiki that are not discussed until later in the book, so I will not dwell on it now; but to get a preview, log in as WikiSysop (or use whichever name you chose), and then go to the following page:

```
http://127.0.0.1/wiki/index.php/Special:Specialpages
```

The list of pages will be familiar to you, but if you scroll down to the bottom of the page, you will see a heading labeled Restricted Special Pages, followed by links to the following Special pages:

❏   Block user

❏   Import pages

❏   Unwatched pages

❏   User rights management

❏   View deleted pages

Of all the options that are available, User rights management is the one we will focus on now. Clicking User rights management will take you to a page where you can add or remove groups for any user.

Changing Permissions

MediaWiki grants permissions to users based upon the group to which they were assigned. The permission granted reflects the capability to perform one or more actions, which are discussed in the next section.

There are two ways to change permissions. You already learned about the first: Assign a user to a different group by using the `Special:Userrights` pages, only accessible by members of the Bureaucrat group. You can also change the default permissions granted to groups by updating the information in `LocalSettings.php`. The following code shows the default permissions defined in `DefaultSettings.php`.

```
/**
 * Permission keys given to users in each group.
 * All users are implicitly in the '*' group including anonymous visitors;
 * logged-in users are all implicitly in the 'user' group. These will be
 * combined with the permissions of all groups that a given user is listed
 * in in the user_groups table.
 *
 * Functionality to make pages inaccessible has not been extensively tested
 * for security. Use at your own risk!
 *
 * This replaces wgWhitelistAccount and wgWhitelistEdit
 */
$wgGroupPermissions = array();

// Implicit group for all visitors
$wgGroupPermissions['*'    ]['createaccount']   = true;
$wgGroupPermissions['*'    ]['read']            = true;
$wgGroupPermissions['*'    ]['edit']            = true;
$wgGroupPermissions['*'    ]['createpage']      = true;
$wgGroupPermissions['*'    ]['createtalk']      = true;

// Implicit group for all logged-in accounts
$wgGroupPermissions['user' ]['move']            = true;
$wgGroupPermissions['user' ]['read']            = true;
$wgGroupPermissions['user' ]['edit']            = true;
$wgGroupPermissions['user' ]['createpage']      = true;
$wgGroupPermissions['user' ]['createtalk']      = true;
$wgGroupPermissions['user' ]['upload']          = true;
$wgGroupPermissions['user' ]['reupload']        = true;
$wgGroupPermissions['user' ]['reupload-shared'] = true;
$wgGroupPermissions['user' ]['minoredit']       = true;

// Implicit group for accounts that pass $wgAutoConfirmAge
$wgGroupPermissions['autoconfirmed']['autoconfirmed'] = true;

// Implicit group for accounts with confirmed email addresses
// This has little use when email address confirmation is off
$wgGroupPermissions['emailconfirmed']['emailconfirmed'] = true;

// Users with bot privilege can have their edits hidden
// from various log pages by default
$wgGroupPermissions['bot'  ]['bot']             = true;
$wgGroupPermissions['bot'  ]['autoconfirmed']   = true;
$wgGroupPermissions['bot'  ]['nominornewtalk']  = true;

// Most extra permission abilities go to this group
$wgGroupPermissions['sysop']['block']           = true;
$wgGroupPermissions['sysop']['createaccount']   = true;
$wgGroupPermissions['sysop']['delete']          = true;
$wgGroupPermissions['sysop']['deletedhistory']  = true; // can view deleted
    history entries, but not see or restore the text
```

```
$wgGroupPermissions['sysop']['editinterface']    = true;
$wgGroupPermissions['sysop']['import']           = true;
$wgGroupPermissions['sysop']['importupload']     = true;
$wgGroupPermissions['sysop']['move']             = true;
$wgGroupPermissions['sysop']['patrol']           = true;
$wgGroupPermissions['sysop']['autopatrol']       = true;
$wgGroupPermissions['sysop']['protect']          = true;
$wgGroupPermissions['sysop']['proxyunbannable']  = true;
$wgGroupPermissions['sysop']['rollback']         = true;
$wgGroupPermissions['sysop']['trackback']        = true;
$wgGroupPermissions['sysop']['upload']           = true;
$wgGroupPermissions['sysop']['reupload']         = true;
$wgGroupPermissions['sysop']['reupload-shared']  = true;
$wgGroupPermissions['sysop']['unwatchedpages']   = true;
$wgGroupPermissions['sysop']['autoconfirmed']    = true;
$wgGroupPermissions['sysop']['upload_by_url']    = true;
$wgGroupPermissions['sysop']['ipblock-exempt']   = true;

// Permission to change users' group assignments
$wgGroupPermissions['bureaucrat']['userrights'] = true;

// Experimental permissions, not ready for production use
//$wgGroupPermissions['sysop']['deleterevision'] = true;
//$wgGroupPermissions['bureaucrat']['hiderevision'] = true;

/**
 * The developer group is deprecated, but can be activated if need be
 * to use the 'lockdb' and 'unlockdb' special pages. Those require
 * that a lock file be defined and creatable/removable by the web
 * server.
 */
# $wgGroupPermissions['developer']['siteadmin'] = true;
```

When you want to change permissions, you simply need to assign the value in the `LocalSettings.php` file. For example, if you were to add the following line to `LocalSettings.php`, then unregistered users would no longer be able to edit pages:

```
$wgGroupPermissions['*'    ]['edit']             = false;
```

Note that you did not have to copy all of the permissions over from `DefaultSettings.php` to `LocalSettings.php`, just the one permission that you wanted to change. When anonymous users are denied editing privileges, instead of seeing the Edit tab at the top of the page, they see a View Source tab that will show them the raw wikitext.

Actions

When users interact with a MediaWiki wiki, they do so through actions. For example, when users click a link to view a page in a wiki, they are telling the MediaWiki application to perform the *view* action. The action being undertaken is usually evident in the URL (with the exception of view, as that is the default action), but you usually don't type action URLs into your browser in order to perform them. They are almost always made available through MediaWiki's user interface.

The following is a list of potential actions. Not all of them are available in every instance. In some cases they need to be enabled in `LocalSettings.php`. If you want to see all the available actions, you need to dig into the code of `Wiki.php`.

- ❏ view
- ❏ watch
- ❏ unwatch
- ❏ delete
- ❏ revert
- ❏ rollback
- ❏ protect
- ❏ unprotect
- ❏ info
- ❏ markpatrolled
- ❏ render
- ❏ deletetrackback
- ❏ purge
- ❏ print
- ❏ dublincore
- ❏ creativecommons
- ❏ submit
- ❏ edit
- ❏ history
- ❏ raw

The URL that is used to access pages contains at least two variables in the query string, specifying the title of the page and the action to be performed on the page. The typical URL for the front page of a wiki is something like this:

```
http://127.0.0.1/wiki/index.php?title=Main_Page
```

When no action is specified, the default is the view action. This means that the previous URL is functionally equivalent to the following:

```
http://127.0.0.1/wiki/index.php?title=Main_Page&action=view
```

Likewise, following the same pattern, you can edit a page by specifying the edit action in the URL:

```
http://127.0.0.1/wiki/index.php?title=Main_Page&action=edit
```

The raw action displays the plain, unparsed wikitext:

```
http://choate.local/mysql/index.php/Main_Page?action=raw
```

In effect, it's almost like View Source except that instead of viewing the HTML, you view the wikitext used to generate the page. You'll learn all about wikitext in the next chapter. An example of raw output follows:

```
<big>'''MediaWiki has been successfully installed.'''</big>

Consult the [http://meta.wikimedia.org/wiki/Help:Contents User's Guide]
    for information on using the wiki software.

== Getting started ==

*
    [http://www.mediawiki.org/wiki/Help:Configuration_settings
  Configuration settings list]
* [http://www.mediawiki.org/wiki/Help:FAQ MediaWiki FAQ]
* [http://mail.wikimedia.org/mailman/listinfo/mediawiki-announce MediaWiki
    release mailing list]

Welcome to my new wiki, for my book [[Professional Wikis]].
```

The info action is not enabled by default. In order to use it, you must first enable it in `LocalSettings.php`:

```
/** Allow the "info" action, very inefficient at the moment */
$wgAllowPageInfo = true;
```

Once that is done, you can call it with the following URL:

```
http://127.0.0.1/wiki/index.php/Main_Page?action=info
```

Here are the results of calling the info action:

```
Number of watchers: 0
Number of edits (article): 6
Number of distinct authors (article): 4
```

Another interesting action is the credits action, which can be called as follows:

```
http://127.0.0.1/wiki/index.php/Main_Page?action=credits
```

This action returns information about when the page was last modified, who modified it, and so on:

```
This page was last modified 19:43, 16 April 2007 by ProfWikis - MySQL user
    WikiSysop. Based on work by Professional Wikis and Anonymous user(s) of
    ProfWikis - MySQL.
```

These are just a few examples of the available actions. There are other actions, such as delete, that you will study in more detail in Chapter 6.

Custom Views with Parameters

Whenever a new version of a document is created, it is assigned a new id. This means that if you ever want to refer to a particular version of an article, you can include a reference to the id. Generally speaking, this is something I rarely do because I usually want to link to the most recent version.

For example, there is a Permanent Links link on many of the pages of Wikipedia, and it is included by default in the MediaWiki installation. If you are on the main page of your MediaWiki installation and you click on it, you will be taken to a page with a link similar to this one:

```
http://127.0.0.1/wiki/index.php?title=Main_Page&oldid=2
```

In addition to the title `Main_Page`, the URL also references `oldid`, which is how MediaWiki refers to document ids. This URL tells MediaWiki to show the version of `Main_Page` that had the id of 2, rather than any of the other ids. Every time a new version of `Main_Page` is saved, a new id is assigned to it, so you can link to any one of those versions.

A similar URL is used to compare two different versions. In the following example, MediaWiki is being told to compare the `Main_Page` with a document id of 2 with the version of `Main_Page` that has a document id of 1:

```
http://127.0.0.1/wiki/index.php?title=Main_Page&diff=2&oldid=1
```

Summary

In this chapter, you learned how to update some of MediaWiki's default settings and were introduced to the different kinds of pages that you will encounter as a user of MediaWiki. This chapter also introduced you to users and roles, and described the default permissions available to users, as well as how to change them for your own needs.

In the next chapter, you will focus exclusively on writing and editing content on MediaWiki. There is a lot of important information to cover in this chapter. MediaWiki uses a special markup language called *wikitext* to author pages. While WYSIWYG editing is available, it's only available as an extension. Although some users do not like wikitext because it reminds them of writing code, it is an extremely powerful and versatile tool. You will also learn how to extend MediaWiki by adding a WYSIWYG editing tool.

4

Writing and Editing Content

In this chapter, you will learn about writing and editing content on MediaWiki using wikitext. Wikitext is a shorthand form of HTML, intended to be easier (and quicker) to type than HTML. As a consequence, the more you know about HTML, the easier it will be to begin using wikitext. This chapter assumes you have a basic knowledge of HTML, so it does not provide a detailed explanation about how to write HTML. If you are a complete newcomer, a good starting place is Jon Duckett's *Beginning Web Programming with HTML, XHTML, and CSS* (Wrox, 2004).

MediaWiki provides a wide array of tools to edit and customize pages. This chapter focuses on wikitext, but this is only the beginning. In Chapter 6, you will learn advanced methods of managing pages, such as how to move and delete pages, how to protect them from unwanted editing, and how to add additional functionality to them through extensions or external applications. In Chapter 8, you will learn how to use MediaWiki's magic words and templates, as well how to define your own skins for MediaWiki, which also means more advanced skills for determining the style and presentation of your content.

Prior to jumping into the nuts and bolts of writing wikitext, I'll share some thoughts about writing for the Web in general in order to provide some context for the discussion of wikitext itself.

Writing for the Web

Writing for the Web is different from writing something that will spend its life on paper. People read differently on a computer screen than they do on the printed page, primarily because of the nature of modern computer screens — they are backlit and lack the resolution of a printed page. This is gradually changing as e-paper technologies are beginning to emerge, but do not expect major changes anytime soon. People read more slowly onscreen, and they have a greater tendency to scan the text, rather than read it in great detail.

The pace of reading is an ergonomic issue; a more interesting difference relates to the nature of hypertext. Writing for print is primarily a linear activity. When you write for the Web, you are writing in three dimensions. Designers and authors inexperienced with Web production often mistakenly believe that they can control their readers' actions and ensure that readers navigate their site in a certain order, or see it in a certain way.

Site visitors do not always start on the home page of a site. In fact, the home page may be one of the least frequently visited pages on your site. Eye-tracking studies also show that readers often avoid graphics; some analysts theorize that this is because readers quickly train themselves to avoid advertisements and tend to interpret all graphics as banner ads.

The three-dimensionality of hypertext is due to links. The author can link from one page to another at any time and any place in the document. Individual pages are not distinct. They exist within a context (a website is one such grouping of related, interlinked pages). This interlinking is not limited to a given domain, because pages can link to any other page (in any other format) as long as that page is available on the Internet.

Some of this may be rudimentary information if you are experienced with writing online. Nevertheless, it is necessary to frame what is truly creative and empowering about wikis: they make it easy to create links between pages. They have specialized approaches for internal links, external links, and links between other wikis.

In Apple Computer's user-interface guidelines, WYSIWYG (what you see is what you get) is defined as the image on the screen being representative of the output that is printed. WYSIWYG, by definition, assumes a printed page. Everything is different now. First, most content will never be printed. Second, it will be available on monitors of all different sizes, and on different devices, from handheld computers to mobile phones and screen readers. Finally, users can opt to use their own stylesheet, to change the colors on a page, to hide the images, to view it in their RSS aggregator, and so on. What you see is not what you get. WYSIWYG is convenient, but it gives a false sense of security and detracts from the true business of writing on the Web, which is worrying about the connections between content.

Because of reader behavior, and the unique characteristics of hypertext, there are two basic rules of thumb for writing effectively for the Web:

❑ Use headings liberally and make plenty of use of bulleted (or numbered) lists. This helps readers skim your work faster.

❑ Link richly, adding links to other sections of your site, or to your references or related material. Organize content in a way that does not assume a sequential reading.

Wikitext versus WYSIWYG

There is a certain amount of disagreement among the user community about wikitext versus the more traditional WYSIWYG interfaces. One thing is certain: most users prefer WYSIWYG, especially if they are nontechnical and not used to thinking about writing in terms of codes. If you are implementing a wiki for such a group, then you should consider a WYSIWYG interface.

Despite user preferences, there is an argument to be made in favor of wikitext, and my position is that there is substantial value in encouraging authors to use wikitext because it provides an opportunity to create content that is more structured and thereby more easily searchable and leveraged in other contexts.

Wikitext was born of a need to enable writers to easily create links to other pages, and to apply basic formatting to pages edited through a Web browser. Wikitext is a markup language. The "through the Web" requirement meant that the user did not have the benefit of a WYSIWYG interface.

Following are the benefits of a wikitext editing interface:

- ❑ Low barriers to entry; everybody with a browser can edit with it.

- ❑ WYSIWYG editors give authors too much flexibility (something that seems to be most often exploited by those authors who are design-impaired, leading to a tossed salad of fonts and colors without any consistent semantic meaning).

- ❑ In my experience, WYSIWYG editors do a lousy job of making it easy to link to different pages within the wiki. There really isn't an easier way of doing it than that used by wikis, which usually involves the simple wrapping of a page title with double brackets, like so: [[A Title of a Wiki Page]].

The negatives of wikitext editing are as follows:

- ❑ Users almost universally prefer WYSIWYG editors, because they are more familiar with them.

- ❑ The lack of syntax highlighting makes wikitext hard to read. You cannot easily scan for section headings, for example.

An excellent discussion of this topic can be found on CMSWatch at `www.cmswatch.com/Feature/79-Writers,-XML,-and-CMS`

There are three different approaches to resolving the editing problem:

- ❑ Wikitext (or some other text-oriented markup language such as Textile, Markdown, etc.)

- ❑ WYSIWYG interfaces, like those used in word processors

- ❑ Syntax highlighting, similar to what is used by software programmers in Integrated Development Environments (IDEs). You get the benefit of visual feedback as you type, but you also have absolute control over the HTML that is generated.

The biggest problem with WYSIWYG interfaces is that they link the visual design of a site with the content in an environment where the separation of content from design is seen as an asset. Because content published online can be viewed in multiple browsers on a variety of different platforms (from cell phones to televisions to 50-inch plasma television screens), the WYSIWYG interface does not really provide the author with meaningful information. In fact, it might even shield the author from important structural issues that are not apparent when the page on the computer screen is supposed to be an accurate representation of the expression of that page on paper.

Philosophically speaking, markup used in HTML should be semantically meaningful; references to visual representations are resisted. For example, the HTML element `<strong>` is preferred to the HTML element `<b>`. Both elements are displayed in bold, but the use of `<strong>` explicitly states that the author wants to provide a strong emphasis to this word, whereas the use of `<b>` only makes that information implicit, and all you know for certain is that the author wanted to make the word bold — perhaps for purely aesthetic reasons.

The reason for this distinction is that content will appear on different platforms, now and in the future, and there may be different visual representations of the same idea of strong emphasis used on those platforms. For example, how does one render a bold word when read by a screen-reader application intended for the visually impaired? It is much easier to imagine a screen reader strongly emphasizing a word or phrase by changing the tone of the voice.

Another reason why wikitext is important can best be illustrated with an example. MediaWiki, the application that runs Wikipedia, allows the user to assign a category to a page, the details of which are discussed in the next section. MediaWiki categories are the functional equivalent of the tags used by Flickr. We won't get into the details now, but what is important to understand at this point is that MediaWiki categories are used to group and organize pages, so the text used to designate a category needs to be identifiable by the software application because it will ultimately be used to provide an alternative means of navigation for the user. Even if you have a WYSIWYG editor for your wiki, the user will still need to use some form of markup to identify a category. In this instance, wikitext makes it possible to apply structure to a document as you write, and this can be a very powerful feature.

Wiki Content

There appear to be two broad applications for wikis used by organizations. The first application is as a collaborative tool, most often used to manage projects, as a replacement for e-mail. In this sense, it represents a middle ground between e-mail and more formal project management tools. The second application is as a knowledge management platform. The ease of use inspires organizations to capture tacit employee knowledge and other details that tend to never be documented.

First and foremost, a wiki engine is a content management system, and many organizations use wiki engines for anything you would use a content management system for — more than likely in an intranet. Wikis are an excellent entry-level content management system because they are easy to edit and require very little training and no specialized software (other than the browser and the Web server).

Wiki engines can also be used as a project management tool. In many cases, users report that they are employing wikis as a replacement for e-mail. Consider two e-mail-related issues. The first is mailbox clutter. So much information (and clutter) crowds the typical professional's mailbox these days that messages are easily lost (overlooked or inadvertently routed to junk mail folders by overly eager spam filters). The second issue with e-mail relates to document management and versioning.

Many organizations use Microsoft Word for a number of different purposes. Word's internal version tracking is often used, which can be very powerful and quite handy at times. Unfortunately, e-mail works by spawning innumerable copies of Word documents (constrained only by the number of intended recipients). Unless carefully managed, each document can represent a fork of the original document, with changes made to different copies of the same document, leading to a nightmare merge scenario, not to mention the mere difficulty of knowing with relative assurance that you are viewing the most recent version of the document. (You can view the most recent version of your copy of the document, but you don't know if your copy is the latest copy.)

Wikis nicely present the very latest version of every page (plus a history of edits and who made the edits). The wiki becomes the authoritative source of the document to be managed by the project. Mailboxes are decluttered (and reduced in size) and documents are easier to find.

Writing and Editing

The base content is saved in the database as wikitext. When you edit a page in MediaWiki, you can't edit every aspect of the page. Much of it is generated by the skin. You can only edit the primary content of the page — the text of the article, for example, but not content that appears in the left-hand column, or in the heading. In order to change that information, you must change the skin first, a topic that is covered in Chapter 8.

Much of the writing on Wikipedia is defined by convention, rather than programmatically enforced. Wikipedia has extensive article-naming guidelines, and rules for how to structure pages. This can be a good starting point for your own wiki. It is important to remember that wikis are relatively unstructured sites, so a user can do a lot with what's available — and it may not always look pretty.

Editing Pages

As you learned in the previous chapter, new pages are created by embedding a wiki link into a page. For example, if you wanted to create a page called "Brand New Page," then you could create a link to it from the main page of my wiki by clicking the Edit tab at the top of the page (assuming you have privileges, of course). Figure 4-1 shows a screen shot of the edit field for the wiki's main page. There are a few things to note here: First, no one is logged in (which you can tell because an IP address is displayed in the upper right-hand corner of the page, rather than a username). As a consequence, there are only four tabs across the top of the page: article, discussion, edit, and history. The primary heading on the page is "Editing Main Page," and below that is a row of icons. This is the toolbar, which provides some editing shortcuts, which you will learn more about later in this chapter.

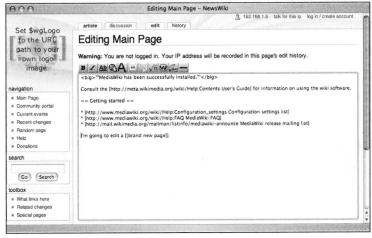

Figure 4-1: Editing the Main page

Beneath the toolbar is the edit field where wikitext is entered into the page. In addition to the text that is displayed on that page by default when you first install MediaWiki, the following code shows an additional sentence:

```
<big>'''MediaWiki has been successfully installed.'''</big>

Consult the [http://meta.wikimedia.org/wiki/Help:Contents User's Guide] for
    information on using the wiki software.

== Getting started ==
```

```
    * [http://www.mediawiki.org/wiki/Help:Configuration_settings|Configuration
      settings|list]
    * [http://www.mediawiki.org/wiki/Help:FAQ MediaWiki FAQ]
    * [http://mail.wikimedia.org/mailman/listinfo/mediawiki-announce
      MediaWiki release mailing list]

    I'm going to edit a [[brand new page]]
```

An empty line separates the new text that has been entered (the line about creating a brand-new page) and the text that was already on the page. This is the first rule of wikitext: *a blank line separates paragraphs*. At this point, you have the option of saving the page, showing a preview of the page, showing changes, and canceling my edits. When you click the Save Page button, you are returned to the main page, where you will see that the new text you entered has now been converted to HTML. The text [[brand new page]] has been converted to a link, and if you are using the default skin that comes with MediaWiki, the link will be colored red, which indicates that the page does not exist. If you click on the red link, then you will automatically be taken to the editing page for the Brand New Page page, as shown in Figure 4-2.

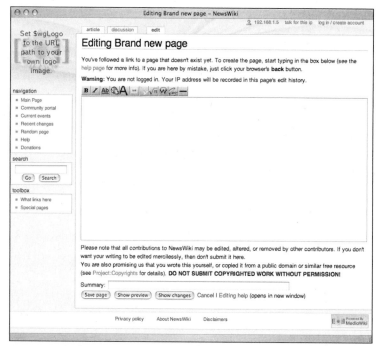

Figure 4-2: Editing the "Brand new page" page in MediaWiki

Previewing Changes

Pressing the Show Preview button enables you to see the raw wikitext alongside the rendered HTML, in order to ensure that it is converted as intended (see Figure 4-3).

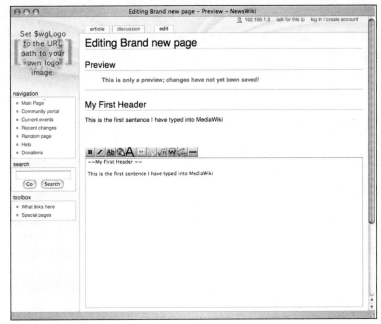

Figure 4-3: Preview the changes you have made before saving them

Summary Field

MediaWiki also provides a summary field in which you can enter information about the changes you've made before saving them. This can be particularly helpful when several people are collaborating on a document. The text of the summary is displayed in the page's history.

History

The history of changes made to a document can be viewed by clicking the History tab (see Figure 4-4).

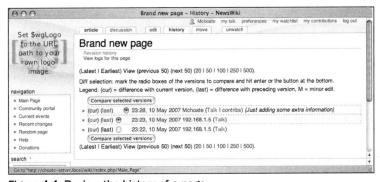

Figure 4-4: Review the history of a page

Options for Logged-in Users

If you are a registered user, the editing interface gives you two more options: a This Is a Minor Edit checkbox, and a Watch This Page checkbox.

Minor Edits

The first option allows you, as a registered user, to mark an edit as a *minor edit*. A minor edit is an edit that fixes a typo or makes a small cosmetic adjustment that doesn't otherwise substantively change the meaning of the underlying article.

This privilege is reserved for registered users because it is used by sysops and others who review the site — they don't want to be bothered with checking a recently changed page if the change only reflects a spelling correction. As a registered user, you are presumably a little more trustworthy, so others can focus their monitoring efforts on changes made by unregistered users, which are always checked.

Watch This Page

The second option allows you to watch the page, which means that it will show up in the user's watched pages list. You need to be a registered user to have a watched pages list, so that is why it is restricted from unregistered users.

Creating Links

In my opinion, creating links is the most important part of wikitext. This is because linking to other pages can be the most tedious part of writing content for the Web. In most other writing environments, the interface to creating a link is cludgy, and typically involves a pop-up window in which you enter the link data. Once a link is established (as in Microsoft Word), it becomes difficult to edit because if you mistakenly click on the word in the wrong way, the application assumes you want to follow the link; and the next thing you know a Web browser is loading a page, when all you wanted was to edit the text, or see exactly where the link was directed.

In MediaWiki terms, there are three basic varieties of link: internal links (also called *wiki links*), external links, and interwiki links. The following sections describe about each one.

Wiki (Internal) Links

A wiki link is used to link one page from a wiki to another page in the same wiki. Because every page title in a wiki is unique, you can readily create links to other pages, as long as you know the title of the page. A wiki link is created when a word or phrase that corresponds to a page title is surrounded by a pair of brackets, like so: `[[Main Page]]`. If you were to type this into the edit field of your wiki, it would create a link that takes you to the main page of your wiki.

This is also the way a new page is created. You can place a word or phrase in a pair of brackets, whether a page actually exists or not. Once you save this page, MediaWiki will check to see whether the page designated in the brackets already exists. If it does not exist, then the link is displayed in red (when using the default monospace skin), and links to the edit page for the currently unwritten page.

Wiki Links

For example, the following is an example of wikitext that includes basic wiki links:

```
==Wiki links==

This links to the [[Main Page]].

This links to the [[Main page]].

This links to the [[main Page]].

This links to the [[Help:Link]] page.
```

The first three links all go to the Main Page of the wiki, but you will notice that the capitalization is different for each one. When you examine the HTML that is produced, you will notice that the first link and third link to the Main Page works, but the second link is treated as a link to a completely different page. This is because MediaWiki automatically treats the first character of a page title as uppercase.

In the third link, main is changed to Main and everything works fine. The reason the second link does not work is because the second word is in lowercase, and MediaWiki will not modify the second word, so it does a case-sensitive search for a title whose second word is : rather than Page and doesn't find it. You can also see in this example that MediaWiki treats namespaces just like any other link:

```
<h2>Wiki links</h2>

<p>This links to the <a href="/wiki/index.php/Main_Page"
    title="Main Page">Main Page</a></p>

<p>This links to the <a
    href="/wiki/index.php?title=Main_page&action=edit"
    class="new" title="Main page">Main page</a>.</p>

<p>This links to the <a href="/wiki/index.php/Main_Page"
    title="Main Page">main Page</a>.</p>

<p>This links to the <a
    href="/wiki/index.php?title=Help:Link&amp;action=edit"
    class="new" title="Help:Link">Help:Link</a> page.</p>
```

Piped Links

Piped links are links that use the | character, which, when inserted inside a wiki link, enables you to define text displayed in the browser that is different from the title of the document. In the following example, the first link is a standard example of how pipe links typically appear. Note the remaining four links in the example: The wiki link ends with a pipe character and no information follows. In these examples, the pipe is a shorthand notation that converts the links according to a particular set of rules. The rules are as follows:

❑   If a pipe character follows a page with a namespace, then the namespace is dropped from the text that is displayed in the browser.

❑   If the title contains a parenthetical word or phrase that is followed by a single pipe, then the parenthetical phrase will be dropped from the text displayed in the browser.

❑   If the title contains a comma that is followed by a single pipe, then the text following the comma will be dropped from the text that is displayed in the browser.

```
==Piped Links==

This links to the [[Main Page | home page]].

This is how to  [[Help:Link|]] to the help section.

A link to Dylan's [[Ain't No Man Righteous (No Not One)|]]

A link to Dylan's [[It's Alright, Ma (I'm only bleeding)|]]

The pipe character is [[pipes||]].
```

You can see an example of how these links are displayed in Figure 4-5. In the following output, you can see the HTML that is produced from the wikitext, and how the special pipe rules are manifested:

```
<h2>Piped Links</h2>

<p>This links to the <a href="/wiki/index.php/Main_Page"
   title="Main Page">home page</a>.</p>

<p>This is how to <a
   href="/wiki/index.php?title=Help:Link&amp;action=edit"
   class="new" title="Help:Link">Link</a> to the help
   section.</p>

<p>A link to Dylan's <a
   href="/wiki/index.php?title=Ain%27t_No_Man_Righteous_%28
   No_Not_One%29&amp;action=edit" class="new" title="Ain't
   No Man Righteous (No Not One)">Ain't No Man
   Righteous</a></p>

<p>A link to Dylan's <a
   href="/wiki/index.php?title=It%27s_Alright%2C_Ma_%28I%27
   m_only_bleeding%29&amp;action=edit" class="new"
   title="It's Alright, Ma (I'm only bleeding)">It's
   Alright, Ma</a></p>

<p>The pipe character is <a
   href="/wiki/index.php?title=Pipes&amp;action=edit"
   class="new" title="Pipes">|</a>.</p>

<div class="editsection" style="float:right;margin-
   left:5px;">
  [<a
   href="/wiki/index.php?title=Wikilink_examples&amp;action
   =edit&amp;section=3" title="Edit section: Special
   case">edit</a>]
</div>
```

Special Cases

Finally, there is one special case worth mentioning. Good link style suggests that you embed links in the normal flow of text, so that it reads like a sentence, and that you should avoid constructions such as the phrase "click here" to insert a link into text. Sometimes, however, grammatical constructs makes this a little awkward. For example, sometimes a word needs to be written as a plural, even though the title of the page that you will be linking to is singular. The following wikitext example shows two different ways to approach this:

```
==Special case==

How many [[Main Page]]s are there?

How many  [[Main Page]]<nowiki>s</nowiki> are there?
```

When this wikitext is rendered as HTML, the trailing *s* in the first link is included in the link that is displayed in the browser (see Figure 4-5 for an example), whereas in the second example the *s* is left outside the link. The image in Figure 4-5 is in black and white, but if it were in color, you would see that the *s* in the first link is blue, whereas the *s* in the second link is black.

```
<p><a name="Special_case" id="Special_case"></a></p>

<h2>Special case</h2>

<p>How many <a href="/wiki/index.php/Main_Page" title="Main
    Page">Main Pages</a> are there?</p>

<p>How many <a href="/wiki/index.php/Main_Page" title="Main
    Page">Main Page</a>s are there?</p>
```

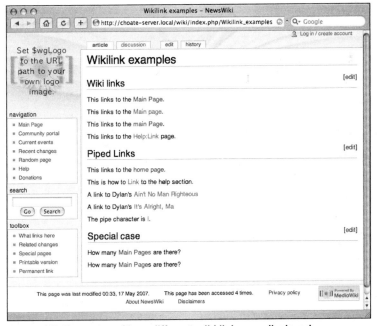

Figure 4-5: Examples of how different wiki links are displayed

External Links

External links are those that link to websites on the Internet that are not part of your wiki. There are three basic forms for external links:

```
[http://choate.info/]
[http://choate.info This is a link to my site]
http://choate.info
```

Each form results in a different look on the final HTML page, which is displayed as shown in Figure 4-6.

Figure 4-6: External links are shown in three different ways.

The first link is treated almost like a footnote. The second (predictably) shows the text that follows the URL, as well as the arrow icon indicating that it's an external link. The final format simply repeats the URL as the text of the link, also followed by the arrow icon.

If you wrap the external links in a `<span>` element, and assign it the class `plainlink`, then the arrow icon will not be displayed:

```
<span class="plainlinks">[http://choate.info]</span>

<span class="plainlinks">[http://choate.info This is a link to my site.]</span>

<span class="plainlinks">http://choate.info</span>
```

This is not really a MediaWiki feature. It leverages cascading stylesheets that can control whether an element is displayed or not. You could just as easily decide that external links should be bold, and create a class that does that within your stylesheet:

```
<span class="bold">[http://choate.info]</span>
```

Alternately, you can embed the style information in the HTML in the `style` attribute. In the following example, the text is bold and underlined:

```
<span style="font-weight:bold; text-
    decoration:underline">http://choate.info</span>
```

Characters at the end of external links are not automatically added, as they are with internal wiki links.

Interwiki Links

Interwiki links demonstrate the benefits of having a flat namespace, as wikis do. An interwiki link is an external link that links to another wiki (any kind of wiki will do, as long as its URL structure is predictable). When MediaWiki is installed, an interwiki table is established in the database. The table defines a prefix and a URL (the columns `iw_prefix` and `iw_url`, respectively). The prefix serves as a substitute for the full URL so that the URL can be typed onto a page conveniently.

One example is an interwiki link that links to the wiki run by Ward Cunningham. The prefix `wiki` is replaced by `http://c2.com/cgi/wiki?$1`, and the `$1` variable is replaced by the word or words that follow the prefix in the link. For example, `[wiki: WikiWikiWebFaq]` is translated into the following:

```
http://c2.com/cgi/wiki?WikiWikiWebFaq
```

One thing you should be aware of is that MediaWiki translates what it considers to be titles according to its own rules, but not every wiki uses the same guidelines. Originally, wikis used CamelCase links (two or more words joined together, with an uppercase letter used on the first letter of each distinct word). The preceding link takes you to a wiki from the Portland Pattern Repository, and it uses CamelCase links. In order for the link to work, you have to use CamelCase as well. MediaWiki replaces spaces with underscore (_) characters, but Portland Pattern Repository does not.

Formatting and Styles

A principle concept for Web development is the separation of content from design. The underlying realities of this idea have already been discussed earlier in the chapter. In practice, this separation is typically implemented in HTML by the use of cascading stylesheets (CSS). While it is possible to format a document in HTML, it is considered bad form. Instead, HTML should focus on the structure of your document, and a separate stylesheet should define how that structure appears on different kinds of devices. For example, you might have one stylesheet for print and another one for viewing on a screen.

That said, you do have some control over styles using wikitext, but bear in mind that most of the style information is documented in stylesheets. MediaWiki uses skins (I really wish they'd use a different name), which is a combination of templates and stylesheets that together comprise a site's look and feel.

Customizing your wiki's skin is discussed in great detail in Chapter 8.

The fastest way to understand this is to see some examples. You can break down these elements into two basic categories. The first group is called *inline elements*, because they can be applied to individual words or phrases within a paragraph or block of text. The second group is called *block-level elements*, and these are used to apply style information to an entire block of text, such as a paragraph. The following code samples illustrate all the wikitext and HTML tags that can be used to format inline text.

The wikitext is identified by a cluster of apostrophes. In order to make a word appear in italic type, you have to surround it with a pair of apostrophes, like so:

```
This word is ''italic''.
```

Likewise, to make the word appear in bold text, you surround it with three apostrophes:

```
This word is '''bold'''.
```

Finally, to display the word both in italic and bold, you use five apostrophes:

```
This word is '''''bold and italic'''''.
```

In addition to this wikitext markup, also available are several HTML elements that you can embed in your wikitext document, and which work just like regular HTML. The following wikitext example demonstrates all of the inline wikitext and HTML elements available to you:

```
Wikitext lets you set text to ''italic'', '''bold''' and
    '''''bold and italic''''' using wikitext, and I can set
    text to <i>italic</i>, <b>bold</b> and <b><i>bold and
    italic</i></b> using html, too. I can even
    <u>underline</u> it. Don't forget
    <strong>strong</strong> and <em>emphasis</em>, either.

This text is <tt>teletype</tt> and this text is for a <var>variable</var>

I can make text <big>big</big> and I can make text <small>small</small>.

I can <s>strike</s> text I no longer need.

I can <strike>strike</strike> text I no longer need this way, too.

I can write H<sub>2</sub>O, if I want, as well as E=mc<sup>2</sup>.

I do not recommend setting the <font face="Palatino">font
    to "Palatino"</font>, because not all computers use that font.

Here is a code example:<code>2+2=5</code>

Feel free to <cite>cite me in your code</cite>.
```

The preceding passage will be translated into the following HTML:

```
<p>Wikitext lets you set text to <i>italic</i>, <b>bold</b>
    and <i><b>bold and italic</b></i> using wikitext, and I
    can set text to <i>italic</i>, <b>bold</b> and
    <b><i>bold and italic</i></b> using html, too. I can
    even <u>underline</u> it. Don't forget
    <strong>strong</strong> and <em>emphasis</em>, either.</p>

<p>This text is <tt>teletype</tt> and this text is for a <var>variable</var></p>

<p>I can make text <big>big</big> and I can make text <small>small</small>.</p>

<p>I can <s>strike</s> text I no longer need.</p>

<p>I can <strike>strike</strike> text I no longer need this way, too.</p>
```

```
<p>I can write H<sub>2</sub>O, if I want, as well as E=mc<sup>2</sup>.</p>

<p>I do not recommend setting the <font face="Palatino">font
    to "Palatino"</font>, because not all computers use that font.</p>
```

As you can see, the original HTML elements that were used in the wikitext remained as is when the entire passage was converted to HTML. Figure 4-7 shows how the converted wikitext will be displayed in the viewer's browser.

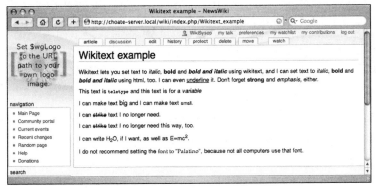

Figure 4-7: Wikitext is converted to HTML

In order to write italicized text, you must wrap the text in two apostrophes. (If you create the text in Microsoft Word and paste it into the editing field of MediaWiki, expect unexpected results. Microsoft Word usually converts apostrophes to "smart quotes," which is not read by MediaWiki.)

Comments

HTML comments are also allowed in wikitext:

```
<!-- Comment goes here  -->
```

A comment in wikitext is created in the same way as a comment in HTML, but with one important difference. Just as in regular HTML, MediaWiki does not display comments in the browser. In fact, MediaWiki doesn't convert a comment into HTML at all. The only time you can see a comment is when you are editing the wikitext. This means that you can leave notes to other editors without having to worry about the general public seeing them (assuming, of course, that the general public doesn't have access to editing your wikitext).

In the following sections you will learn about more complex wikitext constructs, so the examples have wikitext comments to highlight important areas for you to review.

Headings

Headings are used for generating tables of contents. When used, individual [edit] links appear to the right of the heading so that users can edit a particular section of the page, rather than the entire page.

The following code sample shows the six different heading levels, coded both in wikitext and in HTML:

```
=Heading 1=

<h1>Heading 1 (HTML)</h1>

==Heading 2==

<h2>Heading 2 (HTML)</h2>

===Heading 3===

<h3>Heading 3 (HTML)</h3>

====Heading 4====

<h4>Heading 4 (HTML)</h4>

=====Heading 5=====

<h5>Heading 5 (HTML)</h5>

======Heading 6======

<h6>Heading 6 (HTML)</h6>
```

For the sake of brevity, the following shows only the output of the first four headings:

```
<div class="editsection" style="float:right;margin-left:5px;">
  [<a href="/wiki/index.php?title=Headings&amp;action=edit&amp;section=1"
   title="Edit section: Heading 1">edit</a>]
</div>

<p><a name="Heading_1" id="Heading_1"></a></p>

<h1>Heading 1</h1>

<div class="editsection" style="float:right;margin-left:5px;">
  [<a href="/wiki/index.php?title=Headings&amp;action=edit&amp;section=2"
   title="Edit section: Heading 1 (HTML)">edit</a>]
</div>

<p><a name="Heading_1_.28HTML.29" id="Heading_1_.28HTML.29"></a></p>

<h1>Heading 1 (HTML)</h1>

<div class="editsection" style="float:right;margin-left:5px;">
  [<a href="/wiki/index.php?title=Headings&amp;action=edit&amp;section=3"
   title="Edit section: Heading 2">edit</a>]
</div>

<p><a name="Heading_2" id="Heading_2"></a></p>

<h2>Heading 2</h2>
```

```
<div class="editsection" style="float:right;margin-left:5px;">
  [<a href="/wiki/index.php?title=Headings&action=edit&section=4"
   title="Edit section: Heading 2 (HTML)">edit</a>]
</div>

<p><a name="Heading_2_.28HTML.29" id="Heading_2_.28HTML.29"></a></p>

<h2>Heading 2 (HTML)</h2>
```

MediaWiki treats headings as sections, and it allows users to edit only the section of the page they want to modify. This can be helpful with long pages. As you can see in the HTML output, preceding each heading is a <div> element that links to an editing page for each section. The preceding HTML output contains four sections, numbered one through four, which you can see referred to inside the <div> element.

In addition, as you can see, both the wikitext heading and the HTML heading are formatted the same way. The only difference is the name used for the named anchor. This is a consequence of the fact that you cannot have duplicate named anchors in a document, so MediaWiki creates a unique name. This is why the first heading has a name and id of Heading_1, while the second heading has a name and id of Heading_1_.28HTML.29. These named anchors are used to generate a table of contents for the page, which is displayed at the top of the page. Again, this is helpful when reading long pages. The following code shows the HTML that is produced for the table of contents page. Note that it ends with a bit of JavaScript code that enables users to toggle between displaying or not displaying the table:

```
<table id="toc" class="toc" summary="Contents">
  <tr>
    <td>
  <div id="toctitle">
    <h2>Contents</h2>
  </div>

  <ul>
    <li class="toclevel-1"><a href="#Heading_1"><span class="tocnumber">
  1</span> <span class="toctext">Heading 1</span></a></li>

    <li class="toclevel-1">
      <a href="#Heading_1_.28HTML.29"><span class="tocnumber">2</span> <span
    class="toctext">Heading 1 (HTML)</span></a>

      <ul>
        <li class="toclevel-2"><a href="#Heading_2"><span class="tocnumber">
    2.1</span> <span class="toctext">Heading 2</span></a></li>

        <li class="toclevel-2"><a href="#Heading_2_.28HTML.29"><span
      class="tocnumber">2.2</span> <span class="toctext">Heading
      2 (HTML)</span></a></li>
      </ul>
    </li>
  </ul>
    </td>
  </tr>
</table>
<p><script type="text/javascript">
 if (window.showTocToggle) { var tocShowText = "show"; var
  tocHideText = "hide"; showTocToggle();}
</script></p>
```

By default, the table of contents is only generated for pages with three or more headings. A user can opt not to have any table of contents at all by going to the user preferences page and clicking the Misc tab. One of the options that is selected by default is Show Table of Contents (for pages with more than three headings). Clicking the checkbox toggles that default preference off. You can also set limits on how deep the table of contents can go by adding the following to the `LocalSettings.php` file:

```
/** Maximum indent level of toc. */
$wgMaxTocLevel = 999;
```

By default, the maximum indent level is 999, which is more than enough. In fact, the only really meaningful limit would be something less than six, as the headings only extend six levels deep.

As a stylistic point, bear in mind that the title of the page is displayed using `<h1>` the element, so you should reserve your use of headings in the body of the article to the equivalent of `<h2>` and above. It is also regarded as good style to nest your headings in descending order, without skipping any levels. For example, you do not want to do the following:

```
==This is my first article section==

Some introductory text...

====This is a sub-heading====
```

This example jumps from a level 2 heading to a level 4 heading, rather than use a level 3 heading as the next natural subhead. Figure 4-8 shows the heading levels in MediaWiki.

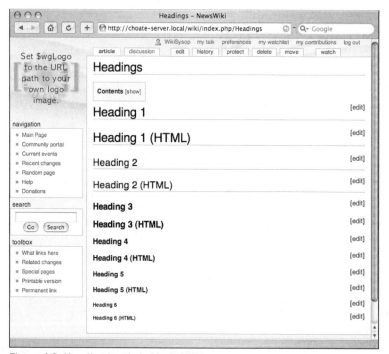

Figure 4-8: Heading levels in MediaWiki

Lines and Breaks

A horizontal rule is simply four hyphens (----). You can also use the `<hr>` HTML element.

The horizontal rule element is one of only a couple of elements that never have any child elements. In HTML, you are allowed to have an element with an opening tag, but not a closing tag. XML forbids this, so XHTML (the XML implementation of HTML) requires a closing tag, or the use of a shorthand notation. Note that MediaWiki accepts both forms of horizontal rule.

The first item in the following example is the old-fashioned HTML version of the horizontal rule, and the second item is the new-fangled XHTML version of the horizontal rule. The only difference is the presence of a / in the second item:

```
<hr width="50%">
<hr width="50%"/>
```

One of the advantages of using the HTML version, rather than the wikitext version, is that you get access to all the attributes of horizontal rules. In the previous example, I have set the width of the rule to be 50% of the size of the page on which it is displayed. Without the intervention of cascading stylesheets (CSS), this is not possible with the wikitext version.

When you want to insert a line break into a document without establishing another paragraph, you can use the `<br>` element. Like the horizontal rule, it doesn't have any children, so MediaWiki takes two forms of it as well:

```
<br>
<br/>
```

Block-Level Elements

Technically speaking, heading elements are block-level elements too, as they apply to the entire paragraph of text. Nevertheless, they have special attributes that warrant a separate treatment. By definition, a block-level element stands alone with space before it and after it (see Figure 4-9). Unlike inline elements, you'll never see two block-level elements displayed side by side. The wikitext addition to the HTML is simple: A blank line designates a new paragraph, as shown in the following example:

```
A blank line separates paragraphs.

You can also use HTML tags to establish paragraphs.

<p>This is a paragraph</p>

<div>This is a block of text</div>

<blockquote>Yes, you can quote me on this</blockquote>

And a caption: <caption>This is my caption.</caption>
```

The wikitext is converted to the following HTML:

```
<p>A blank line separates paragraphs.</p>

<p>You can also use HTML tags to establish paragraphs.</p>
```

```
<p>This is a paragraph</p>

<center>
   This is a centered paragraph
</center>

<div>
   This is a block of text
</div>

<blockquote>
   Yes, you can quote me on this
</blockquote>
<p>And a caption:</p>

<table>
   <caption>
        This is my caption.
   </caption>
</table>
```

Note that when MediaWiki encounters a `<caption>` element, it automatically assumes that it is part of a table, and inserts it between `<table>` tags.

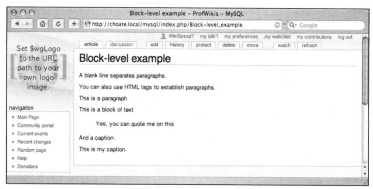

Figure 4-9: The block-level elements

Preformatted Text

There are times when you do not want your wikitext converted to HTML. There are three ways to do this in MediaWiki. The following code shows all three methods:

```
== Pre-formatted text==

===Example 1: &lt;nowiki&gt; ===

<nowiki>
# First item
## This item should be indented
# The final item
```

```
</nowiki>

----

===Example 2: &lt;pre&gt; ===

<pre>
# First item
## This item should be indented
# The final item
</pre>

===Example 3: Preceding space===

 # First item
 ## This item should be indented
 # The final item
```

The first example uses the `<nowiki>` tag. The second example uses `<pre>` , which should be familiar if you know HTML. Figure 4-10 shows an example of how these are displayed. In the final example, a space has been inserted at the front of each line. The following code shows the HTML that is rendered:

```
<div class="editsection" style="float:right;margin-left:5px;">
  [<a href="/wiki/index.php?title=Pre-formatted_text_example&amp;action=edit&amp;
   section=1" title="Edit section: Pre-formatted text">edit</a>]
</div>

<p><a name="Pre-formatted_text" id="Pre-formatted_text"></a></p>

<h2>Pre-formatted text</h2>

<div class="editsection" style="float:right;margin-left:5px;">
  [<a href="/wiki/index.php?title=Pre-formatted_text_example&amp;action=edit&amp;
   section=2" title="Edit section: Example 1: &amp;lt;nowiki&amp;gt;">edit</a>]
</div>
<p><a name="Example_1:_.3Cnowiki.3E" id="Example_1:_.3Cnowiki.3E"></a></p>

<h3>Example 1: &lt;nowiki&gt;</h3>

<p># First item ## This item should be indented # The final item</p>
  <hr>

<div class="editsection" style="float:right;margin-left:5px;">
  [<a href="/wiki/index.php?title=Pre-formatted_text_example&amp;action=edit&amp;
   section=3" title="Edit section: Example 2: &amp;lt;pre&amp;gt;">edit</a>]
</div>

<p><a name="Example_2:_.3Cpre.3E" id="Example_2:_.3Cpre.3E"></a></p>

<h3>Example 2: &lt;pre&gt;</h3>
  <pre>
# First item
## This item should be indented
```

```
# The final item
</pre>
<div class="editsection" style="float:right;margin-left:5px;">
  [<a href="/wiki/index.php?title=Pre-formatted_text_example&amp;action=edit&amp;
   section=4" title="Edit section: Example 3: Preceding space">edit</a>]
</div>
```

```
<p><a name="Example_3:_Preceding_space"
   id="Example_3:_Preceding_space"></a></p>
```

```
<h3>Example 3: Preceding space</h3>
  <pre>
# First item
## This item should be indented
# The final item
</pre>
```

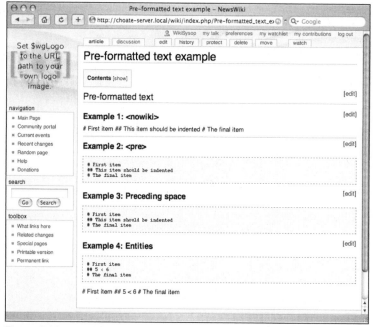

Figure 4-10: <nowiki> and <pre> links displayed by MediaWiki

Lists

There are three kinds of lists: ordered lists, unordered lists (bulleted lists), and definition lists. An ordered list uses numbers of different formats to identify each list item, whereas an unordered list uses bullets. The actual numeric format and bullet are ultimately decided by stylesheets. Definition lists are lists of terms, along with their definitions, such as a glossary.

As you might guess, there is both a wikitext method of creating lists and an HTML method. The following code shows examples of both methods:

```
==Wikitext ordered list==

# first list item
# second list item

==HTML ordered list==

<ol>
   <li> first list item</li>
   <li> second list item</li>
</ol>

==Wikitext unordered list==

* first list item
* second list item

==HTML unordered list==

<ul>
   <li> first list item</li>
   <li> second list item</li>
</ul>

definition lists:

;Glossary
;Wikitext : Markup used for MediaWiki
;HTML: Hypertext Markup Language

<dl><dt>Glossary
<dt>Wikitext 
<dd> Markup used for MediaWiki
<dt>HTML<dd> Hypertext Markup Language
</dl>
```

One important difference between the wikitext method and the HTML method is that the wikitext method limits list items to a single paragraph. This is due to a limitation in the parser. If your list items need to be more than one paragraph, then you should use the HTML method.

You may have noticed that the HTML used in the last example for the definition list does not use closing tags — that is, there is no < /dt> or </dl> . That's because, for some reason, the parser does not interpret them properly and they end up being displayed on the page. When they are removed, the parser converts the text to proper HTML and it is formatted appropriately when displayed. This kind of shorthand is based on SGML-based HTML which allows tags to not be closed. In most cases, this chapter doesn't focus on that syntax because it is nonstandard XHTML and there is simply not enough space to address every possible variation (the MediaWiki parser is actually quite accommodating). In this case, the example used here was chosen because the XHTML method does not work.

Figure 4-11 illustrates three lists displayed as HTML.

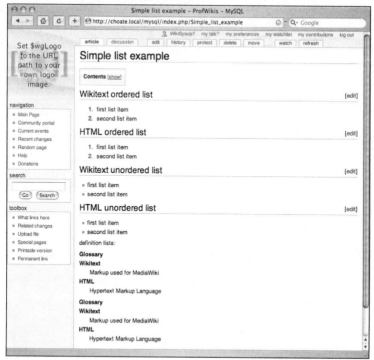

Figure 4-11: An ordered list, an unordered list, and a definition list in MediaWiki

Nested Lists

So far, the examples have been simple, but you can do more complicated, interesting things with your lists. For example, you can create nested lists. The following example shows you how to make a nested, ordered list:

```
==Nested lists==
# first list item
## first sub item
## second sub item
# second list item

<ol>
  <li> first list item
    <ol>
      <li> first sub item</li>
      <li> second sub item</li>
    </ol>
  </li>
  <li> second list item</li>
</ol>
```

Mixed Nested Lists

In the previous example, one ordered list was nested inside another ordered list. You might be tempted to use the following wikitext to nest an unordered list inside an ordered list:

```
==Bad mixed nested list==
# first list item
** first sub item
** second sub item
# second list item

==Good mixed nested list==

# first list item
#* first sub item
#**first sub sub item
#* second sub item
# second list item
## first numbered sub item

==Another good mixed nested list==

# first list item
#* first sub item
#*#first sub sub item
#* second sub item
# second list item
## first numbered sub item
```

In the preceding examples, the first list attempts to nest an unordered list inside an ordered list. If you do this, however, you will get the following output, which is likely not what you expect:

```
<ol>
  <li> first list item</li>
</ol>
<ul>
  <li>
    <ul>
      <li> first sub item</li>
      <li> second sub item</li>
    </ul>
  </li>
</ul>
<ol>
  <li> second list item</li>
</ol>
```

Instead of finding an unordered list nested inside an ordered list, you find an ordered list followed by an unordered list, followed by yet another ordered list. Figure 4-12 illustrates how this list will be displayed by MediaWiki.

The two examples that follow the first example show the proper way to do nesting. You were shown the wrong way to do it first because the wrong way seems to be the intuitive way (to me, at least), and the correct way isn't that intuitive.

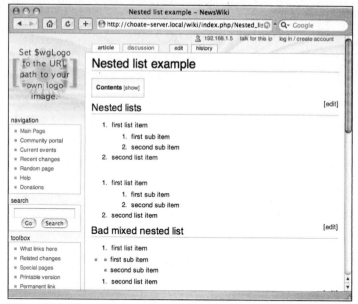

Figure 4-12: Three lists in sequence, rather than nested as expected

Figure 4-13 shows both examples of acceptable nested lists.

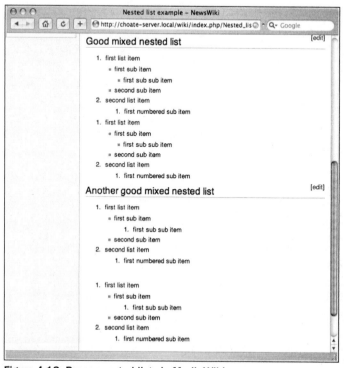

Figure 4-13: Proper nested lists in MediaWiki

Tables

Tables are difficult to implement under any circumstances. Wikitext provides a non-WYSIWYG way to create tables, but it is less than ideal. As a matter of fact, it allows you to use three different approaches to creating tables. Because the first approach is simply to code it in XHTML, I focus my examples on the other two approaches: simplified HTML and a piped table. Either way, each system requires a thorough understanding of how to create tables in HTML. The piped table merely substitutes | characters for certain HTML constructs, so if you don't understand what's being replaced, you may find it confusing.

Basic Tables

The following wikitext examples show three different ways of making a basic table in MediaWiki. Tables are divided into rows and columns, and the intersection of a row and a column is a cell. The first table is created using familiar HTML syntax:

```
<table>
  <tr>
    <th>Row 1, Heading 1</th>
    <th>Row 1, Heading 2</th>
  </tr>
  <tr>
    <td>Row 2, Cell 1</td>
    <td> Row 2, Cell 2</td>
  </tr>
</table>
```

This is the wikitext version of the same table:

```
{|
! Row 1, Heading 1
! Row 1, Heading 2
|-
| Row 2, Cell 1
| Row 2, Cell 2
|}
```

The following example shows an alternative equivalent. Instead of each cell being written on its own line, the following example shows the cells of each row displayed on the same line. In order to separate cells using table headers, the line must start with an exclamation mark (!), and each cell must be separated by two exclamation marks (!!). Likewise, table data rows start with a pipe (|), and each cell in the row is separated by two pipes (||):

```
{|
! Row 1, Heading 1!! Row 1, Heading 2
|-
| Row 2, Cell 1 || Row 2, Cell 2
|}
```

All three of the preceding table examples are rendered the same way in MediaWiki, as shown in Figure 4-14.

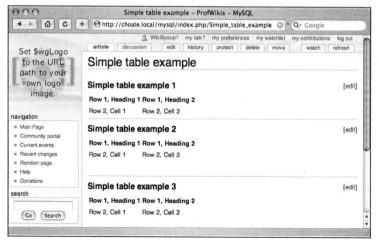

Figure 4-14: Basic tables in MediaWiki

Table Attributes

If you enter the table example into the edit field of MediaWiki, it will be published as is, with no changes to the code you entered. If you do this, you'll see that the table is formed, but difficult to read. In order to fix that, you need to modify some attributes of the table. When testing or writing a new table, one of the best things to do is display the borders of the cells. The space between the cells is defined by the `cellpadding` and `cellspacing` attributes.

Padding refers to the space between the text within the cell and the edge of the cell, while *spacing* refers to the space between the cells. The following two examples display the same table from the previous example, but with a border that is 1-pixel wide, and with cell padding of 2 pixels and cell spacing of 6 pixels. Figure 4-15 shows a simple table with various attributes added. In addition to the border, a caption is added as well:

```
===Simple table (with attributes) example 1===

<!-- You can create tables in plain HTML -->

<table border="1" cellpadding="2" cellspacing="6">
  <caption>This is my caption</caption>
  <tr>
    <th>Row 1, Heading 1</th>
    <th>Row 1, Heading 2</th>
  </tr>
  <tr>
    <td>Row 2, Cell 1</td>
    <td> Row 2, Cell 2</td>
  </tr>
</table>

===Simple table (with attributes) example 2===
```

```
<!-- The following table is equivalent to the previous
HTML table-->

{| border="1" cellpadding="2" cellspacing="6"
|+ This is my caption
! Row 1, Heading 1
! Row 1, Heading 2
|-
| Row 2, Cell 1
| Row 2, Cell 2
|}
```

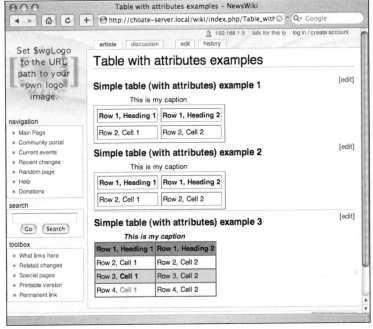

Figure 4-15: Tables with attributes in MediaWiki

Attributes can be used on rows and cells, too. The following example builds on the previous one by adding color to two of the rows of the table, and by adding a wikilink in the first cell of row 4:

```
===Simple table (with attributes) example 3===

<!-- This is a slightly more complex table, that
sets attributes on rows and individual cells -->

<!-- Set the space between the cells (cellspacing) to 0-->
{| border="1" cellpadding="2" cellspacing="0"
<!-- I want the caption to be bold and italic-->
|+ '''''This is my caption'''''
<!-- Set the header background color to gray-->
|- bgcolor="gray"
```

```
! Row 1, Heading 1
! Row 1, Heading 2
|-
| Row 2, Cell 1
| Row 2, Cell 2
<!-- This row uses a different way to define the color-->
|- bgcolor="#cccccc"
<!-- Regular wikitext can be used in cells, too-->
| Row 3, '''Cell 1'''
| Row 3, Cell 2
|-
<!--Wiki links work as well-->
| Row 4, [[Cell 1]]
| Row 4, Cell 2
|}
```

Colspan and Rowspan

You can also combine cells, across rows or columns. The following examples show both the HTML and the wikitext method of joining cells:

```
===Colspan and rowspan example 1===

====HTML colspan====
<table border="1">
  <tr>
  <!-- The header will span two columns -->
    <th colspan="2">Row 1, Heading 1</th>
  </tr>
  <tr>
    <td>Row 2, Cell 1</td>
    <td> Row 2, Cell 2</td>
  </tr>
</table>

----

====Wikitext colspan====

{| border="1"
|+ This is my caption
! colspan="2" |Row 1, Heading 1
|-
| Row 2, Cell 1
| Row 2, Cell 2
|}


===Colspan and rowspan example 2===

====HTML rowspan====
```

```
<table border="1">
  <tr>
    <!--The following cell spans two rows-->
    <th rowspan="2">Row 1, Heading 1</th>
    <th>Row 1, Heading 2</th>
  </tr>
  <tr>
    <td> Row 2, Cell 2</td>
  </tr>
</table>

----

====Wikitext rowspan====


{| border="1"
|+ This is my caption
! rowspan="2"| Row 1, Heading 1
! Row 1, Heading 1
|-
| Row 2, Cell 2
|}
```

Figure 4-16 shows how the different colspan and rowspan options are displayed.

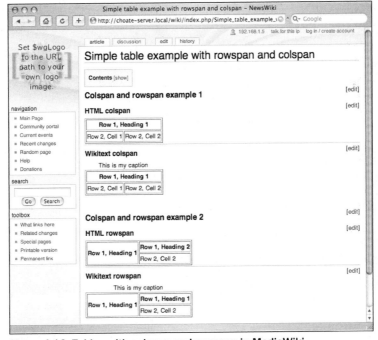

Figure 4-16: Tables with colspan and rowspan in MediaWiki

Combining Tables and Lists

A more complicated construct occurs when combining tables and lists. The following wikitext is an example of embedding a list inside a cell of a table:

```
===Tables and lists example===

{|border=1 cellpadding=0 cellspacing=0
|+ Resume
|- valign="top"
! Experience
|
<!-- The "NASA" item has a space in front of it, causing it to
be displayed incorrectly-->
 # NASA
# CIA
|- valign="top"
<!-- The list items need to be on their own line -->
! Goals
|
# Get a job
# Lose weight
|}
```

The following code shows the HTML that is output. Two lists are used in the table: The first list is used to display a list of organizations for which the applicant has worked in the past, and the second list is a record of personal goals for the applicant. The first list is not displayed as expected because an extra space has been inserted before the # NASA phrase, which MediaWiki assumes should be converted into a <pre> tag. It is then followed by an ordered list with one item, CIA. The list of goals is displayed properly.

```
<div class="editsection" style="float:right;margin-left:5px;">
  [<a href="/wiki/index.php?title=Table_with_embedded_lists&amp;action=edit&amp;
    section=1" title="Edit section: Tables and lists example">edit</a>]
</div>

<p><a name="Tables_and_lists_example" id="Tables_and_lists_example"></a></p>

<h3>Tables and lists example</h3>

<table border="1" cellpadding="0" cellspacing="0">
  <caption>
        Resume
  </caption>

  <tr valign="top">
        <th>Experience</th>
        <td>
<pre>
# NASA
</pre>
```

```
                    <ol>
                        <li>CIA</li>
                    </ol>
            </td>
        </tr>

        <tr valign="top">
            <th>Goals</th>
            <td>
                    <ol>
                        <li>Get a job</li>
                        <li>Lose weight</li>
                    </ol>
            </td>
        </tr>
</table>
```

The output of this HTML is shown in Figure 4-17.

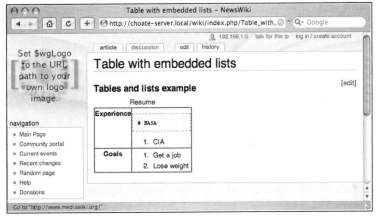

Figure 4-17: Table with embedded list output

HTML on Wiki Pages

Despite the convenience of wikitext, many users prefer to use HTML, and MediaWiki obliges that wish by providing several options for placing HTML on the page. However, it does so with its own idiosyncrasies.

Character and Entity References

MediaWiki deviates from the XML standard in handling numeric character references and character entity references. The goal is to avoid collisions with special characters used in XML markup.

For example, if you were to refer to a < character in the text of a document, an XML parser would mistake that for the beginning of an XML tag. In order to avoid that, you use a reference instead. When you enter < in your text, it is rendered by the browser as a < character. XML defines the character entity references shown in the following table, along with the character that is displayed in the browser.

Entity References	Displayed Character
&amp;	&
&lt;	<
&gt;	>
&quot;	"
&apos;	'

MediaWiki supports all of these entities except '. All of the others work just like they do in XML, but any use of ' in text will be converted to &apos;, which is displayed as "'". In other words, it is displayed in the browser just as it's written in wikitext.

In addition to the XML character entity references, HTML defines a total of 252 character entity references. These are defined in the global variable $wgHtmlEntities by Sanitizer.php.

Whenever you want the characters defined in this list to display in the browser, you need to use the entity references. One possible source of confusion is that you can enter the characters directly into the edit field:

ˆ øπ'''æ...¬°Δ˙©ƒ

When you select Preview, the characters will be displayed as is, without being converted. However, when you are ready to save the changes to the page, a blank page is returned — the raw UTF-8 characters are neither converted to entities nor displayed in the browser. The reason for this has to do with how different languages are handled by MediaWiki, a topic reviewed later in the book.

Sanitizing

MediaWiki allows you to use a wide range of HTML instead of wikitext. All such HTML is run through the Sanitizer.php script, which ensures that the HTML is well formed, and converts HTML 4.x tags to XHTML tags (performing tasks such as changing <br> to < br/> and making the element names lowercase). It also encodes values in attributes that would confuse the MediaWiki parser. Any characters with special meaning to the parser are converted into entities, as shown in the following snippet of code pulled from Sanitizer.php:

```
'<'    => '&lt;',    // This should never happen,
'>'    => '&gt;',    // we've received invalid input
'"'    => '&quot;',  // which should have been escaped.
'{'    => '&#123;',
'['    => '&#91;',
'"'    => '&#39;&#39;',
```

```
'ISBN' => '&#73;SBN',
'RFC'  => '&#82;FC',
'PMID' => '&#80;MID',
'|'    => '&#124;',
'__'   => '&#95;_',
```

It also cleans up any CSS included in style attributes, removing JavaScript expressions (from Internet Explorer 5.0+) and all URLs.

If you choose not to have this level of security (and concomitant restrictions), you can opt to allow unrestricted HTML to be entered by users (a risky proposition), by setting the global variable $wgRawHtml to true. Likewise, you can disable HTML altogether, by setting the global variable $wgUserHtml to false.

The following example shows wikitext handling of entities. The result of this wikitext will be a table that displays the entity markup in the first column, and the entity output in the second column. In order to do this, the entities in the first column are escaped:

```
<h2>Tables and Entities</h2>
{|border="1" width="80%" cellpadding="4px" cellspacing="0px"
|+ This table illustrates the use of entities in wikitext
|- bgcolor="gray"
! Entity !! Character
|-align="center"
|&amp;amp;|| &amp;
|-
|&amp;amp;|| &
|-
|&amp;gt;|| &gt;
|-
|&amp;gt;|| >
|-
|&amp;lt;|| &lt;
|-
|&amp;lt;|| <
|-
|&amp;copy;|| &copy;
|-
|&amp;#34;|| &#34;
|-
|&amp;quot;|| &quot;
|-
|&amp;#34;|| "

|}
```

The wikitext is converted to the following HTML. Pay special attention to how the entities are converted:

```
<div class="editsection" style="float:right;margin-left:5px;">
  [<a href="/wiki/index.php?title=Table_example&amp;action=edit&amp;
   section=1" title="Edit section: Tables and Entities">edit</a>]
</div>
```

107

```
<p><a name="Tables_and_Entities" id="Tables_and_Entities"></a></p>

<h2>Tables and Entities</h2>

<table border="1" width="80%" cellpadding="4px" cellspacing="0px">
  <caption>
          This table illustrates the use of entities in wikitext
  </caption>
  <tr bgcolor="gray">
          <th>Entity</th>
          <th>Character</th>
  </tr>
  <tr align="center">
          <td>&amp;amp;</td>
          <td>&amp;</td>
  </tr>
  <tr>
          <td>&amp;amp;</td>
          <td>&amp;</td>
  </tr>
  <tr>
          <td>&amp;gt;</td>
          <td>&gt;</td>
  </tr>
  <tr>
          <td>&amp;gt;</td>
          <td>&gt;</td>
  </tr>
  <tr>
          <td>&amp;lt;</td>
          <td>&lt;</td>
  </tr>
  <tr>
          <td>&amp;lt;</td>
          <td>&lt;</td>
  </tr>
  <tr>
          <td>&amp;copy;</td>
          <td>©</td>
  </tr>
  <tr>
          <td>&amp;#34;</td>
          <td>"</td>
  </tr>
  <tr>
          <td>&amp;quot;</td>
          <td>"</td>
  </tr>
  <tr>
          <td>&amp;#34;</td>
          <td>"</td>
  </tr>
</table>
```

Figure 4-18 shows how MediaWiki displays a complex table of entities.

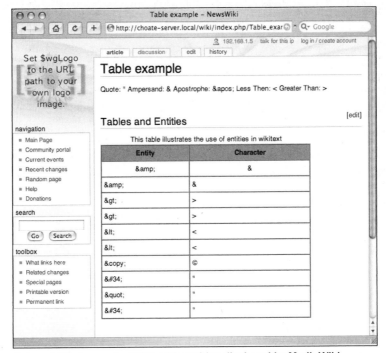

Figure 4-18: A complex table with entities displayed by MediaWiki

Ruby text, for East Asian languages

The final group of HTML elements usable in MediaWiki are those used for rubies, a typographical technique used in Japanese writing:

```
<rb>
<rp>
<rt>
<ruby>
```

Footnotes

Footnotes are not part of the base MediaWiki installation, but there is an extension that you can easily install that adds this feature. All extensions are installed inside the extensions folder. The first step is to create a Cite folder inside the extensions folder. Then, download Cite.php and Cite.i18n.php from MediaWiki's Subversion repository:

```
http://svn.wikimedia.org/viewvc/mediawiki/trunk/extensions/Cite/Cite.php?view=co
http://svn.wikimedia.org/viewvc/mediawiki/trunk/extensions/Cite/
   Cite.i18n.php?view=co
```

Once the files are downloaded, you need to update `LocalSettings.php` by adding the following line:

```
require_once( "{\$IP}/extensions/Cite/Cite.php" );
```

That's all there is to adding this extension. It enables two new XML tags to be used in the text: `<ref>` `</ref>` and `<references/>`. The text for the footnote is inserted between the `<ref>` tags. `<references/>` is a placeholder that you type at the bottom of the page, where the actual reference will be displayed. The following snippet shows how a reference is entered into the document:

```
A reference goes here <ref>Professional Wikis by Mark Choate</ref>.

more text....


<references/>
```

The preceding reference is translated into the following HTML:

```
A reference goes here <sup id="_ref-0" class="reference"><a
   href="#_note-0" title="">[1]</a></sup>.

more text...

<ol class="references">
  <li id="_note-0"><a href="#_ref-0" title="">$\uparrow$</a> This is
  a reference</li>
</ol>
```

The footnotes themselves are automatically numbered. This example contains one footnote, and it's numbered 1. The code is also smart enough to know when references are repeated, so it will combine footnotes if more than one footnote refers to the same text.

Figure 4-19 shows how the references are displayed.

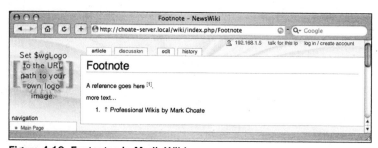

Figure 4-19: Footnotes in MediaWiki

Signatures

If you want to sign your name to a post, MediaWiki offers three shortcuts. Signatures are used primarily on pages in the Talk namespace, to identify the person making the post. Typically, articles in the main namespace do not use signatures because they are collaboratively authored.

```
<!--Three tildes display your username-->
~~~
<!--Four tildes display your username and the current date-->
~~~~
<!--Five tildes display the current date-->
~~~~~
```

Figure 4-20 shows how the three different variations are displayed on the page.

Figure 4-20: Three different signatures

Editing Alternatives

Wikitext and HTML are not your only editing options. MediaWiki also provides a toolbar that can be used to assist with the composition of wikitext, and some WYSIWYG alternatives are available too.

Toolbar

The toolbar displayed above the edit field offers some shortcuts that can help you avoid typing wikitext. It offers at least some of the ease of using a WYSIWYG editor. The following table shows you the wikitext that is generated if you click one of the buttons while no text is selected in the edit field is selected.

The buttons insert some placeholder text, which can be useful if you've forgotten the syntax of a particular item. If you have text selected in the field, then pressing the button wraps the selected text in the appropriate wiki tags in order to apply the proper formatting.

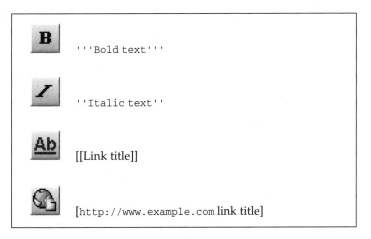

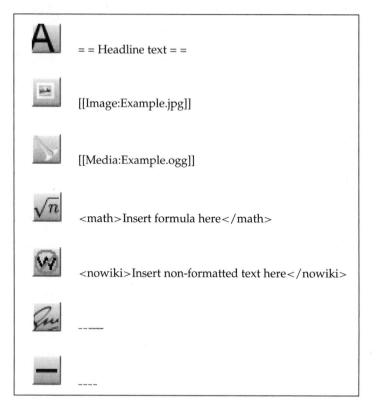

You can find information online about different approaches to editing MediaWiki, including instructions for embedding a WYSIWYG interface, as well as how to use external editors. This chapter does not cover these in any detail, for a few reasons.

First, many of the approaches were developed specifically for Wikipedia, so the process of customizing them for your own needs is somewhat complex, and certainly beyond the scope of this book. Second, in almost all cases, specialized approaches mean limiting users to certain browsers. Finally, all of the approaches tested for this book simply didn't work very well, or they didn't work at all. None of them are core parts of the MediaWiki distribution, and they are not implemented by the MediaWiki developers.

Summary

In this chapter, you learned how to create and edit pages using wikitext and some basic HTML markup. In the next chapter, you will build on this knowledge and learn how to upload images and display them on wiki pages, as well as how to upload files that can be downloaded by users.

5

Images and Files

In the previous chapter, you learned how to create and edit pages using wikitext, but that just skimmed the surface of the kind of content you can add to a wiki page. In this chapter, you will learn how to configure MediaWiki so that files can be uploaded, as well as how to control what kinds of files can be uploaded. You will also learn how to link to images, embed images in pages, and create thumbnails, as well as how to make image galleries. The chapter concludes with a discussion of uploading different file types and how you can use this feature as a simple document management tool.

File Uploads

MediaWiki can be configured to allow users to upload files of any type. By default, this feature is used primarily to upload images, but it can also be used to upload documents in formats such as Microsoft Word, Adobe PDF, and so on. By default, file uploading is disabled, so the first step is to enable it.

Enabling Uploads

There are three steps to enabling file uploads. The first step is to make sure that PHP is configured to allow file uploads. This is set in the php.ini file:

```
file_uploads = On
```

The second step is to make sure that $wgFileUploads is set to true in LocalSettings.php:

```
$wgFileUploads=true
```

By default, MediaWiki installs all files inside the images folder of your MediaWiki installation.

The third step is to make sure that the images directory in your MediaWiki installation is writeable by the Web server because that is where the uploaded files will reside.

Uploading Images

Files are uploaded using the `Special:Upload` page. If you have the privileges to upload files, then a link to this page will appear in the toolbox of your wiki (in the left-hand column in the default design). You can also go directly to the page at the following URL (changing the address to match yours, of course):

```
http://127.0.0.1/wiki/index.php/Special:Upload
```

If you click on the `Special:Upload` page and you have not enabled file uploads, then you will be notified that uploads are disabled.

Another way to get to the `Special:Upload` page is to put an image link in another page, just as you put wiki links into pages in order to create new pages (see "Image Linking and Embedding" later in this chapter to learn about the syntax of creating image links). After you add a link to an image, the link to that image will appear as a hyperlink on the page, which, when clicked, will take the user to the `Special:Upload` page.

The `Special:Upload` page (shown in Figure 5-1) enables you to select the file to upload by clicking the Choose File button. Once a file is selected, its name appears next to the button. You can also choose to give the file a different name when it is uploaded. You might want to do this if there is already a file with the same name that you do not want to overwrite. (MediaWiki saves copies of all uploaded files, so you can always revert to a previous version of the file if you inadvertently overwrite another file.)

You should also write a summary of the file in the Summary field — the summary appears in several places and helps to identify the image without having to actually view it. Finally, you are given the option to watch the page, which you invoke by checking the Watch This Page checkbox. You can also select the option to Ignore Any Warnings, which you should only do if you truly know what you are doing. The warnings include messages that you are about to overwrite a file, that the file is larger than is preferred, or that it's not of a type that MediaWiki wants you to upload. The parameters that trigger the warnings about file size and file type are all configurable in `LocalSettings.php` and are discussed in more detail later in this chapter.

Figure 5-1: The Special:Upload page

To see a list of images that have already been uploaded, you can visit the `Special:Imagelist` page.

If you upload an image with the same name as an image that has already been uploaded, then it will overwrite the original image. The old version of the file (or image) is saved, however, and you will be able to revert to the file if needed. Chapter 7 provides more details about MediaWiki's version control facilities and how to revert to earlier versions of pages and files.

The Image Page

Once a file is uploaded, MediaWiki creates a page for that file known as an *image description page* (it would be more accurate to call it a file description page). The page that it creates is a page like any other page (see Figure 5-2). If the file is an image, then the image is embedded in the page. If the file is not an image, then an icon for that file is displayed if MediaWiki knows the file's MIME type.

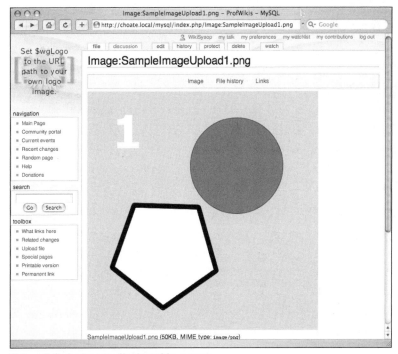

Figure 5-2: An image displayed in a page

User Preferences

The image shown in Figure 5-2 is rather large, large enough that the entire length of the page could not be viewed on my computer without scrolling. Because users of wikis have different monitor sizes, and different connection speeds, MediaWiki enables users to set some preferences for how these images are displayed. In the preferences section of MediaWiki, users can specify how large an images should be displayed.

The following code excerpt from `DefaultSettings.php` shows the available settings from which users can choose. The first array determines the size of the image as displayed on the image description page. The second array sets the width of image thumbnails, which are explained in the section "Image Linking and Embedding" later in this chapter.

```
/**
 * Limit images on image description pages to a user-selectable limit. In order
 * to reduce disk usage, limits can only be selected from a list. This is the
 * list of settings the user can choose from:
 */
```

```
$wgImageLimits = array (
        array(320,240),
        array(640,480),
        array(800,600),
        array(1024,768),
        array(1280,1024),
        array(10000,10000) );

/**
 * Adjust thumbnails on image pages according to a user setting. In order to
 * reduce disk usage, the values can only be selected from a list. This is the
 * list of settings the user can choose from:
 */
$wgThumbLimits = array(
        120,
        150,
        180,
        200,
        250,
        300
```

Figure 5-3 shows an example of an image description page displaying the same image shown in Figure 5-2, except that here the image width has been modified.

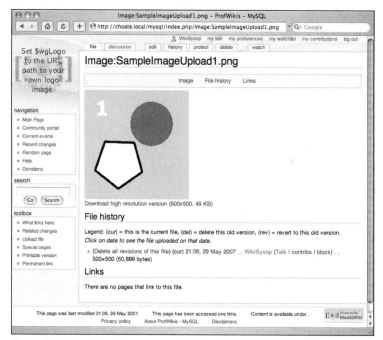

Figure 5-3: File upload page, with user preferences set

Now that we have a more manageable image size, we can turn to the other information that is on the page. The first section is a section about the file's history. Every time you upload a new file with the same name as this file, a new entry in the history list will be added. This enables you to revert to older versions of the image (or document). This is followed by a list of pages that link to this image.

This page can be edited, just like any other page, by clicking the Edit tab at the top of the page. Your copy will appear above the file history section, right below the image thumbnail. Anything you do on a regular MediaWiki page can be done here, too.

File Types

The following code listing shows the default configuration of MediaWiki with respect to file uploads. The $wgFileExtensions variable is a list of file extensions that MediaWiki allows. This is followed by $wgFileBlacklist, which is an array of extensions that MediaWiki explicitly does not allow because of security concerns. For example, MediaWiki won't let you upload HTML files, JavaScript files, or any files associated with scripting languages or executables. The variable $wgCheckFileExtensions must be set to true for this to have any effect.

In addition to testing by file extension, MediaWiki also maintains a blacklist based on MIME type, as the file extension is no guarantee of what is in the file. In order for this to work, $wgVerifyMimeType must be enabled.

```
/**
 * This is the list of preferred extensions for uploading files. Uploading files
 * with extensions not in this list will trigger a warning.
 */
$wgFileExtensions = array( 'png', 'gif', 'jpg', 'jpeg' );

/** Files with these extensions will never be allowed as uploads. */
$wgFileBlacklist = array(
        # HTML may contain cookie-stealing JavaScript and web bugs
        'html', 'htm', 'js', 'jsb',
        # PHP scripts may execute arbitrary code on the server
        'php', 'phtml', 'php3', 'php4', 'php5', 'phps',
        # Other types that may be interpreted by some servers
        'shtml', 'jhtml', 'pl', 'py', 'cgi',
        # May contain harmful executables for Windows victims
        'exe', 'scr', 'dll', 'msi', 'vbs', 'bat', 'com', 'pif', 'cmd', 'vxd', 'cpl' );

/** Files with these MIME types will never be allowed as uploads
 * if $wgVerifyMIMEType is enabled.
 */
$wgMIMETypeBlacklist= array(
        # HTML may contain cookie-stealing JavaScript and web bugs
        'text/html', 'text/javascript', 'text/x-javascript',
    'application/x-shellscript',
        # PHP scripts may execute arbitrary code on the server
        'application/x-php', 'text/x-php',
```

```
        # Other types that may be interpreted by some servers
        'text/x-python', 'text/x-perl', 'text/x-bash', 'text/x-sh', 'text/x-csh',
        # Windows metafile, client-side vulnerability on some systems
        'application/x-msmetafile'
);

/** This is a flag to determine whether or not to check file extensions on upload. */
$wgCheckFileExtensions = true;
```

The previous settings defined file types that are allowed, as well as file types that are disallowed, but there are a lot more file types than what is defined in these settings. In order to address all of the other file types that are not explicitly addressed in the previous configuration variables, MediaWiki also introduces $wgStrictFileExtensions, which by default is set to true. When this is set to true, MediaWiki won't let you upload any file, unless it is explicitly configured to do so. For example, you will not be able to upload a PDF file with the default configuration, nor will you be able to upload a TIFF file.

If this parameter is set to false, the user will see a warning when trying to upload a file that is not on the list, but will be allowed to continue and post it anyway.

```
/**
 * If this is turned off, users may override the warning for files not covered
 * by $wgFileExtensions.
 */
$wgStrictFileExtensions = true;
```

A better alternative to setting $wgStrictFileExtensions to true is to explicitly add whatever file types you want to the list. Again, placing these settings in LocalSettings.php and modifying them will address the issue. If you want your users to be able to upload PDF files, then you need to have the following line in LocalSettings.php:

```
$wgFileExtensions = array( 'png', 'gif', 'jpg', 'jpeg', 'pdf' );
```

Finally, you can warn users if the files they upload are too large, which, by default, is 150 kilobytes:

```
/** Warn if uploaded files are larger than this (in bytes)*/
$wgUploadSizeWarning = 150 * 1024;
```

Image Linking and Embedding

Once you upload an image, you can link to two different things. You can link directly to the image file itself or you can link to an image description page that is automatically created by MediaWiki.

When a file is uploaded, it is accessible using either the Image or Media namespace.

After file uploading, MediaWiki automatically generates a page for the file, which works much like any other page in MediaWiki except that it is accessible through the Image namespace. If you want to link directly to the file itself, you must use the Media namespace.

By default, when you add an image link to a page, the image is embedded, or displayed, in the page itself, but you can also put links to images that appear like normal hyperlinks, which the user can click on in order to be taken directly to either the image itself or the image description page.

The Image Namespace

Basic image links work just like wiki links, except that the filenames are accessed through the Image namespace. When you use the Image namespace, the image is embedded in the page. The following table shows the wikitext markup to use alongside the HTML into which MediaWiki converts that text.

Wikitext	HTML Output
`[[Image:SampleImageUpload.png]]`	`<p><a href="/mysql/index.php/Image:SampleImageUpload.png" class="image" title="Image:SampleImageUpload.png"> <img src="/mysql/images/b/b5/SampleImageUpload.png" alt="Image:SampleImageUpload.png" width="253" height="254" longdesc="/mysql/index.php/Image:Sample ImageUpload.png"></a></p>`
`[[Image:SampleImageUpload.png| This is a sample image]]`	`<p><a href="/mysql/index.php/Image:SampleImage Upload.png" class="image" title="Some ALT text"> <img src="/mysql/images/b/b5/SampleImageUpload.png" alt="Some ALT text" width="253" height="254" longdesc="/mysql/index.php/Image:SampleImage Upload.png"></a></p>`

As you can see in the table, you can use the pipe (|) character with image links in a similar way that you do in wiki links. The difference is that the text that follows the | is used as the Alt text of the image. This should be a descriptive phrase or sentence about the image that screen readers can use to describe the image for people with disabilities, or it can also be displayed as a tooltip when a user holds the mouse over the image. Figure 5-4 shows an example of how these two kinds of image links are displayed. In the second image, you can see the tooltip for the image.

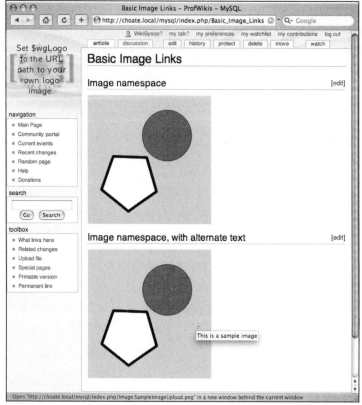

Figure 5-4: Basic image links

The Media Namespace

Sometimes you may not want to embed an image in a page, but you still want to link to the image. In other cases, you may want to link to a file for which there is no image to embed (other than an icon). When you want to link directly to any uploaded file, you need to use the Media namespace, rather than the Image namespace. The following table shows the wikitext and corresponding HTML output of two links using the Media namespace.

Wikitext	HTML Output
`[[Media:SampleImageUpload.png]]`	`<p><a href="/mysql/images/b/b5/SampleImageUpload.png" class="internal" title="SampleImageUpload.png">media:Sample ImageUpload.png</a></p>`
`[[Media:SampleImageUpload.png|Some descriptive text]]`	`<p><a href="/mysql/images/b/b5/SampleImage Upload.png" class="internal" title="SampleImageUpload.png">Some descriptive text</a></p>`

Much like the previous example that used the Image namespace, you can use the pipe (|) character in Media namespace links as well. In this case, instead of generating Alt text, it creates the text that is displayed by the link, just like it does when you use the same text in a wiki link.

Figure 5-5 shows how the two links are displayed on a Web page. You can see that the text for the first link is just the name and namespace of the link, whereas the second link uses the "Some descriptive text" phrase to serve as the link text.

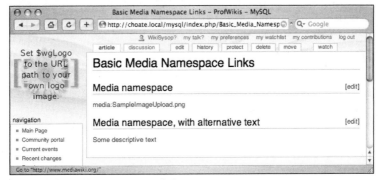

Figure 5-5: Media namespace links

Linking to the Image Description Page

In addition to embedding an image in a page, or linking directly to the image, there is a third option: linking directly to the image description page (without embedding the image). In order to link to the image description page, you need to prepend a colon to the image link, as illustrated here:

```
[[:Image:SampleImageUpload.png]]
```

The colon forces the link to be in the default namespace, which is why it links to the description page itself, rather than the file. You can use the | character here as well, with the expected results.

Using an Image as a Link

Another thing you might want to do is use an image in place of text in a link. In other words, you might want to have an image embedded in a page that, when clicked on, goes to some other wiki page, rather than the image description page. In order to use an image as a link to a different page, you need to use a template or install an extension. Templates are discussed in detail in Chapter 8, where you will find an example of how to do this.

Extended Image Syntax

It is at this point that image links begin to part ways from common wiki links. Technically speaking, the extended image syntax is an example of a parser function, and it allows additional properties about an image to be decided by the author.

> Parser functions, like templates, are discussed in Chapter 8.

Pay special attention to the HTML that is output when using the extended image syntax, because MediaWiki implements the actual look and feel of these images through stylesheets, so setting a parameter primarily affects the name of the class that is assigned to surrounding elements. It does not necessarily apply the values to legal HTML attributes of the <img> element. This is important to know, because it means that you can entirely change the way the image looks on the page simply by changing the underlying stylesheet. This is covered in more detail in Chapter 8, "Magic Words, Templates, and Skins."

With extended image syntax, you can set the image display width, image alignment and float properties, and instruct MediaWiki to display an image thumbnail.

Image Display Width

The following table is an example of how to set the display width of an image in MediaWiki. In this case, the image width is set to 150 pixels across. MediaWiki automatically calculates the height of the image, which can be seen in the HTML output in the adjacent column.

Wikitext	HTML Output
`[[Image:SampleImageUpload.png|` `150px|An image with a width of 150px.]]`	`<p>` `<a href="/mysql/index.php/Image:SampleImage Upload.png" class="image" title="An image with a width of 150px."><img src="/mysql/images/thumb/b/b5/SampleImage Upload.png/150px-SampleImageUpload.png" alt="An image with a width of 150px." width="150" height="151" longdesc="/mysql/index.php/Image:Sample ImageUpload.png"></a>` `</p>`

Image Alignment

Image alignment is determined by setting the CSS float value of the containing element. The element can either float left, right, or not float at all. There is also another alignment option: You can center the element, but that is not accomplished through a CSS float value (there is no float:center property); instead, it uses the CSS text-align property.

The important thing to remember about floats is that in addition to determining where an image is placed on a page, they also determine how text flows (or does not flow) around the image. If an image floats to the left, then text will flow to the right of the image. Likewise, if an image floats to the right, then text will flow to the left of the image. If an image is centered, and is not floating, or if its float value is simply set to none, then the text does not flow on either side of the image. Instead, the text before the image in the HTML file stops above where the image is located on the page, and the text following the image in the HTML document starts below the image, with no text appearing on either side. Figure 5-6 shows examples of these image alignment options.

In the following examples, you can see that MediaWiki controls the float property by assigning different classes to each wrapping <div> element: floatleft, floatright, floatnone and so on. There are corresponding CSS class selectors that define the float properties.

Wikitext	HTML Output

`[[Image:SampleImageUpload.png|left]]`	`<div class="floatleft">`
	`<span>`
	`<a`
	`href="/mysql/index.php/Image:SampleImage`
	`Upload.png" class="image" title="Float left">`
	`<img src="/mysql/images/thumb/b/b5/`
	`SampleImageUpload.png/100px-Sample`
	`   ImageUpload.png"`
	`alt="Float left" width="100"`
	`height="100"`
	`longdesc="/mysql/index.php/Image:Sample`
	`   ImageUpload.png">`
	`</a>`
	`</span>`
	`</div>`

`[[Image:SampleImageUpload.png|right]]`	`<div class="float right">`
	`   <span><a`
	`href="/mysql/index.php/Image:SampleImage`
	`Upload.png" class="image" title="Float right">`
	`<img src="/mysql/images/thumb/b/b5/SampleImage`
	`Upload.png/100px-SampleImageUpload.png"`
	`alt="Float right" width="100" height="100"`
	`longdesc="/mysql/index.php/Image:Sample`
	`ImageUpload.png"></a></span>`
	`</div>`

`[[Image:SampleImageUpload.png|none]]`	`<div class="floatnone">`
	`   <span><a href="/mysql/index.php/Image:Sample`
	`ImageUpload.png" class="image" title="Float`
	`none"><img`
	`src="/mysql/images/thumb/b/b5/SampleImage`
	`Upload.png/100px-SampleImageUpload.png"`
	`alt="Float none" width="100" height="100"`
	`longdesc="/mysql/index.php/Image:SampleImage`
	`Upload.png"></a></span>`
	`</div>`

`[[Image:SampleImageUpload.png|center]]`	`<div class="center">`
	`      <div class="floatnone">`
	`         <span><a`
	`href="/mysql/index.php/Image:SampleImage`
	`Upload.png" class="image" title="Some`
	`centered text"><img`
	`src="/mysql/images/thumb/b/b5/SampleImage`
	`Upload.png/100px-SampleImageUpload.png"`
	`alt="Some centered text" width="100" height="100"`
	`longdesc="/mysql/index.php/Image:Sample`
	`ImageUpload.png"></a></span>`
	`   </div>`
	`</div>`

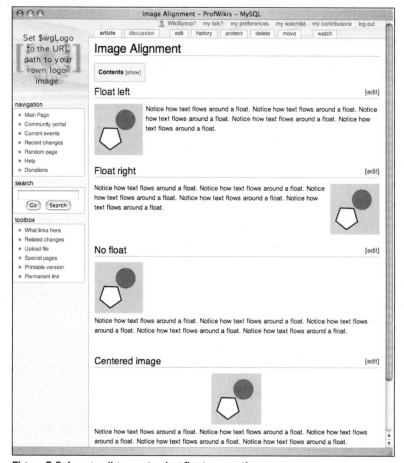

Figure 5-6: Image alignment using float properties

Clearing Elements

In some situations, you may not want text to continue to float around an image. For example, there may be text that applies to the image that is followed by an unrelated section. If you do not want that unrelated content to appear directly beside the image, but instead want it to start below it, then you can use the
 HTML element, which is a line break. If you place the following code directly above the content you do not want to appear next to the image, then it will be pushed down and will only appear beneath the image, as if the float property were not set.

A visual example is probably the best way to illustrate this. The following snippet of wikitext takes an example from the previous table and inserts `<br clear="all"/>` between the image and the text that was flowing next to the image:

```
[[Image:SampleImageUpload.png|100px|left|Float left]]

<br clear="all"/>

Notice how text flows around a float. Notice how text
    flows around a float. Notice how text flows around a float.
    Notice how text flows around a float.
Notice how text flows around a float.
```

As shown in Figure 5-7, the text no longer flows around the image. Instead, it starts beneath it.

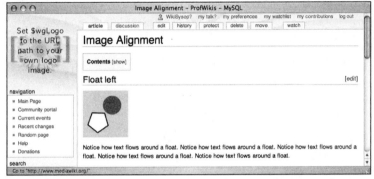

Figure 5-7: The use of `<br clear="all"/>` to keep text from wrapping around an image

Thumbnails and Frames

Thumbnails and frames are two similar ways of displaying an image in a wiki page. The following wikitext code shows how the two formats can be used. The difference between them is that an image with the `thumb` parameter set automatically scales the image to the size selected by the user in their user preferences, whereas the `framed` parameter displays the image in either its natural size or in the size specified (in this case, it's 175 pixels wide):

```
== Image thumbnail ==

[[Image:SampleImageUpload.png|thumb|An image with the "thumb" parameter set.]]

<br clear="all"/>
```

```
==Framed==

[[Image:SampleImageUpload.png|175px|framed|Some framed centered text]]

Notice how text flows around a float. Notice how text flows
    around a float. Notice how text flows around a float.
    Notice how text flows around a float.
Notice how text flows around a float.
```

The thumbnailed image link produces the following HTML:

```
<div class="thumb tright">
        <div class="thumbinner" style="width:122px;">
            <a href="/mysql/index.php/Image:SampleImageUpload.png"
    class="internal" title="An image with the &quot;thumb&quot; parameter set.">
    <img src="/mysql/images/thumb/b/b5/SampleImageUpload.png/
    120px-SampleImageUpload.png" alt="An image with the &quot;thumb&quot;
    parameter set." width="120" height="120"
    longdesc="/mysql/index.php/Image:SampleImageUpload.png" class="thumbimage"></a>

            <div class="thumbcaption">
                <div class="magnify" style="float:right">
                    <a href="/mysql/index.php/Image:SampleImageUpload.png"
    class="internal" title="Enlarge"><img src="/mysql/skins/common/images/
    magnify-clip.png" width="15" height="11" alt=""></a>
                </div>An image with the "thumb" parameter set.
            </div>
        </div>
    </div>
```

The framed HTML output is displayed next. It looks exactly like the thumbnail version, except that the image isn't thumbnailed:

```
<div class="thumb tright">
        <div class="thumbinner" style="width:255px;">
            <a href="/mysql/index.php/Image:SampleImageUpload.png"
    class="internal" title="Some framed centered text">
    <img src="/mysql/images/b/b5/SampleImageUpload.png"
    alt="Some framed centered text" width="253" height="254"
    longdesc="/mysql/index.php/Image:SampleImageUpload.png" class="thumbimage"></a>

            <div class="thumbcaption">
                Some framed centered text
            </div>
        </div>
    </div>
```

Figure 5-8 shows the page produced by the preceding HTML. You can see the similarities in presentation between the two formats (a gray box around the image and a light-gray background) as well as the differences. The thumbnail contains a graphic indicating that it's a thumbnail and can be clicked on to see a larger image.

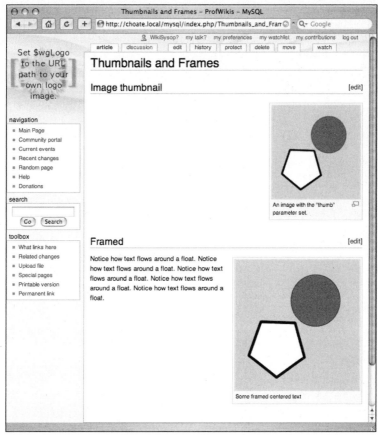

Figure 5-8: Thumbnails and framed images

Specifying a Specific Image for the Thumbnail

MediaWiki also enables you to substitute an image of your choice to be used as the thumbnailed image. Consider the following wikitext:

```
==Thumbnail==

[[Image:SampleImageUpload.png|thumb|An image with the "thumb" parameter set.]]

<br clear="all"/>

==Selected Thumbnail==

[[Image:SampleImageUpload.png|thumb=Closedfolder.gif|An
   image with the "thumb" parameter set.]]
```

Note that the second image link includes `thumb=Closedfolder.gif`, which means that the `Closedfolder.gif` file will be used as the thumbnail image, rather than an automatically generated thumbnail. In both cases, if you click on the thumbnail image, you will go to the same place. The only difference is the thumbnailed image. Keep in mind that you must use an image that has already been uploaded as a thumbnail replacement.

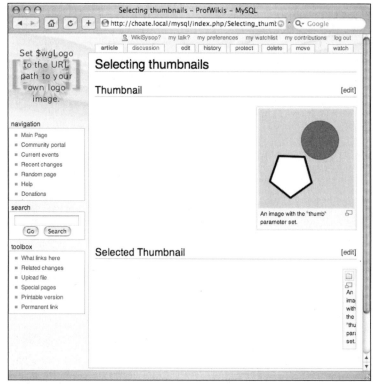

Figure 5-9: Setting a custom thumbnail image

Thumbnail Alignment

As you can see from the preceding examples, thumbnails are automatically generated so that they float right, but that can be overridden by explicitly specifying the thumbnail to float left, as shown in the following code:

```
[[Image:SampleImageUpload.png|100px|left|thumb|An image with the "thumb"
    parameter set and a width of 100px.]]
```

The HTML output follows. Note the use of the class `tleft` in the outer `<div>` element:

```
<div class="thumb tleft">
    <div class="thumbinner" style="width:102px;">
        <a href="/mysql/index.php/Image:SampleImageUpload.png"
    class="internal" title="An image with the &quot;thumb&quot;
    parameter set and a width of 100px."><img src="/mysql/images/thumb/b/b5/
    SampleImageUpload.png/100px-SampleImageUpload.png"
```

```
alt="An image with the &quot;thumb&quot; parameter set
and a width of 100px." width="100" height="100" longdesc="/mysql/index.php/
Image:SampleImageUpload.png" class="thumbimage"></a>

        <div class="thumbcaption">
                <div class="magnify" style="float:right">
                        <a href="/mysql/index.php/Image:SampleImageUpload.png"
        class="internal" title="Enlarge"><img
        src="/mysql/skins/common/images/magnify-clip.png"
        width="15" height="11" alt=""></a>
                </div>An image with the "thumb" parameter set and a width of 100px.
        </div>
    </div>
</div>
```

Image Galleries

You can add an entire gallery of images to a page using the following syntax. In MediaWiki version 1.9.3, the only attribute you can set is the gallery — a thumbnail size of 120 pixels is hard-coded into the ImageGallery.php file that handles generation of the gallery. You may still find some references to more detailed syntax on the MediaWiki.org website, but it won't work. The following is a sample of a basic image gallery:

```
<gallery caption="Sample gallery">
Image:SampleImageUpload1.png
Image:SampleImageUpload2.png
Image:SampleImageUpload3.png
Image:SampleImageUpload4.png
</gallery>
```

The HTML produced by this tag is as follows:

```
<table class="gallery" cellspacing="0" cellpadding="0">
  <tr>
        <td class="galleryheader" colspan="4"><big>Sample gallery</big></td>
  </tr>

  <tr>
        <td>
                <div class="gallerybox">
                        <div class="thumb" style="padding: 13px 0;">
                                <a href="/mysql/index.php/Image:SampleImageUpload1.png"
        title="Image:SampleImageUpload1.png"><img src="/mysql/images/thumb/9/99/
        SampleImageUpload1.png/120px-SampleImageUpload1.png"
        width="120" height="120" alt=""></a>
                        </div>

                        <div class="gallerytext">
                                This is the first image
                        </div>
                </div>
        </td>
```

```
            <td>
                    <div class="gallerybox">
                            <div class="thumb" style="padding: 13px 0;">
                                    <a href="/mysql/index.php/Image:SampleImageUpload2.png"
title="Image:SampleImageUpload2.png"><img src="/mysql/images/thumb/d/d3/
SampleImageUpload2.png/120px-SampleImageUpload2.png" width="120"
height="120" alt=""></a>
                            </div>

                            <div class="gallerytext"></div>
                    </div>
            </td>

            <td>
                    <div class="gallerybox">
                            <div class="thumb" style="padding: 13px 0;">
                                    <a href="/mysql/index.php/Image:SampleImageUpload3.png"
title="Image:SampleImageUpload3.png"><img src="/mysql/images/thumb/6/64/
SampleImageUpload3.png/120px-SampleImageUpload3.png" width="120"
height="120" alt=""></a>
                            </div>

                            <div class="gallerytext"></div>
                    </div>
            </td>

            <td>
                    <div class="gallerybox">
                            <div class="thumb" style="padding: 13px 0;">
                                    <a href="/mysql/index.php/Image:SampleImageUpload4.png"
title="Image:SampleImageUpload4.png"><img src="/mysql/images/thumb/3/30/
SampleImageUpload4.png/120px-SampleImageUpload4.png" width="120"
height="120" alt=""></a>
                            </div>

                            <div class="gallerytext"></div>
                    </div>
            </td>
    </tr>
</table>
```

Because the basic gallery tag is so limited, you may find it better to create your own galleries using wikitext table syntax. The following code produces a similar gallery, with a few notable exceptions. First, by using a table, you can control how many images appear on each row. In this case, there are two images per row. In order to ensure that the thumbnail images appear correctly in the table, you have to make sure they don't float left or right, so you need to use the none parameter.

You also need to hard-code a width of 120 pixels. Note that in the example, the class of the table element is set to gallery, and the class of the caption row is set to galleryheader. This ensures that the table will share common design elements with the table produced automatically by the gallery tag.

```
==Table gallery==

{| class="gallery"
|+
!class="galleryheader" style="border:none" colspan="2"| <big>Sample Gallery</big>
|-
| [[Image:SampleImageUpload1.png|120px|none|thumb| This is the first image]]
| [[Image:SampleImageUpload2.png|120px|none|thumb]]
|-
| [[Image:SampleImageUpload3.png|120px|none|thumb]]
| [[Image:SampleImageUpload4.png|120px|none|thumb]]
|}
```

The HTML output of this table is as follows:

```
<table class="gallery">
  <tr>
        <th class="galleryheader" style="border:none" colspan="2"><big>Sample
  Gallery</big></th>
  </tr>

  <tr>
        <td>
              <div class="thumb tnone">
                    <div class="thumbinner" style="width:122px;">
                          <a href="/mysql/index.php/Image:SampleImageUpload1.png"
  class="internal" title="This is the first image"><img
  src="/mysql/images/thumb/9/99/SampleImageUpload1.png/
  120px-SampleImageUpload1.png"
  alt="This is the first image" width="120" height="120"
  longdesc="/mysql/index.php/Image:SampleImageUpload1.png"
  class="thumbimage"></a>

                          <div class="thumbcaption">
                                <div class="magnify" style="float:right">
                                      <a
  href="/mysql/index.php/Image:SampleImageUpload1.png" class="internal"
  title="Enlarge"><img src="/mysql/skins/common/images/magnify-clip.png"
  width="15" height="11" alt=""></a>
                                </div>This is the first image
                          </div>
                    </div>
              </div
        </td>

        <td>
              <div class="thumb tnone">
                    <div class="thumbinner" style="width:122px;">
                          <a
  href="/mysql/index.php/Image:SampleImageUpload2.png" class="internal"
```

```
title=""><img src="/mysql/images/thumb/d/d3/SampleImageUpload2.png/
120px-SampleImageUpload2.png" alt="" width="120" height="120"
longdesc="/mysql/index.php/Image:SampleImageUpload2.png" class="thumbimage"></a>
                              <div class="thumbcaption">
                                    <div class="magnify" style="float:right">
                                          <a
href="/mysql/index.php/Image:SampleImageUpload2.png"
class="internal" title="Enlarge"><img
src="/mysql/skins/common/images/magnify-clip.png" width="15" height="11"
alt=""></a>
                                          </div>
                                    </div>
                              </div>
                        </div>
                  </td>
            </tr>

            <tr>
                  <td>
                        <div class="thumb tnone">
                              <div class="thumbinner" style="width:122px;">
                                    <a
href="/mysql/index.php/Image:SampleImageUpload3.png" class="internal"
title=""><img src="/mysql/images/thumb/6/64/SampleImageUpload3.png/120
px-SampleImageUpload3.png" alt="" width="120" height="120"
longdesc="/mysql/index.php/Image:SampleImageUpload3.png" class="thumbimage"></a>
                              <div class="thumbcaption">
                                    <div class="magnify" style="float:right">
                                          <a
href="/mysql/index.php/Image:SampleImageUpload3.png" class="internal"
title="Enlarge"><img src="/mysql/skins/common/images/magnify-clip.png"
width="15" height="11" alt=""></a>
                                          </div>
                                    </div>
                              </div>
                        </div>
                  </td>

                  <td>
                        <div class="thumb tnone">
                              <div class="thumbinner" style="width:122px;">
                                    <a
href="/mysql/index.php/Image:SampleImageUpload4.png" class="internal"
title=""><img src="/mysql/images/thumb/3/30/SampleImageUpload4.png/120
px-SampleImageUpload4.png" alt="" width="120" height="120"
longdesc="/mysql/index.php/Image:SampleImageUpload4.png"
class="thumbimage"></a>
```

```
                    <div class="thumbcaption">
                            <div class="magnify" style="float:right">
                                    <a
    href="/mysql/index.php/Image:SampleImageUpload4.png" class="internal"
    title="Enlarge"><img src="/mysql/skins/common/images/magnify-clip.png"
    width="15" height="11" alt=""></a>
                                    </div>
                            </div>
                    </div>
            </td>
    </tr>
</table>
```

Figure 5-10 shows an example of both galleries. Note the design similarities between the two, because they both use the same classes in the wikitext table version as that automatically generated using the gallery tag. They both share a gray border around the table, and the "Sample gallery" text is the same font, size, and alignment. In Chapter 8, you will learn how to change the CSS directly in order to change the look and feel of any of the HTML produced by MediaWiki.

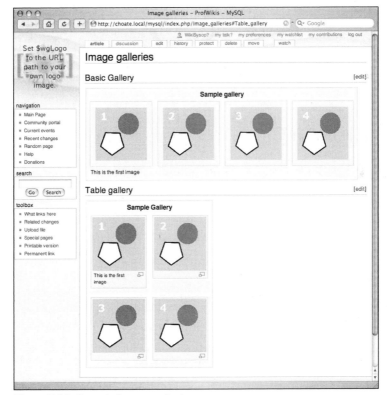

Figure 5-10: Sample image galleries

Uploading Documents

On Wikipedia, images seem to be what is uploaded most often, but don't forget that this MediaWiki feature enables you to upload any kind of document, as long as you have configured it properly. Many organizations use wikis on their intranet, both for basic knowledge management and as a way to share files. While you may wish that everyone would enter their content directly to the wiki, you will find that many Word documents and PDF files need to be shared as well.

MediaWiki's facilities for tracking changes to any file that has been uploaded can be used to track changes in a Microsoft Word document, for example.

The image in Figure 5-11 shows the so-called image description page for an uploaded PDF file. In order to enable this, you have to add the PDF extension to the list of files that MediaWiki would accept for uploading. In `DefaultSettings.php`, the legal extensions are as follows:

```
$wgFileExtensions = array( 'png', 'gif', 'jpg', 'jpeg' );
```

In order to enable PDF files, you need to put the following line in `LocalSettings.php`:

```
$wgFileExtensions = array( 'png', 'gif', 'jpg', 'jpeg', 'pdf' );
```

Once you make this change, you can upload a PDF file just like you uploaded images before.

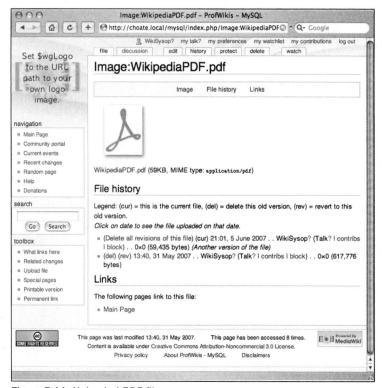

Figure 5-11: Uploaded PDF file

The ins and outs of tracking changes to the uploaded files are discussed in the next chapter, but you can already see the potential for using MediaWiki as a basic document management system.

This author once consulted with a small nonprofit scientific research firm that was in the process of standardizing all of their internal processes (a necessary evil that results from growth). They were creating standard operating procedure (SOP) documents in Microsoft Word and posting them to a shared drive on which everyone in the office could access them.

The problem was that they had no way of knowing whether they were viewing the latest copy, and no way to make comments on the documents as they went through the editing process. MediaWiki was recommended as a viable solution to such a problem because it has some distinct advantages. The documents could be made available through a Web browser, as opposed to through the file system, and anyone could look at the different versions of the document that existed, including who uploaded the latest version. If there was a question about one of the SOPs, then it could be posted on the talk page for that image. Not only is it a very simple solution, it's also very inexpensive (effectively free), and a significant improvement on the previous method they were using.

Summary

In this chapter, you learned how to enable images and how to use wikitext to embed images in your pages and link to images. You also learned how to create and work with image galleries. In the next chapter, you will build on that knowledge and learn about more advanced editing features. For example, you will learn how to move, delete, and protect pages, followed by learning how to perform advanced editing functions using what the developers of MediaWiki call *magic words*. You will also learn how MediaWiki handles version control for both regular pages and images, and how you can control access to certain page functions.

6

Page Actions and Version Control

In the previous two chapters, you learned how to edit pages with wikitext, as well as how to upload images. There is a lot more that you can do with a page (or to a page). Some of the concepts have been touched on in previous chapters, but this chapter focuses on two closely related topics: what MediaWiki calls actions, and MediaWiki's approach to version control.

You've already been exposed to actions in previous chapters. Viewing a page is an action, for example, as is editing a page, moving a page, or deleting a page. Beyond that, you can perform actions such as protecting pages, reverting to earlier revisions, comparing changes, and so on.

Technically speaking, an action is invoked by passing a parameter in the URL of an HTTP GET request to MediaWiki's index.php file. There are also some activities that fall under the same conceptual category of actions that I have included in this chapter that rely on Special Pages to implement, such as importing and exporting pages. While technically not actions, these topics fit best in the context of this chapter, which is why they are discussed here.

Before we get to the actions themselves, there is some background information to review. First, you will get a very brief overview of some aspects of the HTTP protocol that you should know in order to help you understand the semantics of actions. This is followed by a more detailed look at how pages are implemented in MediaWiki, including a look at the underlying database tables and how different revisions of pages are managed. With this background information in place, you will then learn about the actions themselves, as well as how MediaWiki handles permissions and limits actions to specific user groups.

How Pages Work

For eleven years, while I was working at a newspaper, every day there was a distinct moment when work on the content for that day's newspaper stopped and the printing and distribution of the newspaper began. This is the moment when a newspaper is published, when ink is pressed against paper. It's also the last step of a very long process of newsgathering, writing, and editing (a process that was once described by a colleague as the most remarkable series of coincidences that have to occur every day to get the paper out).

Sometimes newspaper people refer to this moment as "putting the paper to bed." There was (and is) a sense of permanence to it. For every story that appeared in the paper, the writing and editing process was completed once the paper was put to bed. While references to earlier stories or corrections to stories may appear in future editions, the story as published on that day will stay that way forever, a permanent record of the state of the world on that particular day.

Editing and content management in the world of printing presses is discrete and clearly delineated, like black ink on white paper; a wiki, more than any other kind of website, smudges those edges, leaving smears of gray. In the world of printing presses, stories are drafted, edited, and revised in an iterative process that culminates in publication. In the wiki world, there is no such thing as a draft. Every modification to the content of a page is immediately published once the changes are submitted by the author.

In MediaWiki, a page is a series of revisions. The current revision does have greater import than previous revisions, and it is the closest thing to the idea of a published, finished work, but the next revision and all the earlier revisions are always just a few clicks away. In theory, with each revision, the article should be better (except for the occasional act of vandalism), but each revision is still provisional, preserving its privileged status only until the next revision is made that replaces it.

Because MediaWiki defers all editorial oversight until after a change has been made, the ability to track, monitor, and roll back changes is of utmost importance. In order to understand how MediaWiki manages pages, you need to understand how MediaWiki manages revisions.

Components of a Page

Content — in this case, a page — consists of a collection of revisions and variants. The term variant isn't an official MediaWiki designation, but it is one that can be used when discussing content management issues in a more precise way. One revision replaces a previous revision. A variant is another form of the same document, either in a different context or format (such as wikitext versus HTML) or in another language. Any given page can be displayed in the following variants:

- ❏ In a different skin, with different navigational elements
- ❏ As HTML without any navigational elements at all
- ❏ As raw wikitext
- ❏ In a different language

All of these different variants of a page (with the exception of the last one) can be triggered by using an action in MediaWiki.

A page is broadly divided into a content area and a navigation area (see Figure 6-1). The content area displays the content that is unique to a given page — the content that is written for an article, or was written by users. The navigation area contains a variety of different kinds of information, such as the site logo, copyright information, and links to other parts of the site. The actual layout and structure of the overall page is determined by the skin, which is composed of PHP code and stylesheets. By default, users can select which skin to use, but the name of the default skin is "monotone" (which is also the skin in use in all the screen shots used in this book so far).

> **In Chapter 8, you will learn how to customize the skin for your requirements.**

While the skin determines the layout of the page, it does not control the text that is displayed. Bear in mind that MediaWiki is designed to be a multilingual site, which means that all the content in the navigation area of the page is dependent upon the language in use at the site. The default language of a site is determined in `LocalSettings.php`, but it can be overridden in user preferences. All the screen shots thus far have been in English, but they could easily be changed to French, German, or even Hebrew, by modifying your preferences. This chapter does not go into much detail about language localization.

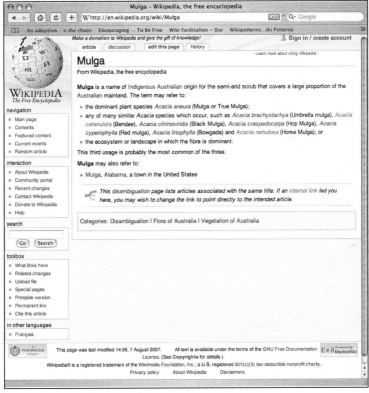

Figure 6-1: A wiki page can be divided into a navigation area and a content area

Revisions

When you visit a page, you are actually viewing the current revision of the page. While the default behavior is to view the current revision, the default behavior can be overridden, making it possible for any user to view any version of a page as long as the user knows the revision ID of that page. This enables the user to view the history of the page, to roll back changes to previous versions, to find out who made what changes to a page at any given time, and so on. The following URL causes the revision of the Main Page with the ID of 1 to be displayed, rather than the current revision:

```
http://127.0.0.1/mysql/index.php/Main_Page?action=view&oldid=1
```

The version tracking of MediaWiki is not as sophisticated as what you find in a version control system like Subversion. The primary difference is that MediaWiki keeps a complete copy of each version, even when there are only minor differences between the two versions. Version control systems, on the other hand, only keep a record of the differences between two versions of a document, which saves a lot of space (and network traffic). Old versions of pages can be compressed when archived, but that is still not quite as good as version control (arguably, it doesn't really matter, as storage space is cheap, but it does seem inelegant, at least).

For a typical page, three different tables track its current state: page, revision, and text. (If you chose to use a prefix when installing MediaWiki, then the tables will be named prefix_page, prefix_revision, etc.) There is one record per page in the page table.

The page table (MySQL)

The following code shows the SQL used to generate the page table in MySQL, and includes the comments provided by MediaWiki developers.

The table is indexed on the page_namespace and page_title fields.

The table also tracks whether the page is a redirect, and whether it is new (which is defined as a page with only one edit), what the restrictions are for the page, and when the page was last touched. A random number is also stored in the table that is used by the Special:Random page to randomly display a page to a user. The page also maintains the page_latest field, which points to the rev_id field of the revision table, which serves as the id of the current revision. Finally, the length of the current text of the page is stored.

```
-- Core of the wiki: each page has an entry here which identifies
-- it by title and contains some essential metadata.
--
CREATE TABLE /*$wgDBprefix*/page (
  -- Unique identifier number. The page_id will be preserved across
  -- edits and rename operations, but not deletions and recreations.
  page_id int(8) unsigned NOT NULL auto_increment,

  -- A page name is broken into a namespace and a title.
  -- The namespace keys are UI-language-independent constants,
  -- defined in includes/Defines.php
  page_namespace int NOT NULL,

  -- The rest of the title, as text.
  -- Spaces are transformed into underscores in title storage.
  page_title varchar(255) binary NOT NULL,

  -- Comma-separated set of permission keys indicating who
  -- can move or edit the page.
  page_restrictions tinyblob NOT NULL,
```

```
-- Number of times this page has been viewed.
page_counter bigint(20) unsigned NOT NULL default '0',

-- 1 indicates the article is a redirect.
page_is_redirect tinyint(1) unsigned NOT NULL default '0',

-- 1 indicates this is a new entry, with only one edit.
-- Not all pages with one edit are new pages.
page_is_new tinyint(1) unsigned NOT NULL default '0',

-- Random value between 0 and 1, used for Special:Randompage
page_random real unsigned NOT NULL,

-- This timestamp is updated whenever the page changes in
-- a way requiring it to be re-rendered, invalidating caches.
-- Aside from editing this includes permission changes,
-- creation or deletion of linked pages, and alteration
-- of contained templates.
page_touched char(14) binary NOT NULL default '',

-- Handy key to revision.rev_id of the current revision.
-- This may be 0 during page creation, but that shouldn't
-- happen outside of a transaction... hopefully.
page_latest int(8) unsigned NOT NULL,

-- Uncompressed length in bytes of the page's current source text.
page_len int(8) unsigned NOT NULL,

) TYPE=InnoDB;
```

The revision table

The revision table links the page record in the page table with the different revisions in the text table. Each page has a page_id and a revision_id.

The revision table's function is primarily to serve as a link between a page record and a text record. Each page can have many revisions, but each revision is linked to only one text record. In addition to the rev_page field, which holds the page ID, and the rev_text_id field, which holds the ID of the text record, the revision table also tracks the username and ID of the person responsible for the revision, any comments the user made while making the revision, and a timestamp. If the user has designated this revision as a minor one, then that fact is tracked in the rev_minor_edit field.

```
-- Every edit of a page creates also a revision row.
-- This stores metadata about the revision, and a reference
-- to the text storage backend.
--
CREATE TABLE /*$wgDBprefix*/revision (
  rev_id int(8) unsigned NOT NULL auto_increment,

  -- Key to page_id. This should _never_ be invalid.
  rev_page int(8) unsigned NOT NULL,

  -- Key to text.old_id, where the actual bulk text is stored.
```

```
    -- It's possible for multiple revisions to use the same text,
    -- for instance revisions where only metadata is altered
    -- or a rollback to a previous version.
    rev_text_id int(8) unsigned NOT NULL,

    -- Text comment summarizing the change.
    -- This text is shown in the history and other changes lists,
    -- rendered in a subset of wiki markup by Linker::formatComment()
    rev_comment tinyblob NOT NULL,

    -- Key to user.user_id of the user who made this edit.
    -- Stores 0 for anonymous edits and for some mass imports.
    rev_user int(5) unsigned NOT NULL default '0',

    -- Text username or IP address of the editor.
    rev_user_text varchar(255) binary NOT NULL default '',

    -- Timestamp
    rev_timestamp char(14) binary NOT NULL default '',

    -- Records whether the user marked the 'minor edit' checkbox.
    -- Many automated edits are marked as minor.
    rev_minor_edit tinyint(1) unsigned NOT NULL default '0',

    -- Not yet used; reserved for future changes to the deletion system.
    rev_deleted tinyint(1) unsigned NOT NULL default '0',

    PRIMARY KEY rev_page_id (rev_page, rev_id),
) TYPE=InnoDB;
```

The text table

MediaWiki never deletes the text to a page on its own, so the text table contains all the different versions of the page that are in existence. The text table stores the raw wikitext, so when a page is viewed, that wikitext is rendered into HTML (or pulled from the cache). Different revision records can point to the same text record (in the event of rollbacks to a previous version, for example). When a page is rolled back to a previous version, a new revision record is created so that the entire history is preserved.

The fields in this table are prefixed with old as a legacy from early versions of MediaWiki. There are only three fields in the table: old_id, old_text, and old_flags, which mark as old the text ID, the actual text of the revision, and some flags about the nature of the content of the text field, respectively.

```
    --
    -- Holds text of individual page revisions.
    --
    -- Field names are a holdover from the 'old' revisions table in
    -- MediaWiki 1.4 and earlier: an upgrade will transform that
    -- table into the 'text' table to minimize unnecessary churning
    -- and downtime. If upgrading, the other fields will be left unused.
    --
    CREATE TABLE /*$wgDBprefix*/text (
      -- Unique text storage key number.
      -- Note that the 'oldid' parameter used in URLs does *not*
```

```
    -- refer to this number anymore, but to rev_id.
    --
    -- revision.rev_text_id is a key to this column
    old_id int(8) unsigned NOT NULL auto_increment,

    -- Depending on the contents of the old_flags field, the text
    -- may be convenient plain text, or it may be funkily encoded.
    old_text mediumblob NOT NULL,

    -- Comma-separated list of flags:
    -- gzip: text is compressed with PHP's gzdeflate() function.
    -- utf8: text was stored as UTF-8.
    --        If $wgLegacyEncoding option is on, rows *without* this flag
    --        will be converted to UTF-8 transparently at load time.
    -- object: text field contained a serialized PHP object.
    --        The object either contains multiple versions compressed
    --        together to achieve a better compression ratio, or it refers
    --        to another row where the text can be found.
    old_flags tinyblob NOT NULL,
    ) TYPE=InnoDB;
```

In the previous chapter, when you edited a page, the text stayed the same regardless of what happened, unless it was edited again, or a page that it linked to was changed in some way. Images are a special case. Like every other page, information about the image is stored in the page, revision, and text tables. Unlike other pages, though, there is also an image table that contains information pertinent to the image file.

There are also pagelink and imagelink tables, that track which pages link to each other so that when a page changes (e.g., is deleted, etc.), all the other pages that link to it can be updated.

Actions

Most of the user interaction with MediaWiki is mediated by the index.php page. Whenever the index.php page is called, MediaWiki performs an action. The type of action is determined by parameters that are passed as part of the URL in the query string. If no parameters are passed, then the default action is view.

Many of the actions are oriented toward viewing different aspects of the page, such as the page metadata, or the raw wikitext, and so on. The rest refer to actions that are done to a page, such as editing, moving, and deleting the page.

As a user of the site, you do not necessarily need to bother yourself much with actions, other than knowing what basic things you can do to or with a page, as well as knowing how the actions are restricted to certain user groups. If you plan on doing any customization of MediaWiki, then more detailed knowledge of how the different actions are triggered is essential.

Permissions

Every action is paired with a set of permissions that determines which user groups are allowed to perform the action. Out of the box, MediaWiki is set up so that anonymous users can read, create, and edit pages, as well as create their own accounts and their own talk page. As a wiki operator, you may not want anonymous users to be able to perform such operations, and you can control that by changing the settings in `LocalSettings.php`.

Every user must belong to one of five explicit groups:

❑ The * group refers to all anonymous visitors to the site — basically, readers who have not logged in.

❑ The user group represents all logged in accounts.

❑ The bureaucrat is a special group that affords members the privilege of setting other people's privileges.

❑ The sysop group is the primary administrative group, which is given the most powers to manipulate pages, including the capability to move pages, delete them, roll back edits, and so forth.

❑ The bot group is designated to represent scripts that automate tasks in MediaWiki. The script logs into MediaWiki as a user in the bot group. Because most of the reason for using a bot is to make wholesale changes, it's helpful to be able to know whether a change was made by a bot or a human being. In addition, bot actions are not logged.

The following code snippet is the PHP array used by MediaWiki to track privileges. The first element in the array identifies the group, and the second element identifies what action the group member is allowed to take:

```php
$wgGroupPermissions = array();

// Implicit group for all visitors
$wgGroupPermissions['*'    ]['createaccount']   = true;
$wgGroupPermissions['*'    ]['read']            = true;
$wgGroupPermissions['*'    ]['edit']            = true;
$wgGroupPermissions['*'    ]['createpage']      = true;
$wgGroupPermissions['*'    ]['createtalk']      = true;

// Implicit group for all logged-in accounts
$wgGroupPermissions['user' ]['move']            = true;
$wgGroupPermissions['user' ]['read']            = true;
$wgGroupPermissions['user' ]['edit']            = true;
$wgGroupPermissions['user' ]['createpage']      = true;
$wgGroupPermissions['user' ]['createtalk']      = true;
$wgGroupPermissions['user' ]['upload']          = true;
$wgGroupPermissions['user' ]['reupload']        = true;
$wgGroupPermissions['user' ]['reupload-shared'] = true;
$wgGroupPermissions['user' ]['minoredit']       = true;

// Implicit group for accounts that pass $wgAutoConfirmAge
$wgGroupPermissions['autoconfirmed']['autoconfirmed'] = true;

// Implicit group for accounts with confirmed email addresses
// This has little use when email address confirmation is off
$wgGroupPermissions['emailconfirmed']['emailconfirmed'] = true;

// Users with bot privilege can have their edits hidden
```

```
// from various log pages by default
$wgGroupPermissions['bot'  ]['bot']              = true;
$wgGroupPermissions['bot'  ]['autoconfirmed']    = true;
$wgGroupPermissions['bot'  ]['nominornewtalk']   = true;

// Most extra permission abilities go to this group
$wgGroupPermissions['sysop']['block']            = true;
$wgGroupPermissions['sysop']['createaccount']    = true;
$wgGroupPermissions['sysop']['delete']           = true;
$wgGroupPermissions['sysop']['deletedhistory']   = true; // can view deleted
    history entries, but not see or restore the text
$wgGroupPermissions['sysop']['editinterface']    = true;
$wgGroupPermissions['sysop']['import']           = true;
$wgGroupPermissions['sysop']['importupload']     = true;
$wgGroupPermissions['sysop']['move']             = true;
$wgGroupPermissions['sysop']['patrol']           = true;
$wgGroupPermissions['sysop']['autopatrol']       = true;
$wgGroupPermissions['sysop']['protect']          = true;
$wgGroupPermissions['sysop']['proxyunbannable']  = true;
$wgGroupPermissions['sysop']['rollback']         = true;
$wgGroupPermissions['sysop']['trackback']        = true;
$wgGroupPermissions['sysop']['upload']           = true;
$wgGroupPermissions['sysop']['reupload']         = true;
$wgGroupPermissions['sysop']['reupload-shared']  = true;
$wgGroupPermissions['sysop']['unwatchedpages']   = true;
$wgGroupPermissions['sysop']['autoconfirmed']    = true;
$wgGroupPermissions['sysop']['upload_by_url']    = true;
$wgGroupPermissions['sysop']['ipblock-exempt']   = true;

// Permission to change users' group assignments
$wgGroupPermissions['bureaucrat']['userrights'] = true;
```

As you can see from the preceding code, the sysop has the broadest level of discretion in terms of what he or she can do. If your wiki is available on the Internet, and not behind a company firewall, you should disable edits by the general public, unless you are prepared to monitor the pages intensively to identify spam. It's easily done. If you want only registered users to be able to edit pages, then you merely need to insert the following line in LocalSettings.php:

```
$wgGroupPermissions['*'   ]['edit']              = false;
```

Another common permissions setting is to disable anonymous users' ability to create their own account, by entering the following line in LocalSettings.php:

```
$wgGroupPermissions['*'   ]['createaccount']         = false;
```

If the wiki is on a local intranet, then the IT department may want to create user accounts, or have users use existing usernames and passwords (MediaWiki supports LDAP and ActiveDirectory). This is both a convenience item and a security item. If users are able to create their own accounts, then it makes it difficult to have a solid audit trail of changes made to the site. In many cases, you need to be able to definitively associate a user ID with a real person, and the only way to do that is to place controls on account creation.

In addition to the explicit permissions, there are two other groups, autoconfirmed and emailconfirmed.

The autoconfirmed permission refers to a security measure MediaWiki has in place to track new users and limit, to some degree, spammers. When a user creates an account, the user has limited privileges until a period of time specified by the $wgAutoConfirmAge value in LocalSettings.php. The default value is 0, which means that no time is required. The following code snippet comes from DefaultSettings.php:

```
/**
 * Number of seconds an account is required to age before
 * it's given the implicit 'autoconfirm' group membership.
 * This can be used to limit privileges of new accounts.
 *
 * Accounts created by earlier versions of the software
 * may not have a recorded creation date, and will always
 * be considered to pass the age test.
 *
 * When left at 0, all registered accounts will pass.
 */
$wgAutoConfirmAge = 0;
//$wgAutoConfirmAge = 600;      // ten minutes
//$wgAutoConfirmAge = 3600*24;  // one day
```

As this example shows, the duration is tracked in terms of seconds.

When MediaWiki was originally configured, you had the option of requiring e-mail confirmation. The emailconfirmed permission tracks whether a user has confirmed his or her e-mail address after registering.

These permission settings are from MediaWiki 1.9.3. In MediaWiki 1.10, which was released during the production of this book, additional permission settings are available. Be sure to check the latest documentation to know what's available.

Viewing Pages

View is the default action. As such, it does not necessarily appear in the URL request for the page. Recall that the URL can take two forms, so this chapter will show you two different examples of how the action view is triggered when viewing a page. The basic URL looks like the following:

```
http://127.0.0.1/mysql/index.php?title=Main_Page&action=view
```

If you are using Apache, you can have pretty URLs that drop the question mark after the index.php portion of the URL. As you will see in the following example, if you are using pretty URLs, then you have to treat the action = view portion of the URL as the very first part of the query string and prepend a ?. Web servers treat everything after the question mark as part of the query string; and even though Apache allows you to eliminate the ? for the first parameter, you still need it for those that follow.

```
http://127.0.0.1/wiki/index.php/Main_Page?action=view
```

From here on out, the examples use the plain version of the URL, as it works in all cases. You will see that the pattern action = {action word} is repeated throughout the examples.

Viewing Specific Versions

By default, the view action displays the current revision of a page, but you also have the option of requesting a specific revision of a page. This most commonly comes into play when viewing the history of the page — MediaWiki enables you to compare different revisions of any given page, and in order to do that MediaWiki needs to be able to generate links to particular revisions. The following example shows a link to a page with a revision ID of 76:

```
http://127.0.0.1/mysql/index.php?title=Main_Page&action=view&oldid=76
```

Note that because the default action is view, you can drop that parameter and use the following equivalent URL:

```
http://127.0.0.1/mysql/index.php?title=Main_Page&oldid=76
```

Viewing the Raw Wikitext of a Page

View shows the page rendered along with the user interface of the wiki's skin. Sometimes you want to be able to view the raw wikitext before it is converted to HTML, and it is for that reason that the raw action exists. To view the raw wikitext of your wiki's main page, you can use the following URL:

```
http://127.0.0.1/wiki/index.php?title=Main_Page&action=raw
```

If you paste this URL into your browser, then instead of getting the complete page, you get only the wikitext, as shown in the following sample:

```
<big>'''MediaWiki has been successfully installed.'''</big>

Consult the [http://meta.wikimedia.org/wiki/Help:Contents User's Guide]
    for information on using the wiki software.

== Getting started ==

*
    [http://www.mediawiki.org/wiki/Help:Configuration_settings Configuration
    settings list]
* [http://www.mediawiki.org/wiki/Help:FAQ MediaWiki FAQ]
* [http://mail.wikimedia.org/mailman/listinfo/mediawiki-announce MediaWiki
    release mailing list]
```

Viewing the Wikitext Rendered as HTML

Sometimes you want to see how the wikitext text is rendered, but you are not that interested in having all the extra navigation and logos that surround the main content area displayed. In order to do that, you need to use the render action:

```
http://127.0.0.1/wiki/index.php?title=Main_Page&action=render
```

Figure 6-2 shows how just the content itself is rendered as HTML, and not every item on the typical page.

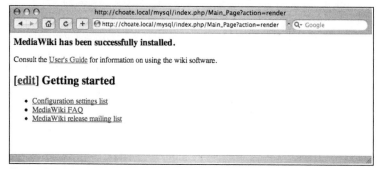

Figure 6-2: Rendered wikitext

Editing and Modifying Pages

Editing a page is a two-step process. First, you go to the edit page, where a text field is displayed in which you can edit the wikitext. Then, once you have edited the page, you can submit the edits, which then become the current revision for that page.

Edit/Submit

On the surface, the editing action is simple enough, but some interesting things take place in the background that you need to know. First, to get to the edit page itself, you click on a URL that takes the following form:

```
http://127.0.0.1/mysql/index.php?title=Main_Page&action=edit
```

This will display the edit page. Once you are finished editing, you can submit the page, but MediaWiki needs to ensure that malicious users can't just submit edits to any page willy-nilly, so when the editing form is presented to the user, it contains a hidden field, #wpEditToken, which in the following example is set to the value of 70c50ff7beee7423276b639a3877c227\. This token is then resubmitted when the user submits the edits to the page, so MediaWiki knows that it is a legitimate edit. When the changes are submitted, they are posted to the following URL (which is displayed as a relative URL, as that is how it is coded on the page:

```
/mysql/index.php?title=Main_Page&action=submit
```

The value for the token is POSTed, which is how form data is sent to a Web server. This means that it is not displayed in the URL as it is with typical GET requests. In practice, this means that some of the values used by MediaWiki are passed in the URL, while others are passed as form data.

The following is an example of the edit form generated by MediaWiki. Toward the end of the code, you can see the token:

```
<form id="editform" name="editform" method="post" action="/mysql/index.php?
   title=Main_Page&amp;action=submit" enctype="multipart/form-data">
      <input type='hidden' value="" name="wpSection">
```

```
    <input type='hidden' value="20070604194308" name="wpStarttime">
    <input type='hidden' value="20070601194849" name="wpEdittime">
    <input type='hidden' value="" name="wpScrolltop" id="wpScrolltop">

    <textarea tabindex='1' accesskey="," name="wpTextbox1" id="wpTextbox1"
rows='25' cols='80'>

    Text to edit goes here

    </textarea>

    <div id="editpage-copywarn">
        Copyright info goes here
    </div><span id='wpSummaryLabel'><label for='wpSummary'>Summary:
</label></span>

    <div class='editOptions'>
        <input tabindex='2' type='text' value="" name='wpSummary' id='wpSummary'
maxlength='200' size='60'><br>
        <input tabindex='3' type='checkbox' value='1' name='wpMinoredit'
accesskey='i' id='wpMinoredit'> <label for='wpMinoredit' title='Mark this as a
minor edit [alt-i]'>This is a minor edit</label> <input tabindex='4'
type='checkbox' name='wpWatchthis' accesskey="w" id='wpWatchthis'>
<label for='wpWatchthis' title="Add this page to your watchlist [alt-w]">
Watch this page</label>

        <div class='editButtons'>
            <input id="wpSave" name="wpSave" type="submit" tabindex="5"
value="Save page" accesskey="s" title="Save your changes [alt-s]">
<input id="wpPreview" name="wpPreview" type="submit" tabindex="6"
value="Show preview" accesskey="p" title="Preview your changes,
please use this before saving! [alt-p]"> <input id="wpDiff"
name="wpDiff" type="submit" tabindex="7" value="Show changes"
accesskey="v" title="Show which changes you made to the text. [alt-v]">
<span class='editHelp'><a href="/mysql/index.php/Main_Page"
title="Main Page">Cancel</a> | <a target="helpwindow"
href="/mysql/index.php/Help:Editing">Editing help</a>
(opens in new window)</span>
        </div><!-- editButtons -->
    </div><!-- editOptions -->

    <div class="mw-editTools"></div>

    <div class='templatesUsed'></div><input type='hidden'
value="70c50ff7beee7423276b639a3877c227\" name="wpEditToken">
<input name="wpAutoSummary" type="hidden"
value="d41d8cd98f00b204e9800998ecf8427e">
  </form>
```

Previous Versions

Manipulating previous versions is an important part of MediaWiki. You can view the history
of pages, compare revisions, and revert to previous revisions. Figure 6-3 shows the history of a page

called A New Page. You get to this page by clicking the History tab on the article page, or you can enter the following URL directly:

```
http://127.0.0.1/wiki/index.php?title=A_new_page&action=history
```

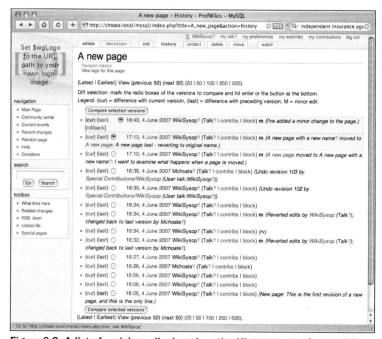

Figure 6-3: A list of revisions displayed on the History page of an article

The History page displays a list of information about each revision for that particular page, each displayed on its own line. It also enables you to compare different revisions of the same page by viewing what is called a *diff*, a graphical representation of the differences between the two files. You can compare a page with any previous version, not just the one immediately preceding it. You can also compare two older versions.

In order to use this page effectively, it is helpful to take a closer look at the information that is displayed. Each line represents a revision, and it consists of text, links to pages with more information, and radio buttons for selecting pages to compare.

Figure 6-4 is a close-up of the top line from the previous figure. Each item is numbered to illustrate the specific meaning of each column.

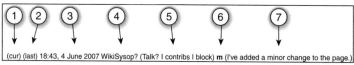

Figure 6-4: Information about an individual revision on the History page

1. This link (cur) compares the current revision (which is always the first one listed) with the revision represented by this row. The link is disabled on the first row, as it makes no sense to compare a revision with itself.

2. The second link in the row compares this revision with the previous revision, which is the revision in the row directly beneath it.

3. The date reflects the date on which that particular revision was made, and if you click on it, you are taken to a page that displays the revision. Whenever you view an earlier revision of a page, the user is notified at the top of the page that they are reading an earlier version of the document so that they will know they are potentially reading outdated information.

4. This is the user who created the revision.

5. The next three links all contain information pertaining to the user who created this revision. There is a link to the Talk page for this user, a link to a list of this user's other contributions, and a link to a page that enables you to block this user from making additional revisions (see the section called "Blocking" later in this chapter).

6. The m signifies a minor edit.

7. The comments made by the user when submitting the edit are displayed here. It's a good idea to have a policy regarding what kind of comments users should place here when submitting an edit. When the user describes the edit in some detail, it can make it easier to review. For example, if all you did was fix the spelling of one word, then it is helpful to note that fact in the comments so that the next reviewer will know what was changed.

In addition to the links, there are radio buttons you can use to make an ad hoc selection. The left radio button selects the earlier of the two revisions to be compared, while the right radio button selects a more recent revision.

Diff

When you compare pages, you are taken to a page that displays a diff. Links to view the diff look like the following:

```
http://127.0.0.1/mysql/index.php?title=A_new_page&diff=111&oldid=107
```

The first parameter, diff = 111, refers to the current revision, and oldid = 107 refers to an earlier revision. In terms of radio buttons, the oldid refers to the earlier of the two revisions, which is the radio button in the left-hand column.

The program used to generate the diff is set in LocalSettings.php. Figure 6-5 illustrates a diff as displayed by MediaWiki. The left column represents the earlier revision and the right column represents the more recent revision. The page does not show the complete content from both pages. Instead, it shows the lines where differences exist, plus some additional context that includes the preceding line.

Lines of text preceding by a minus sign (−) are lines that have been deleted (it is displayed in yellow if you are using the default skin). Lines of text preceded by a plus sign (+) are lines that have been added. In this example, line 7 was modified between the two revisions. In the earlier revision, it said, "Not to be outdone, I'm adding a fifth revision." In the later of the two revisions, it says, "Not to be outdone, I'm adding a fifth revision. A minor change." The diff program treats this as if line 7 were deleted from the earlier revision and a new line 7 was added in the more recent revision. The program is smart enough to know that the two lines share a lot of the same text, so only the actual new text is highlighted in red — the phrase "A minor change."

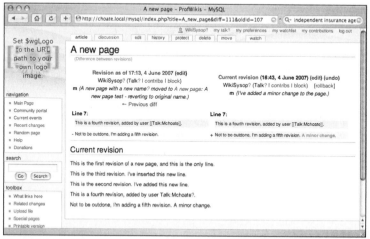

Figure 6-5: A diff comparing two different revisions of the same page

The other links on the page work just like the links on the History page. There are some additional links as well, which are used to revert to previous versions. There are three different ways to return to an earlier version of a page: *rollback*, *revert*, and *undo*. They all do basically the same thing, but in modestly different ways. Here are the definitions:

- ❏ **Undo:** Makes the most recent previous revision the current revision

- ❏ **Revert:** Makes any earlier revision the current revision

- ❏ **Rollback:** Eliminates any edits made by the last user to a page, so that the page that existed prior to that user's edits is once again the current page. From a practical perspective, the purpose of a rollback is to revert a page back to its state prior to being vandalized, which is why you would want to wipe out a series of edits by a user. This privilege is limited to sysops by default and is available from the History page.

Both undo and rollback are triggered by clicking on their respective links. In order to revert to an earlier page, you click the Edit link on the diff page. When you click the link to edit the page, you are taken to the edit page. The edit page displays the following warning: "You are editing an out-of-date revision of this page. If you save it, any changes made since this revision will be lost." You can make any changes you want (or no changes at all) and then click the Save Page button, and this revision will now become the current revision for the page.

The process of returning a page to an earlier revision suffers to some degree from a lack of clarity in the terminology MediaWiki uses to describe the action. In some cases, the interface uses the word revert and in others it uses rollback, and the online documentation isn't particularly helpful in clarifying the difference between reverting to an earlier revision, rolling back to an earlier revision, or undoing to an earlier revision.

Deleting Pages

The delete action deletes the page's record from the page table and inserts the relevant information into the archive table. The text and revision tables are not changed. This makes it possible to restore deleted pages using the `Special:Undelete` page.

The process is similar to editing and submitting changes to a page. When a page is to be deleted, a form is presented asking for confirmation. When the user submits the form, a token (`$wpEditToken`) is passed back to the server.

Deleting Files and Images

Deleting files and images works differently than deleting pages. By default, deleted files are truly deleted, but you can configure MediaWiki to save versions of files as well. You need to set `$wgSaveDeletedFiles` to true in `LocalSettings.php`, and you need to assign the directory in which the deleted files will be stored by setting it in `$wgFileStore` as follows, replacing `directory` with the name of the directory in which you want the files to reside:

```
$wgFileStore['deleted']['directory']
```

Move (Rename)

When you move a page, all you are doing is renaming the page. In the page table, the name is changed, but the page ID isn't changed. This allows the history of the page to remain intact. A new redirect page is created with the original name of the page so that any links to the old name are automatically redirected to the new page location. There are a few important things to keep in mind when moving pages:

❑   Image or category pages cannot be moved.

❑   You should always move a page, rather than simply cut the content from one and paste it into another, because it loses the page history. In some cases this is more important than others — for instance, the license under which Wikipedia content is released requires acknowledgment of all contributors, and the history is how the contributors are tracked.

❑   Moving it back to the original name will result in a warning because it requires the deletion of the redirect page that is created upon the move.

❑   If you change your mind and want to change the name back to what it was, you need to move the page back instead of undoing it or rolling it back — undo and rollback do not work for moves because of the way in which a page's revision history stays connected to the moved page. One confusing aspect of MediaWiki is that you can also go to the log page for the move (click View Logs from the History page). There will be a link called Revert that moves the file back to the original name.

Purge

The purge action is one that can be particularly helpful to Web developers. It clears the cache of a page. Most of the other actions are usually triggered by following a link on a page produced by MediaWiki, but this is one of the rare examples of an action that is usually triggered by manually appending the action information to the end of the URL. The following example shows the URL needed to purge the cache for the main page of your wiki:

```
http://127.0.0.1/wiki/index.php?Main_Page&action=purge
```

If you are not logged in, then you will get a form that asks for confirmation before MediaWiki clears the cache; and only then will the cache be purged.

Protecting Pages

The protect, watch, and patrol actions are related in that they are three different ways that administrators can monitor context on a wiki and ensure that the content is appropriate for the site.

Protect/Unprotect

Protect and Unprotect use $wpEditToken to verify that the request is a valid one. You can set protections against editing and moving a page. You have the option of using the default, restricting unregistered viewers from editing and moving the page, or limiting the ability to edit and move the page only to sysops. Wikipedia uses this feature to protect pages that are particularly controversial and subject to a great deal of vandalism. By limited edits and moves to sysops, access is limited to only trusted members of the community.

Watch/Unwatch

These actions place or remove the page in a user's watchlist. If the page is already in the list, then it is removed. You toggle the value indicating whether a page is watched or not by clicking the Watch tab (labeled Unwatch if the page is already on your watchlist). To view the pages on your watchlist, go to the special page Special:Watchlist. You can find a link to this page in the upper-right corner of the wiki page if you are logged in.

Patrolling

Marking a page as patrolled is limited to sysops, and this is a simple mechanism that notifies other Sysops that a page has been reviewed by a trusted figure. For example, you may decide to review all submissions for nonregistered users. If that's the case, then you will watch for any new revisions by unregistered users and read what has been posted. Afterwards, you mark the page as patrolled so that no one else will check it.

Blocking

Another available option when viewing the list of revisions on the History page is to block a particular user. If you are in the appropriate group (sysop) and you find that a user is making inappropriate edits, you may elect to block that user. To do so, you can click the Block link and you will be taken to the Block User page, illustrated in Figure 6-6.

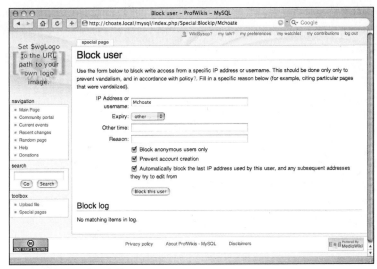

Figure 6-6: The Block User page

As you can see in Figure 6-6, you can block a user for a particular period of time. The drop-down menu provides options ranging from two hours to an infinite amount of time, or you can select Other and enter your own duration. You can also enter the reason why the user was blocked.

You can block a user by IP address or by username. This is an important distinction, and you can fine-tune the results by setting the following values in the form:

❑ **Block anonymous users only:** By selecting this option, you only block anonymous users. This is important when you are blocking an IP address because you may have more than one user coming from the same IP address and you may not want to block registered users who participate in the wiki.

❑ **Prevent account creation:** When you select this option, you are denying account creation to anyone from a particular IP address (if you are blocking by username, then the user in question already has created an account).

❑ **Automatically block the last IP address used by this user, and any subsequent addresses they try to edit from:** This option associates any IP address used by a particular user and blocks it. This can be something of a draconian measure because more than one user can share an IP address (and each user can use more than one IP address). Nevertheless, there may be instances when you want to do this.

You can get a list of blocked users on the `Special:Ipblocklist` page. Figure 6-7 shows a screen shot of this page. In this example, the user was logged into the wiki as WikiSysop, and blocked user Mchoate, selecting all of the options, including to automatically block the last IP address used by Mchoate.

If you look closely at Figure 6-7, you will see that two items are listed in the block IP list. The first is Mchoate, and the second is WikiSysop. How did that happen? Because the user logged into the wiki under both usernames on the same computer, MediaWiki followed the instructions and blocked WikiSysop because WikiSysop was using the same IP address as the user Mchoate, who was blocked.

Figure 6-7: A list of blocked users

Page Metadata

Metadata means data about data. There are a handful of actions that are used to display data about a page, rather than the page itself: `info`, `credits`, `dublincore`, and `creativecommons`.

Info

The `info` action must be enabled by setting `$wgAllowPageInfo` to `true` in `LocalSettings.php`. This is because it requires a lot of effort to generate. The URL for displaying page info is as follows:

```
http://127.0.0.1/wiki/index.php?title=Main_page&action=info
```

The info page tells you the number of watchers the page has, how many edits have been done, and the number of distinct authors, as illustrated in Figure 6-8.

Figure 6-8: Output of the info action

Credits

The `credits` action enables you to see who is responsible for the content on a given page. The URL looks like this:

```
http://127.0.0.1/wiki/index.php/Main_Page?action=credits
```

The output of the page contains the following kind of information:

```
This page was last modified 16:05, 4 June 2007 by ProfWikis - MySQL user
WikiSysop. Based on work by Mark Choate and Professional Wikis and Anonymous
user(s) of ProfWikis - MySQL.
```

dublincore, creativecommons actions

Two actions, dublincore and creativecommons, are closely related. Both have to be enabled in
LocalSettings.php:

```
/** RDF metadata toggles */
$wgEnableDublinCoreRdf = false;
$wgEnableCreativeCommonsRdf = true;
```

The dublincore action is rather simple — it causes Dublin Core metadata to be produced in the Resource
Description Framework (RDF). The Dublin Core refers to a set of primary metadata terms that have been
defined by the Dublin Core Metadata Initiative. The terms are simple, and you will see the basic set in
the following sample output. You can learn more about the Dublin Core at http://dublincore.org.

Type in the following URL:

```
http://127.0.0.1/wiki/index.php?title=Main_page&action=dublincore
```

Instead of an HTML page being returned, you will receive an XML page that expresses the core metadata
for the document in question:

```
<?xml version="1.0" encoding="UTF-8"?>
<!DOCTYPE rdf:RDF PUBLIC "-//DUBLIN CORE//DCMES DTD 2002/07/31//EN"
    "http://dublincore.org/documents/2002/07/31/dcmes-xml/dcmes-xml-dtd.dtd">
<rdf:RDF xmlns:rdf="http://www.w3.org/1999/02/22-rdf-syntax-ns#"
    xmlns:dc="http://purl.org/dc/elements/1.1/">
 <rdf:Description rdf:about="http://127.0.0.1/mysql/index.php/Page_title">
        <dc:title>Page title</dc:title>
        <dc:publisher>ProfWikis - MySQL</dc:publisher>
        <dc:language>en</dc:language>
        <dc:type>Text</dc:type>
        <dc:format>text/html</dc:format>

 <dc:identifier>http://127.0.0.1/mysql/index.php/Page_title</dc:identifier>
        <dc:date>2007-05-30</dc:date>
        <dc:creator>ProfWikis - MySQL user WikiSysop</dc:creator>
        <dc:rights rdf:resource="http://creativecommons.org/licenses/by/3.0/"/>
 </rdf:Description>
</rdf:RDF>
```

The creativecommons action causes the same information to be generated, except that it includes
information about the license under which the content is released, if it has been configured. In order
to configure licensing information, the following variables need to be set in LocalSettings.php:

```
## For attaching licensing metadata to pages, and displaying an
## appropriate copyright notice / icon. GNU Free Documentation
## License and Creative Commons licenses are supported so far.
# $wgEnableCreativeCommonsRdf = true;
```

```
$wgRightsPage = ""; # Set to the title of a wiki page that describes your
    license/copyright
$wgRightsUrl = "http://creativecommons.org/licenses/by/3.0/";
# prepends 'Content is available under a'
$wgRightsText = "Creative Commons Attribution-Noncommercial 3.0 License";
$wgRightsIcon = "http://creativecommons.org/images/public/somerights20.png";
```

MediaWiki knows about certain licenses, and will do interesting things with the licensing information you place here, if it's a license supported by Creative Commons (http://creativecommons.org).

The following licenses are available:

❑ Creative Commons Attribution 3.0 License

❑ http://creativecommons.org/licenses/by/3.0/

❑ Creative Commons Attribution-Noncommercial 3.0 License

❑ http://creativecommons.org/licenses/by-nc/3.0/

❑ Creative Commons Attribution-Share Alike 3.0 License

❑ http://creativecommons.org/licenses/by-sa/3.0/

❑ Creative Commons Attribution-No Derivative Works 3.0 License

❑ http://creativecommons.org/licenses/by-nd/3.0/

❑ Creative Commons Attribution-Noncommercial-Share Alike 3.0 License

❑ http://creativecommons.org/licenses/by-nc-sa/3.0/

❑ Creative Commons Attribution-Noncommercial-No Derivative Works 3.0 License

❑ http://creativecommons.org/licenses/by-nc-nd/3.0/

❑ Creative Commons - GNU GPL 2.0

❑ http://creativecommons.org/licenses/GPL/2.0/

❑ Creative Commons - GNU LGPL 2.1

❑ http://creativecommons.org/licenses/LGPL/2.1/

There are actually three different images you can choose from if you visit Creative Commons and look at their licenses. The image shown in Figure 6-9 is a generic image that simply says some rights have been reserved. The image chosen will appear on the bottom of all of your pages once you have configured the pages to do so.

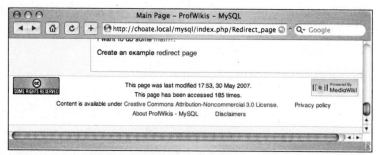

Figure 6-9: Creative Commons license notice

Redirects

There are many cases when you want one page to be redirected to another page. Earlier, when you learned about how to move pages, you saw that once a page was moved, a redirect page was put in place with the original name of the page that pointed to the page with the new name. This means that any links in place that still point to the old page name will automatically be taken to the current version of the page. Another example of when you would want to use a redirect would be to use more than one intuitive name to refer to a particular page.

The following is an example of a redirect page that points to the Main page:

```
#redirect[[Main Page]]
```

You might be wondering how you edit a redirect page, as every time you try to go to the redirect page, you are redirected to some other page. Fortunately, there's an easy solution. Simply append &redirect = no to the end of the URL of the redirect, and you will not be redirected, but taken to the edit page for the redirect.

You can include category tags on a redirect page, although it doesn't make sense to put any categories on the redirect page that are already listed on the target page. When you arrive at a page as a consequence of a redirect, there is a notice at the top of the page content notifying the reader that the page they are viewing is being displayed as a redirect.

It is possible to redirect to a section of a page, by appending the section anchor to the URL. Note one important side effect of doing this, however: the "redirected from" link will not be displayed on the page.

If you rename a page that is the target of a redirect, then the original redirect is automatically updated to reflect the new name of the target page. If the target of a redirect is deleted, then the original redirect is considered broken. You can check for broken redirects using the Special:BrokenRedirects page.

Special Pages

While technically not an action, there are two special pages that let you import and export pages on a wiki. This enables you to export a page on Wikipedia, for instance, and import it into your very own personal wiki.

Importing and Exporting Pages

In order to export the content of a page, you need to use the Special:Export page. The content of pages is exported in a special XML format that optionally contains all the revisions of the page. When you go to the Special:Export page, you are presented with a text field in which you can enter a list of page names you want exported, with one name on each line. A checkbox enables you to check whether to export all the revisions of the page. Once you have listed the pages that you want exported, click the Export button and the exported content will be sent to your browser. Save this file, and you can import it into another wiki.

In order to import a page, go to the Special:Import page, where you will be given the option to select a file to upload. Select a file that has been exported and then this file will be imported to the new wiki.

Summary

In this chapter, you have learned about different page actions that enable you to manage pages in a variety of different ways. As a wiki administrator, you can use this information to decide which groups can perform which actions to pages, as well as to get information about the page itself. The next chapter covers MediaWiki topics related to information architecture, which is the process of organizing a site to make information easier to find. You will learn about ways to manage the organization of your wiki through categories, as well as how to manage MediaWiki's search features.

7

Information Architecture:
Organizing Your Wiki

The objective of information architects is to make information easy to find. They do this in two ways. The first way is by organizing a site, usually in a hierarchical fashion, and using that organizational structure to create a system of navigation that enables users to drill down into the content by following links. The second way is through search engines. Wikis are organized differently than other websites, and in this chapter you will learn how to organize your content on MediaWiki so that users can quickly and easily find the information they are looking for.

How Users Find Information

Typical Wikipedia users find the page they are looking for by searching it by title. In effect, users are guessing the name of the article, because the default search is a title search, which, when found, takes the user directly to the page. Wiki pages can also be grouped into categories, which enables users to browse the site in order to find the content they are looking for.

Site Navigation

The default monotone skin provides a navigation box in the left column of the wiki. The links to the community portal, current events, help, and donations all link to pages that do not exist when the wiki is first set up. The other links, recent changes and random page, are links to special pages. You can either create the pages that are being linked to or you can remove them from the list. For now, it is worthwhile to take a look at the site navigation links themselves and see what they do (see Figure 7-1).

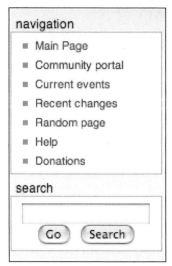

Figure 7-1: Site navigation links

The term "navigation" can be somewhat misleading and should be changed. When you customize your wiki, it is recommended that you remove it (the next chapter will show you how). For example, the title could be changed to something like "Related Information" or "About This Wiki," or something more descriptive because the fact is, you do not use the navigation box to navigate the site. Most true navigation takes place in the search box, which you will learn about next.

Search

True user navigation — the way users actually find the information they are looking for and navigate to it — is handled by the Search box. There are two button options in the search box that provide two different kinds of results. The Go button searches for a page that matches (i.e., has the same title as) the text entered into the Search box. The Search button searches page titles and page body text for any occurrence of the search term(s).

❏   **Go:** When you enter a search term and select Go, MediaWiki checks to see whether a page by that title exists. If the page does exist, the user is redirected to that page directly. The page title has to be an exact match. If a page with that page title does not exist, the user is taken to a Search Results page (see Figure 7-2), as if they had pressed the Search button instead.

❏   **Search:** When a user clicks on the Search button, the search results are displayed on a page that is divided into two sections: Article title matches and Page text matches. If the terms being searched for can be found in the title but aren't an exact match for the title, then those pages are listed under Article title matches. If the terms are in the body text of the article or page, then those pages are listed under Page text matches.

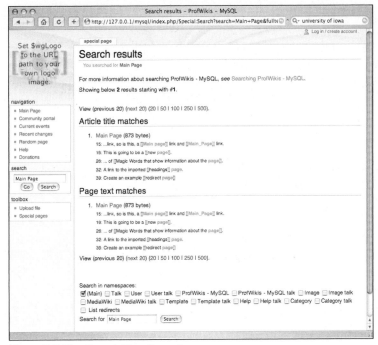

Figure 7-2: The Search Results page

Search Preferences

Users can set certain search preferences that affect how search results are returned. The options are listed under the Search tab in the User Preferences page. The following items can be set:

❑ **Hits per page:** If the user performs a search that returns a large number of results, MediaWiki will page through the results, rather than display them all at once. This setting determines how many results are displayed per page. The default value is 20.

❑ **Lines per hit:** When the search results are returned, each line on which the search term is found is displayed. This setting limits the number of lines that are displayed for each item returned in the search results. The default value is 5.

❑ **Context per line:** When a line is displayed with a search term, MediaWiki displays some of the text around the search term in order to provide context for how the term is being used on the page. You can add to or subtract from the amount of surrounding text that is displayed by setting this value. The default value is 50 characters.

❑ **Default namespaces searched:** On the preferences page, the complete list of namespaces is shown. By default, only the Main namespace is checked, which means that the search only applies to articles contained in the Main namespace. Users can change their preferences so that other namespaces are included as well.

Search Options

MediaWiki implements the site's search feature by default, using the database that was selected during installation, either MySQL or PostgreSQL. While these options work well for many sites, they do present some limitations, especially for large sites.

For example, the MySQL full-text search feature does not scale particularly well because the full-text search indexes are stored in memory (which makes the search very fast when the indexes are not too large). MySQL also has limited features in terms of how the search results are returned. The ranking of search results is determined only by how often a word appears in a document, and it does not calculate things such as *word distance*, which reflects how far apart search terms appear in a given document.

Using Google as Your Search Engine

Because of these limitations, you can decide not to use the default search engines in your wiki. The simplest change to make is to disable MediaWiki's text search by inserting the following text into the `LocalSettings.php` page:

```
$wgDisableTextSearch = true;
```

With this value set, MediaWiki defaults to using Google as the site search, as shown in Figure 7-3. This works well as long as Google has indexed your site. The downside is that you cannot control if, or how often, Google will index your site.

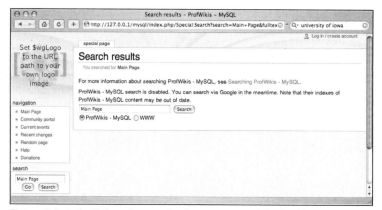

Figure 7-3: Default Google search when text search is disabled

Using an External Search Engine

You also have the option to use any arbitrary external search engine. To do so, in addition to disabling the text search, you also have to tell MediaWiki the URL of the external search engine, as shown here (in `LocalSettings.php`):

```
$wgForwardSearchUrl = 'http://www.google.com/search?q=$1&domains=http://choate
    .info&sitesearch=http://choate.info&ie=utf-8&oe=utf-8';
```

Note that some examples on `MediaWiki.org` mistakenly refer to `$wgSearchForwardUrl` — don't let that confuse you. It should be `$wgForwardSearchUrl`.

When you forward the search URL, you are sending the search to an entirely different server. In the following example, I'm using a search URL for Google, telling it to search my domain `choate.info`. The `$1` value in the query string of the URL will be replaced with the search terms the user entered into the search form. Then the user will be taken directly to the Google site for the search results. If you search for the term "wiki," then the following URL is used:

```
http://www.google.com/search?q=wiki&domains=http://choate
    .info&sitesearch=http://choate.info&ie=utf-8&oe=utf-8
```

Note how `$1` has been replaced by the word `wiki`.

Apache Lucene Search

It is also possible to use Apache Lucene as the full-text search engine. Wikipedia uses Lucene because it is optimized for full-text searching and offers the scalability to accommodate such a large site. Relative to MySQL, Lucene can handle full-text search requests much more efficiently. The implementation used by Wikipedia is Lucene.NET, a .NET port of the original Java Lucene, with code written in C#. The details of using Lucene go beyond the scope of this book, but you can find more detailed information `www.mediawiki.org/wiki/Lucene`.

Category Pages

MediaWiki uses *categories* as a way to organize pages, and groups similar pages together. Different pages can be grouped into a category, and these pages are listed on a special category page. Users can go to a special page, `Special:Catagories`, in order to browse through the pages of the wiki based upon the categories to which they refer. The categories can also be arranged hierarchically, so that a more complex navigation scheme can be developed, with categories and subcategories.

Adding a Page to a Category

Similar to wikilinks, you can create category pages simply by embedding a category link into a page. When you create a category this way, the page containing the category link is automatically added to the category.

```
[[Category: My Category]]
```

Regardless of where you enter the category tag on the page, it is displayed at the bottom of the page so that users can see to which categories a page refers, as shown in Figure 7-4, and follow a link to the category page itself to see other pages in the same category, as shown in Figure 7-5.

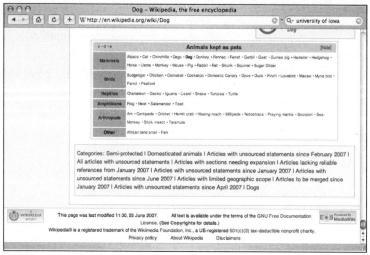

Figure 7-4: Category links appear at the bottom of the page

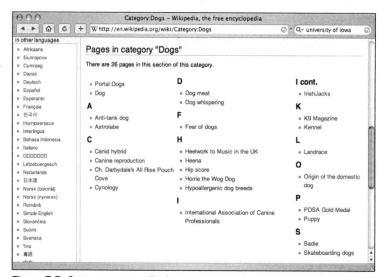

Figure 7-5: Category pages display an alphabetized list of pages for that category

Creating Categories

You can also create a category page directly without automatically adding a page to the category by using the following syntax:

```
[[:Category: My Category]]
```

When you create a category this way, a link to the category appears on the page where you entered the text, but the page with the link isn't added to the category. The category page is created, so you can follow that link to the category page, but you will see that there are no pages in the category.

Linking to Category Pages Using Alternate Text

You can also use this syntax to create a link to a category page that displays alternate text. The following tag links to a category page called Help:Basketball, but only displays the word "Basketball" in the link.

```
[[:Category:Help:Basketball|Basketball]]
```

Sorting Categories

You can control how pages are sorted on category pages. This is useful when you are adding a page that is not in the default namespace to a category. For example, if you have a page in the Help namespace called Help:Basketball and you want to place that page in the Sports category, it normally would be listed under H for Help:Basketball. If, however, you want it listed in the B section, then you could create the category link like this:

```
[[Category:Help:Basketball|Basketball]]
```

The category link at the bottom of the page will still say Help:Basketball. This only affects where the item is listed alphabetically on the category page.

Editing Category Pages

Category pages can be edited like any other page. Any text that you enter will appear above the list of links to pages in that category.

Subcategories

It is also possible to use categories to create a hierarchy of categories and subcategories. There's no such thing as a subcategory per se in MediaWiki, just categories, but you can organize your pages in a hierarchy by virtue of the fact that category pages themselves can be categorized. A category page that is part of another category is a subcategory.

Suppose you're creating a site about sports and you want to include articles about the following topics:

- ❏ Sports
- ❏ College Sports
- ❏ Pro Sports
- ❏ College Basketball
- ❏ Pro Basketball
- ❏ College Football
- ❏ Pro Football

MediaWiki employs a flat hierarchy, and each of these pages will be in the default namespace. One way a user can find these pages is to type the phrase "College Basketball" in the Search field and click the Go button. If the user were looking for information about a particular college basketball player, however, she would need to enter the player's name in the Search field and click the Search button to find any page with the player's name in it.

If the player has a common name, the results might include a list of pages that contain information about other people who share the same name. One way to make the search more efficient would be to group pages about a similar subject together. For instance, it might be a good idea to group all articles about college sports together, all pages about pro sports together, and so on. You might also want to group all articles about college basketball together, and so on. If you were really ambitious, you also might divide college basketball into men's college basketball and women's college basketball, and then separate those into divisions, and then individual teams. All of that is possible with categories.

Whether it is advisable to go into that much detail is another question. There is a delicate balancing act one must perform when categorizing pages. Too much categorization and the site becomes confusing and difficult to maintain. Too little categorization and users might find it hard to find the information they are looking for. There is no hard-and-fast rule, but it is possible to borrow some rules from more traditional content management systems and apply them here.

The hierarchy should be no more than three levels deep, and each category should have only five to seven subcategories. Of course, it's not always possible to fit within these parameters, but they are useful rules of thumb that you can use to help gauge the complexity of your site and spot potential usability issues.

Conceptually, you can group the pages of the example site as shown in Figure 7-6.

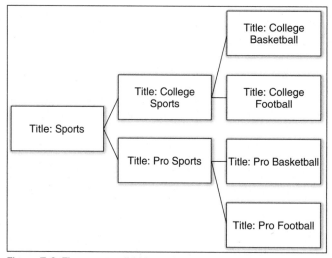

Figure 7-6: The sports wiki hierarchy

Figure 7-6 simply shows how I chose to categorize these pages conceptually. It's easy to understand that Sports is the root node of the tree, that College Sports and Pro Sports are subcategories, and so on. If you want to implement this hierarchy in MediaWiki using categories, you first need to determine the nature of the Sports page, and the College Sports and Pro Sports pages.

Category pages are in a different namespace than article pages, which means that a category page can share the same title as an article page. The question you need to answer is whether these pages are category pages, or whether you will have both category pages and article pages that share the same title. In other words, should you have an article page and a category page called Sports, or just a category page called Sports?

When you are developing a traditional website using traditional content management software, you usually develop the taxonomy first, and then the content is developed to go into the pre-defined categories. Wikis, conversely, often start with the articles first, and only later are the articles added to categories. This is an important difference between a taxonomy and a folksonomy: Folksonomies are created by users after the content has been created. You may find that you already have article pages called Sports, College Sports, Pro Sports, and so on. In that case, you have the option of being able to create category pages with the same name.

In our example, the College Sports article is in the College Sports category, and the College Sports category is a subcategory of Sports. If, however, you simply have the articles College Basketball, College Football, Pro Basketball, and Pro Football, then you can choose to use category pages exclusively for College Sports and Pro Sports, and so on.

Multi-Faceted Categories

The sports example reveals one of the common problems that arises when trying to properly categorize information into categories: There is often more than one sensible way to categorize them. The previous example used college sports and pro sports as subcategories of sports, but you could also just as easily decide to put basketball and football under sports. While people could argue the point both ways, very often the ultimate decision about how to categorize things falls upon the whim or personal preference of the categorizer.

A user of your wiki may have a different preference, or may conceptualize the topic differently than you do. Wouldn't it be nice to be able to organize your content into multi-faceted hierarchies, letting pages exist in different parts of your taxonomy? With MediaWiki, you can. Because any page can be in multiple categories, it's possible to create rather complex, multi-faceted hierarchies.

In order to address the sports problem, all you need to do is add a new category called `Category: Basketball` to the college basketball and pro basketball pages, and one called `Category: Football` to the college and pro football pages. Figure 7-7 shows how the hierarchy looks now (the football pages were omitted for clarity). As you can see, a user can now navigate to basketball-related pages in two different ways: through either the college sports or the pro sports categories, or through the basketball category.

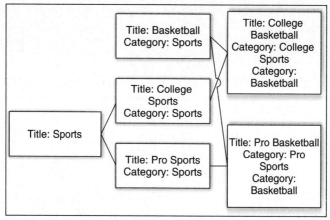

Figure 7-7: Multi-faceted categories

Categories as Folksonomies

In the previous sections, you learned how to organize your content into meaningful hierarchies. There's one important detail (or caveat) you should be aware of: Anybody can add a page to any hierarchy. In other words, one user may categorize pages in one way, while another chooses an entirely different approach. This decentralized categorization is often referred to as a *folksonomy*, in contrast to a *taxonomy*, which is a hierarchy of relationships developed centrally, usually by specialists.

You may be familiar with sites like Flickr that allow users to add *tags* to pages. Conceptually speaking, a tag and a category are very similar — they are both keywords that are used to describe or group a page into some conceptual category or topic. The advantage to this approach is that with many people adding pages to different categories, multiple points of view are represented by the links. What makes sense to one person may not have occurred to another person, and this open-ended approach makes it possible to discover unexpected connections between pages.

Improving Findability

I've already mentioned the importance of using simple, clear page titles to help users find the information they are looking for. Other useful tactics can be employed as well to improve the user experience. Wikipedia has a Manual of Style that establishes consistent ways of formatting pages and other conventions that improve the search experience (see `http://en.wikipedia.org/wiki/Wikipedia:Manual_of_Style`).

Redirects and Synonyms

Clearly, there are often many words or phrases that describe the same thing. The best way to address this with your wiki is with the use of *redirects*. You should select one name per topic, and all variants of that name or phrase should be redirect pages that point to the canonical version. Redirects are discussed in Chapter 6.

Disambiguation Pages

You might run into another problem as well, which results from the fact that one word or phrase may refer to different things. In this case, you can use what is called a *disambiguation page*. A disambiguation page isn't a formal page type in MediaWiki. Rather, it's a standard practice that is used to address this problem. If you have a term that applies to multiple topics, you can create a page with that term and then link from there to the other terms. You can use a template to ensure standard formatting of the disambiguation page.

> **You can read about templates in Chapter 8.**

You can also list the disambiguation page on the MediaWiki:Disambiguations page, and this will ensure that the page is listed on the Special:Disambiguations page. You can view this Wikipedia page at `http://en.wikipedia.org/wiki/MediaWiki:Disambiguationspage`, where you will see a list of templates, discussed in the next chapter.

Wiki Gardening

While it is comforting to think of a wiki as an organic process, with order arising out of chaos naturally, without human intervention or irritating authoritarianism on the part of some consulting taxonomist, it is also naive. Don't get me wrong: Letting the organizational structure of your wiki develop naturally is a good thing, but what emerges needs to be tended in order for it to thrive. Every wiki needs a gardener — someone to pull the weeds, water the plants, and occasionally move a plant from one bed to another.

Several special pages help with the wiki gardening task:

- ❑ **Uncategorized pages** (`Special:Uncategorizedpages`): These are pages that do not have one or more categories assigned. Use this page to ensure that all pages are categorized.

- ❑ **Uncategorized images** (`Special:Uncategorizedimages`): These are image (or file) pages that have not been categorized.

- ❑ **Uncategorized categories** (`Special:Uncategorizedcategories`): Category pages themselves can be categorized. This is useful when building a relatively deep hierarchical structure for your wiki. This special page lists all the category pages that have not been assigned to a category.

- ❑ **Unused categories** (`Special:Unusedcategories`): These are category pages with no pages in them.

- ❑ **Unused files** (`Special:Unusedfiles`): These are files (usually images) that have been uploaded but that are not being linked to.

- ❑ **Wanted categories** (`Special:Wantedcategories`): This page returns a list of categories that have been created but that do not have any content in them. Having no content in them does not mean that there are no pages in the category; it means that the category pages have not been edited and no additional explanatory content has been added.

❑ **Wanted pages** (`Special:Wantedpages`): These are pages for which a wiki link exists but they have not been edited, so they have no content.

❑ **Dead-end pages** (`Special:Deadendpages`): These pages contain no links to other pages in the wiki.

❑ **Long pages and short pages** (`Special:Longpages`, `Special:Shortpages`): Both of these pages function the same way, returning a list of pages ordered either from the smallest to the largest (for short pages) or from the largest to the smallest (for long pages), as measured in bytes. When a page is getting too long, it is often a good idea to break it up into two or more smaller pages. Small pages indicate pages that can possibly be expanded upon.

Summary

In this chapter, you learned how to organize content on your wiki using categories. You also learned how to customize the search engine used by MediaWiki. In the next chapter, you will learn about magic words, templates, and skins. This will enable you to customize the look and feel of your wiki, and add more complex content to your pages.

Magic Words, Templates, and Skins

Magic words and templates provide advanced methods for including content that is dynamic or needs to be standardized across pages. Skins determine the overall look and feel of MediaWiki, as well as standard navigation features, and user tools. All three tools can be customized. This chapter will show you how to create your own templates, and how to modify the default MediaWiki skin to change the look and feel of your wiki. In Chapter 9, you will learn how to install and write extensions to MediaWiki, including how to create your own magic words.

This chapter assumes the reader knows what Cascading Stylesheets (CSS) are and how they work. It also assumes a basic understanding of programming languages, ideally PHP. If you are not familiar with CSS, you should familiarize yourself with it prior to reading the section on MediaWiki skins. An excellent introduction is available on Wikipedia at http://en.wikipedia.org/wiki/CSS. Another good source is Richard York's *Beginning CSS: Cascading Style Sheets for Web Design, Second Edition* (Wrox, 2004).

Magic Words

Magic Words are special words that serve as placeholders for other content that will appear on a wiki page. Some magic words were introduced in Chapter 4, but they weren't called magic words. The XML-style tags `<nowiki>` and `<ref>` are both examples of magic words because they are not raw HTML, and both have an impact on the way the content of the page is parsed and displayed.

There are several different styles of magic words, whose syntax is slightly different. Some magic words are surrounded by a pair of curly brackets ({{and}}), while others are perched between a double underscore character (__), and even others are tagged using XML constructs (such as the `<nowiki>` example already mentioned). The following sections document the most commonly used magic words and provide you with examples of how they are used.

Directives

The first group of magic words is not displayed directly on the page. Instead, they adjust the formatting or display of the page. They are always uppercase, and are surrounded by underscores, like so: __NOTOC__.

These magic words, described in the following table, are typed onto the page when it is being edited. The impact of using the words can be previewed when the page content is previewed.

Magic Word	Description
__TOC__	Causes the table of contents to appear where you want it on the page
__NOTOC__	Keeps the table of contents from appearing, regardless of the number of sections in the page
__FORCETOC__	Forces the table of contents to appear when there are fewer than four sections, or when the user has set preferences so that no tables of content are displayed
__NOEDITSECTION__	Removes the "Edit" links that appear next to section headings on wiki pages
__NEWSECTIONLINK__	New section code ads a " + " tab next to the "edit" tab of a page. This is the default procedure on talk pages, because it allows the reader to automatically create a new section, separate from all the others, gently encouraging posters in talk sections to confine their comments to a section, rather than edit someone else's. The section is appended to the other sections before it, so the most recent posts on a talk page are at the bottom of the page, much like forum or message board words, and not at all the way a blog works, where the latest content appears at the top of the page.
__NOGALLERY__	When used on a page that contains a gallery, the page displays links to the images in the gallery, rather than display the images themselves.

Variables

Variables are magic words that serve as placeholders whose values are replaced when the text is parsed. The replacement value itself varies, depending on the context. There are two basic groups of variables. The first group relates to date and time, and the replacement values are localized, depending on the language used in the site. The second group consists of variables that display information about a page or the wiki itself, such as the total number of articles, and so on. Variables are always in uppercase, and are surrounded by a pair of curly brackets, like so: {{CURRENTMONTH}}.

Date and Time

The following magic words all apply to dates and times, and the output is dependent upon the setting of $wgLanguageCode in LocalSettings.php. This setting determines the language that the wiki uses for all system messages, which are items such as user-interface elements, and so on.

Local times are based on the local time for the wiki and not what is configured in the user's preferences. All other times are based on UTC, otherwise known as Greenwich Mean Time.

The following table shows the relevant magic words and their sample output, based upon an arbitrary date of Tuesday, July 1, 2007, at 20:14 UTC and a four-hour difference between Greenwich and this location.

Magic Word	Output
{{CURRENTMONTH}}	07
{{CURRENTMONTHNAME}}	July
{{CURRENTMONTHNAMEGEN}}	July
{{CURRENTMONTHABBREV}}	Jul
{{CURRENTDAY}}	1
{{CURRENTDAY2}}	01 (displays leading zeros when appropriate)
{{CURRENTDAYNAME}}	Tuesday
{{CURRENTYEAR}}	2007
{{CURRENTTIME}}	20:14
{{CURRENTHOUR}}	20
{{LOCALMONTH}}	07
{{LOCALMONTHNAME}}	July
{{LOCALMONTHNAMEGEN}}	July
{{LOCALMONTHABBREV}}	Jul
{{LOCALDAY}}	1
{{LOCALDAY2}}	01 (displays leading zeros when appropriate)
{{LOCALDAYNAME}}	Tuesday
{{LOCALYEAR}}	2007
{{LOCALTIME}}	16:14
{{LOCALHOUR}}	16
{{CURRENTTIMESTAMP}}	20070701160537
{{LOCALTIMESTAMP}}	20070701120537

Information About the Page

The following group of magic words causes information about the page to be displayed. It serves as a way to refer back and forth between related pages with the same title as the article, but in a different namespace. The sample output is based on a fictitious page called "Magic words that show information about the page." The words come in pairs, such as {{PAGENAME}} and {{PAGENAMEE}}. The extra E at the end means that the output has been escaped and can be used in external links or other places where escaped text is required.

Magic Word	Output
{{PAGENAME}} {{PAGENAMEE}}	Returns the page name. If the page is a subpage, then the complete title is returned, such as Page/Subpage. The unescaped version returns: Magic words that show information about the page The escaped version returns: Magic_words_that_show_information_about_the_page
{{NAMESPACE}} {{NAMESPACEE}}	Returns an empty string when in the default namespace; otherwise, returns the appropriate namespace.
{{TALKSPACE}} {{TALKSPACEE}}	Returns the name of the next odd namespace. If the page is in the default names, then it returns the namespace Talk. If the page is in the Help namespace (number 12), then the title of the namespace 13 is returned, which, in this case, would be Help_talk.
{{SUBJECTSPACE}} {{SUBJECTSPACEE}}	Returns the name of the previous even-numbered namespace. For example, if this magic word is used on a page in the Help_talk namespace (13), then Help is returned (12).
{{FULLPAGENAME}} {{FULLPAGENAMEE}}	Returns the namespace and the name of the page. Unescaped: Help:Magic words that show information about the page Escaped: Help:Magic_words_that_show_information_about_the_page
{{SUBPAGENAME}} {{SUBPAGENAMEE}}	Only returns the name of the subpage, and does not return the parent pages, unlike {{PAGENAME}}).
{{BASEPAGENAME}} {{BASEPAGENAMEE}}	Only returns the name of the parent page of a subpage.
{{TALKPAGENAME}} {{TALKPAGENAMEE}}	Unescaped: Talk:Magic words that show information about the page Escaped: Talk:Magic_words_that_show_information_about_the_page
{{SUBJECTPAGENAME}} {{SUBJECTPAGENAMEE}}	Returns the full page name in the subject namespace. In other words, if you are on the Help page, then you can enter {{SUBJECTPAGENAME}} to get the following: Magic words that show information about the page {{SUBJECTPAGENAMEE}} would return this: Magic_words_that_show_information_about_the_page

Revisions

These magic words return information about the revision status of the containing page.

Magic Word	Output
{{REVISIONID}}	The revision ID of the page.
{{REVISIONDAY}}	The day of the month of the last revision. If the revision was made on August, 1, then the output would be 1.
{{REVISIONDAY2}}	The same as before, but with preceding zeros. August, 1 would be represented as 01.
{{REVISIONMONTH}}	The number of the month the revision took place. If the revision was made in August, it would be 8.
{{REVISIONYEAR}}	Returns the year the revision was made: 2007.
{{REVISIONTIMESTAMP}}	A timestamp in ISO 8601 format. For the date/time of July 11, 2007, at 12:05:35 P.M., it will return 20070711120535.

Statistics

The following magic words provide statistical information about the wiki itself. You will notice that these often occur in pairs as well, such as {{NUMBEROFPAGES}} and {{NUMBEROFPAGES:R}}. The words that end with :R are actually examples of parser functions, rather than variables because the R is a parameter that tells the parser to return raw data, which, in practice, means returning numbers without thousands separators.

Magic Word	Output
{{DIRECTIONMARK}}	‎
{{CONTENTLANGUAGE}}	Returns the language code: en for English, and so on.
{{NUMBEROFARTICLES}} {{NUMBEROFPAGES}} {{NUMBEROFFILES}} {{NUMBEROFUSERS}} {{NUMBEROFADMINS}}	These parser functions are self-descriptive. They return the number of articles in the wiki, the number of pages, files, users, and so on.
{{NUMBEROFARTICLES:R}} {{NUMBEROFPAGES:R}} {{NUMBEROFFILES:R}} {{NUMBEROFUSERS:R}} {{NUMBEROFADMINS:R}}	The parser function version of these magic words returns the same value as the variable versions, except without any thousands separator. For example, if there are 10,000 articles in a wiki, {{NUMBEROFARTICLES:R}} returns 10000.

Magic Word	Output
{{PAGESINNS:ns}}	Returns the count for the number of pages in a given namespace. Replace "ns" with the number or name of the namespace.
{{PAGESINNS:ns:R}}	Same as above, except without thousands separators.
{{CURRENTVERSION}}	For example, 1.9.3.

Parser Functions

According to the MediaWiki documentation, parser functions were originally called *colon functions* by those who first documented them, presumably because of the presence of a colon character separating the function name from the function arguments. In any event, the term colon functions was quickly dumped in favor of the more amenable (and descriptive) phrase "parser functions." There are core parser functions, that are part of the basic MediaWiki distribution, and there are a number of parser functions developed as extensions that can be added to MediaWiki. Whether a core parser function, or an extension, both adhere to the same underlying interface.

String Functions

This group of functions is used to change the case of words on the page, as shown in the following table.

Magic Word	Output
{{lcfirst:WORD}}	wORD
{{ucfirst:word}}	Word
{{lc:WORD}}	word
{{uc:word}}	WORD

URL Functions

The following functions are used to build links to other pages. They work with wikilinks as well as intrawiki links. Note that both fullurl and localurl have escaped versions, but there is no difference in the output.

Magic Word	Output
`{{localurl:Image: Closedfolder.gif}}`	`/wiki/index.php/Image:Closedfolder.gif`
`{{localurl:This is some document title}}`	`/wiki/index.php/This_is_some_document_title`
`{{localurl:This is some document title|action=edit}}`	`/wiki/index.php?title=This_is_some_document_ title&action=edit`
`{{localurle:This is some document title}}`	`/wiki/index.php/This_is_some_document_title`
`{{fullurl:This is some document title}}`	`<a href="http://choate.local/wiki/index.php/This_is_some_ document_title" class="external free" title="http://choate .local/wiki/index.php/This_is_some_document_title" rel="nofollow">http://choate.local/wiki/index.php/This_ is_some_document_title</a>`
`{{fullurle:This is some document title}}`	`<a href="http://choate.local/wiki/index.php/This_is_some_ document_title" class="external free" title="http://choate .local/wiki/index.php/This_is_some_document_title" rel="nofollow">http://choate.local/wiki/index.php/ This_is_some_document_title</a>`
`{{localurl:wiktionary:dog}}`	`<a href="http://en.wiktionary.org/wiki/dog" class="external free" title="http://en.wiktionary.org/wiki/dog" rel="nofollow">http://en.wiktionary.org/wiki/dog</a>`
`{{fullurl:wiktionary:dog}}`	`<a href="http://en.wiktionary.org/wiki/dog" class="external free" title="http://en.wiktionary.org/wiki/dog" rel="nofollow">http://en.wiktionary.org/wiki/dog</a>`
`{{urlencode:This is an encoded URL}}`	This returns an encoded string of text so that it is suitable for use in a URL. The output in this example would be `This+is+an+encoded+URL`
`{{anchorencode:This is a section}}`	This function is used to reference named anchors that are generated for page sections. For example, the wikitext `==This is a section==` results in the following HTML, which includes a named anchor: `<a name="This_is_a_section"></a><h2> <span class="mw-headline">This is a section</span></h2>` This function takes the name of the section and returns the string to use to reference the anchor: `This_is_a_section`.

Namespaces

The ns parser function provides a way to generate namespace text by referring to the namespace number or the name of the namespace itself.

Magic Word	Output
{{ns:-2}}	Media
{{ns:Media}}	Media
{{ns:-1}}	Special
{{ns:Special}}	Special
{{ns:0}}	The default content namespace does not return a value.
{{ns:1}}	Talk
{{ns:Talk}}	Talk
{{ns:2}}	User
{{ns:3}}	User_talk
{{ns:4}}	ProfWikis_-_MySQL (the name of the wiki)
{{ns:project}}	ProfWikis_-_MySQL (the name of the wiki)
{{ns:5}}	ProfWikis_-_MySQL_talk
{{ns:project_talk}}	ProfWikis_-_MySQL_talk
{{ns:6}}	Image
{{ns:7}}	Image_talk
{{ns:8}}	MediaWiki
{{ns:9}}	MediaWiki_talk
{{ns:10}}	Template
{{ns:11}}	Template_talk
{{ns:12}}	Help
{{ns:13}}	Help_talk
{{ns:14}}	Category
{{ns:15}}	Category_talk

Creating Links with Variables and Parser Functions

These variables and parser functions are commonly used to create links to other pages in the wiki, and can be used inside of wikilinks. For example, if you want to refer to the Talk page for a given article from within that article, you could use the following:

```
[[{{TALKPAGENAMEE}}]]
```

Templates

Templates embed the content from one page in another, a process called *transclusion*. Most often, the page that is being embedded is in the Template namespace (although it doesn't have to be).

To see an example of how templates work, create a page called `Template:Test` in your wiki, edit it, and add the following text:

```
This is a sample template page, and it will be transcluded in another page.

<noinclude>None of the text here will be displayed</noinclude>
```

Next, create another page called `ASamplePage`, and edit it as well, entering only {{Test}}.

The page `ASamplePage` now refers to the `Template:Test` page, and the content of the `Template:Test` page will be included in `ASamplePage`. Figure 8-1 shows the output of `ASamplePage`. Note that only the first sentence is displayed, and nothing inside the `<noinclude>` tags is displayed. The `<noinclude>` tags are used to display instructions about how to use the template.

Figure 8-1: The Template:Test page embedded in another page

Parameters

You can use parameters with templates, too. By defining a template that takes parameters, you are able to define a standard way of displaying information. For example, suppose you want people to review websites on your site, and you want to make sure that they all include the same basic kinds of information. A parameterized template works perfectly.

When parameters are used, they can be referred to by their name or by their position. Create another template called `Template:SecondTest` and include the following content:

```
This template uses parameters. The first parameter is {{{1}}}
and the second is {{{2}}}.
```

Note that the numbers surrounded by three curly brackets are numbered sequentially, which corresponds to their position in the template tag when it is called from another page. In the following example, the phrase "First Word" is in the first position, and the phrase "Second Word" is in the second position. This means that `First Word` will replace {{{1}}} in the template, and `Second Word` will replace {{{2}}} in the template:

```
{{Test}}

The second template test follows:

{{SecondTest|First Word|Second Word}}
```

Figure 8-2 shows the output of this new, parameterized template.

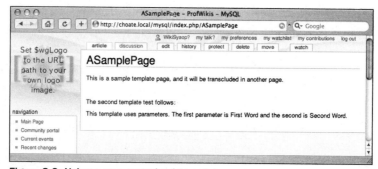

Figure 8-2: Using a parameterized template

Named Parameters

In addition to using parameter position to determine what is replaced, MediaWiki also supports named parameters. Instead of using numbers, you can use words to create placeholders for the information that will be passed to the template. In the following example, the template is expecting two parameters, one named `First` and the other named `Second`. Otherwise, the following is identical to the previous example:

```
This template uses parameters. The first parameter is {{{first}}}
and the second is {{{second}}}.
```

When this template is called, you need to add the name of the parameter to the template tag, as parameter position is no longer being used, as shown in the following example:

```
{{Test}}

The second template test follows:

{{SecondTest|first=First Word|second=Second Word}}
```

The output for this template is identical to the output displayed in the previous example.

Wikipedia uses a lot of templates, and you'll find references to the templates in the help sections on Wikipedia and MediaWiki. Unfortunately, those templates aren't installed by default when you install MediaWiki. It's easy enough to copy a template, however. One common template used on Wikipedia is the Infobox template, which is used to organize related information on a given page. You can see the source of the template by going to `http://en.wikipedia.org/wiki/Template:Infobox`. A screen shot of the Infobox template is shown in Figure 8-3.

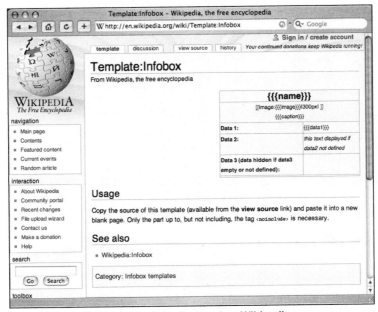

Figure 8-3: The Infobox template displayed on Wikipedia

To access the source, click the Source tab. This is a slightly more complicated template than the previous examples, but the basic structure is the same. Note that this template uses named parameters, which makes it easy for people to remember when dealing with templates with several parameters:

```
{| class="infobox bordered" style="width: 25em; text-align: left; font-size: 90%;"
|-
| colspan="2" style="text-align:center; font-size: large;" | '''{{{name}}}'''
|-
| colspan="2" style="text-align:center;" | [[Image:{{{image}}}|300px| ]]<br>
  {{{caption}}}
|-
! Data 1:
| {{{data1}}}
|-
! Data 2:
| {{{data2|"this text displayed if data2 not defined"}}}
|-
! Data 3 (data hidden if data3 empty or not defined):
| {{{data3|}}}
|-
| colspan="2" style="font-size: smaller;" | {{{footnotes|}}}
|}
```

```
<noinclude>
<!-- TO MAKE A NEW TEMPLATE: copy the source up to, but not including,
    the "noinclude" line into a new page. -->

<br style="clear:both" />
== Usage ==
Copy the source of this template (available from the '''view source''' link) and
paste it into a new blank page.  Only the part up to, but not including, the tag
<code>&lt;noinclude></code> is necessary.

==See also==
*[[Wikipedia:Infobox]]

[[Category:infobox templates| ]]
[[ar:قالب:قالب معلومات]]
[[fa:الگو:داده‌نان]]
[[fr:Modele:Infobox]]
[[zh:Template:Infobox]]
[[ia:Patrono:Infobox]]
</noinclude>
```

Cut and paste this text into a page of your wiki called Template:Infobox and you will immediately be able to use that template on your site. There is a caveat, however. The CSS used in the default MediaWiki distribution does not know about this particular template, causing it to look like it appears in Figure 8-4. In order to make the infobox look the way you want it to look, you need to customize the CSS, which is covered in detail in the "Skins" section.

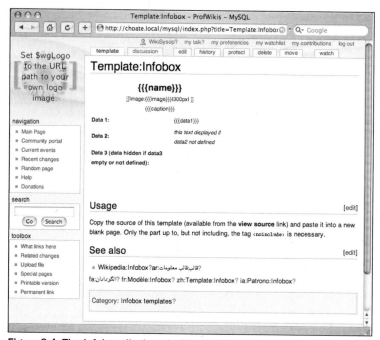

Figure 8-4: The Infobox displayed without CSS

Substitution

When a template is transcluded in a page, it is normally refreshed every time the page is rebuilt, which varies depending on your caching policies. This means that when the template is changed, the pages that include the template will reflect the changes as well. Sometimes you won't want this to happen; to ensure that, use the template modified by subst. The first time a template is included in a page, the content of the template is embedded in the page, so that it will not be changed if the original template is changed later. To substitute our Test template, you would simply change your wikitext to {{subst:Test}} instead of {{Test}}.

User Interface

Magic words, variables, and parser functions are all used in wikitext, primarily in the main content area of each page, but this is not the only place where you can use wikitext. In addition to the article content, other elements on each wiki page make up the user interface, including navigation boxes, sidebars, copyright notices, and so on, and the text of these elements can be changed as well.

There are two ways to change the overall user interface. Minor changes to the text used in the interface can be changed with interface messages. Large-scale changes to the user interface require modification of the wiki's skin. Both techniques are explained in the following sections.

Interface Messages

Interface messages are a kind of system message. MediaWiki handles system messages in a unique way in order to be able to localize the user interface of the wiki and present the interface in the appropriate language for that wiki.

Generally speaking, interface messages consist of all the navigation elements and related text that appear on all the pages. For example, the Sidebar interface message is how the navigation links in the left-hand column of a MediaWiki page are defined (when using the Monospace skin). Specifically, an interface message is a page in the MediaWiki namespace, and this page is used to determine what text to display in different elements of the page.

In order to customize interface messages, $wgUseDatabaseMessages should be set to True in LocalSettings.php. You also must be logged in as an administrator. When logged in as such, the interface message pages are edited just like any other page, and can include wikitext, magic words, parser functions, and so on.

Sidebar

All interface messages are in the MediaWiki namespace. Therefore, the following is the URL for the Sidebar interface message:

```
http://127.0.0.1/mysql/index.php/MediaWiki:Sidebar
```

The Sidebar interface message is responsible for the navigation box in the left-hand column of the Monospace skin.

The navigation elements are defined using a customized version of wikitext in order to specify links. The default content follows:

```
* navigation
** mainpage|mainpage
** portal-url|portal
** currentevents-url|currentevents
** recentchanges-url|recentchanges
** randompage-url|randompage
** helppage|help
** sitesupport-url|sitesupport
```

The first item is the label. It can be another system message, a wiki link, or an external link. MediaWiki checks first to whether a system message with the same name exists. If it does, then the content of the system page is used for the label. In this case, if you visit the page `MediaWiki:Mainpage`, you will find that it contains the text "Main Page," and that is what is displayed for that link.

The second element (the part after the `"|"` character) defines the link for that item. It, too, can be an interface message. The interface messages are converted to the appropriate text prior to the wikitext being parsed by the parser. That's why the line `** mainpage|mainpage` can be used to define a link to the main page of the wiki. In effect, `mainpage` is converted to `"Main Page"`, and `"Main Page"` is then converted to a wiki link to the page titled "Main Page."

The asterisks work similarly to the way they work when creating lists in wikitext, with a few notable differences. First, a single asterisk at the start of a line denotes a new section and causes a new box to be displayed on the page, with the text that follows the asterisk as the label. You can nest items in the list by adding additional asterisks, just as you can with lists. The following example shows how to add a new section to the navigation list, as well as how to use an external link in the navigation list. Note that when you preview the changes, MediaWiki displays the external link incorrectly, but when it is saved, the link is displayed as it should on the page.

```
* navigation
** mainpage|mainpage
** portal-url|portal
** currentevents-url|currentevents
** recentchanges-url|recentchanges
** randompage-url|randompage
** helppage|help
** sitesupport-url|sitesupport
* More stuff
** http://choate.info/|Mark's blog
```

Figure 8-5 shows how the page looks with this modified sidebar.

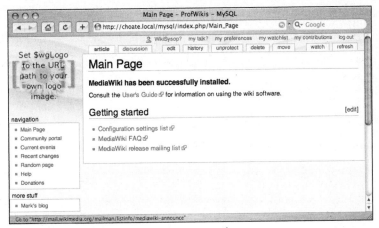

Figure 8-5: The Sidebar now has a new section

Site Notice

Another commonly used interface message is the Sitenotice interface message, which is used to display messages that you want all users to see. It is displayed at the top of the page, as shown in Figure 8-6.

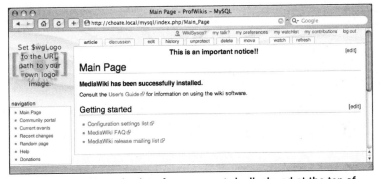

Figure 8-6: The Sitenotice interface message is displayed at the top of every page

The MediaWiki:Sitenotice page must be edited, just like the MediaWiki:Sidebar page was edited. Once done, the notice is displayed sitewide.

Copyright Warning

The copyright warning that is displayed on editing pages is defined in `MediaWiki:Copyrightwarning`. This interface message is different from the previous two examples in that it uses parameters to customize the message for a given context. Go to the `MediaWiki:Copyrightwarning` page and edit it and you will see the following text:

```
Please note that all contributions to {{SITENAME}} are considered to be released
    under the $2 (see $1 for details). If you don't want your writing to be edited
    mercilessly and redistributed at will, then don't submit it here.<br/>
You are also promising us that you wrote this yourself, or copied it from
    a public domain or similar free resource.
<strong>DO NOT SUBMIT COPYRIGHTED WORK WITHOUT PERMISSION!</strong>
```

There are two variables, $1 and $2, and these values are determined based on the settings of the wiki. $1 refers to the name of the license used by the wiki, if that has been configured in `LocalSettings.php`. $2 refers to the link to the wiki page that describes the copyright policy (again, if it has been configured).

> *An up-to-date list of available interface messages can be found at* www.mediawiki.org/wiki/Category:Interface_messages.

Skins

Skins are a collection of resources used to define the overall look and feel of your wiki. The goal of good content management system design is to achieve a separation of application logic and content design. It's never possible to completely separate the two, of course, and a significant amount of application logic in the skin classes shouldn't be meddled with unless you want to change the actual functionality of your wiki.

Skins include a few PHP classes, CSS, JavaScript scripts, and graphical resources. All modern MediaWiki skins are a subclass of the `SkinTemplate` class, and the `QuickTemplate` class, both of which are defined in `/includes/SkinTemplate.php`. The default template for MediaWiki is Monobook, and the Monobook subclasses are defined in `/skins/Monobook.php`. All of the related graphics, CSS, and JavaScript scripts are in the directory `/skins/monobook/` or `/skins/common`.

> *If you create your own skin, you will create your own directory for these files, and you should never overwrite anything in* `/skins/common`.

Displaying a New Logo

The wiki's logo is defined by assigning a URL to the `$wgLogo` variable in `LocalSettings.php`. The default size of the logo should be 135 pixels high and 135 pixels wide. Because you are using a URL, the logo can be a file on a different server, or it can be an image file uploaded into the wiki itself. In order to customize the size of the logo, you need to modify the `Main.css` file in the Monobook skin.

The following excerpt from `Main.css` shows how logo size is defined for the `#p-logo` selector. In order to change the size of the logo, you need to change the values for `height` and `width` to match that of the logo you plan to display. You do not want to change the original `Main.css` stylesheet, because it may be overwritten when you upgrade MediaWiki. See the section "Customizing CSS and JavaScript" later in this chapter to learn how to change stylesheets in an upgrade-proof way. Here is the code defining logo size:

```
#p-logo {
    z-index: 3;
    position:absolute; /*needed to use z-index */
    top: 0;
    left: 0;
    height: 155px;
    width: 12em;
    overflow: visible;
}
```

Skin Settings and Preferences

The default skin is Monobook, but other skins are available, which the user can select if you have not changed the default values. You can change the default skin by setting the $wgDefaultSkin global variable in LocalSettings.php. When you do, use the lowercase version of the skin name. For example, if you wanted to change the default skin to CologneBlue, you would enter the following:

```
$wgDefaultSkin = cologneblue;
```

You can also limit the skins from which users can choose on their preferences page by populating the $wgSkinSkins array in LocalSettings.php. If you do so, every skin listed in this array will be skipped and will not be shown as an option to the user.

```
$wgSkipSkins = array("chick", "cologneblue", "myskin", "nostalgia",
"simple", "standard");
```

If you want to remove all skin options from the user, as well as any trace that it's possible for other skins to exist, then you need to remove the Skins tab in the user's preferences page. In order to do this, edit the /includes/SpecialPreferences.php file. This file is responsible for building the preferences page for the user. Comment out the code that builds the Skin tab (in other words, start each line that refers to the tab with a # character). The code in question is as follows:

```
# Skin
#
$wgOut->addHTML( "<fieldset>\n<legend>\n" . wfMsg('skin') . "</legend>\n" );
$mptitle = Title::newMainPage();
$previewtext = wfMsg('skinpreview');
# Only show members of Skin::getSkinNames() rather than
# $skinNames (skins is all skin names from Language.php)
$validSkinNames = Skin::getSkinNames();
# Sort by UI skin name. First though need to update validSkinNames as sometimes
# the skinkey & UI skinname differ (e.g. "standard" skinkey is "Classic" in the UI).
foreach ($validSkinNames as $skinkey => & $skinname ) {
  if ( isset( $skinNames[$skinkey] ) ) {
        $skinname = $skinNames[$skinkey];
        }
  }
asort($validSkinNames);
```

```
foreach ($validSkinNames as $skinkey => $sn ) {
        if ( in_array( $skinkey, $wgSkipSkins ) ) {
                continue;
        }
        $checked = $skinkey == $this->mSkin ? ' checked="checked"' : '';

        $mplink = htmlspecialchars($mptitle->getLocalURL("useskin=$skinkey"));
        $previewlink = "<a target='_blank' href=\"$mplink\">$previewtext</a>";
        if( $skinkey == $wgDefaultSkin )
                $sn .= ' (' . wfMsg( 'default' ) . ')';
$wgOut->addHTML( "<input type='radio' name='wpSkin' id=\"wpSkin$skinkey\"
    value=\"$skinkey\"$checked /> <label for=\"wpSkin$skinkey\">{$sn}</label>
    $previewlink<br />\n" );
        }
$wgOut->addHTML( "</fieldset>\n\n" );
```

After the preceding code is commented out, users will only be able to use the default skin, as specified by the wiki administrator.

Customizing CSS and JavaScript

The CSS files for Monobook are in /skins/monobook/main.css. If you want to customize the look and feel of your site, you do not want to change this file directly, because it may be overwritten when upgrading to a later version of MediaWiki. In order to work around this potential problem, MediaWiki provides ways to generate site-specific and user-specific CSS that will not be overwritten during an upgrade.

Site JavaScript and CSS

Users in the sysop group can define a new CSS document that will be applied to the entire wiki but that won't overwrite the original CSS files. The same is true for JavaScript files as well. The first step is to enable this feature by entering the following code into LocalSettings.php:

```
$wgUseSiteCss = true;
$wgUseSiteJs = true;
```

Once it is enabled, the sysop should create the following pages in the MediaWiki namespace:

```
MediaWiki:Monobook.css
MediaWiki.Monobook.js
```

After this is done, the sysop can enter style information into the CSS file (or code into the JavaScript file).

In the previous section, the template copied from Wikipedia did not display correctly because the customized CSS required to do so was missing. Using MediaWiki's CSS customization features, it's possible to go to Wikipedia and view the customized CSS. Type the following URL in your browser and you will be taken to the appropriate page:

```
http://en.wikipedia.org/wiki/MediaWiki:Monobook.css
```

In the previous example, the table element used in the Infobox was in the infobox class. You can scroll through the CSS on this page until you find a reference to the infobox class, which, at the time of writing, was as follows:

```
/* Infobox template style */

.infobox {
    border: 1px solid #aaa;
    background-color: #f9f9f9;
    color: black;
}

.infobox.bordered td,
.infobox.bordered th {
    border: 1px solid #aaa;
}

/* styles for bordered infobox with merged rows */
.infobox.bordered .mergedtoprow td,
.infobox.bordered .mergedtoprow th {
    border-top: 1px solid #aaa;
    border-right: 1px solid #aaa;
}

.gallerybox .thumb img {
    background: #F9F9F9;
}

.infobox.bordered .mergedrow td,
.infobox.bordered .mergedrow th {
    border-right: 1px solid #aaa;
}
```

You can copy the preceding CSS and then go back to your wiki and paste it into the MediaWiki: Monobook.css page so that the infoboxes that appear on your page now look exactly like the ones on Wikipedia.

When Monobook.css is customized, it does not eliminate the other CSS files used by the site. If the style is new, and not represented in the default CSS file, then the style is simply added. If the style already exists, then it is overridden by the new style in Monobook.css. This means that you can override the setting for #p-logo in the MediaWiki:Monobook.css page. Simply add the selector to that page and change any of the values you want to change, and that change will then be reflected in the site.

User JavaScript and CSS

The sitewide CSS and JavaScript can only be modified by a sysop, but the same functionality can be implemented for users as well. If you want to let users create their own CSS or JavaScript for the site, you need to enable the following variables in LocalSettings.php:

```
$wgAllowUserCss=true;
$wgAllowUserJs=true;
```

Once the site is configured, users can create their own stylesheets and JavaScript scripts by creating the following pages:

```
Special:Mypage/monobook.css
Special:Mypage/monobook.js
```

The special page Mypage creates a subpage to your user page. Once created, you can now customize to your heart's content.

While there may be some legitimate reasons to let users customize their stylesheets, it is usually better to disable this feature altogether. This is because if you don't know exactly what you are doing, you can make your site unusable. While it's true that any problems would be limited to users who customizes their own CSS, you can avoid the support headache by avoiding the feature altogether. Bear in mind that users can usually override a site's stylesheet in their own browser, which is the best solution for customization.

Skin Output

The following code listing is a sample of a MediaWiki page as generated by the Monobook skin, with most of the content stripped out to make it more legible. References to CSS files and to element classes and IDs are in bold.

The Monobook skin makes liberal use of HTML element IDs, which means that you can easily customize the display of just about every element on the page. The boxes that appear on the left side of the page (when using left-to-right languages) are called *portlets*, and the <div> element that contains them is in the portlets class. Look in the sample HTML and you will see that every list item inside the various portlets contains a unique ID.

Refer to this if you want to customize your site, so that you will know the names of the IDs and classes that you will need to create in your own CSS:

```html
<body class="mediawiki ns-0 ltr page-Main_Page">
<div id="globalWrapper">
  <div id="column-content">
    <div id="content">
      <a name="top" id="top"></a>
      <h1 class="firstHeading">Main Page</h1>

      <div id="bodyContent">
        <h3 id="siteSub">From ProfWikis - MySQL</h3>

        <div id="contentSub"></div>

        <div id="jump-to-nav">
          Jump to: <a href="#column-one">navigation</a>, <a
href="#searchInput">search</a>
        </div>

        <!-- Content goes here -->

        <div class="visualClear"></div>
      </div>
```

```
    </div>
</div>

<div id="column-one">
  <div id="p-cactions" class="portlet">
     <h5>Views</h5>

     <div class="pBody">
       <ul>
         <li id="ca-nstab-main" class="selected"><a
href="/wiki/index.php/Main_Page">Article</a></li>
         <li id="ca-talk" class="new"><a
href="/wiki/index.php?title=Talk:Main_Page&amp;action=edit">Discussion</a></li>
         <li id="ca-edit"><a
href="/wiki/index.php?title=Main_Page&amp;action=edit">Edit</a></li>
         <li id="ca-history"><a
href="/wiki/index.php?title=Main_Page&amp;action=history">History</a></li>
         <li id="ca-unprotect"><a
href="/wiki/index.php?title=Main_Page&amp;action=unprotect">unprotect</a></li>
         <li id="ca-delete"><a
href="/wiki/index.php?title=Main_Page&amp;action=delete">Delete</a></li>
         <li id="ca-move"><a
href="/wiki/index.php/Special:Movepage/Main_Page">Move</a></li>
         <li id="ca-watch"><a
href="/wiki/index.php?title=Main_Page&amp;action=watch">Watch</a></li>
       </ul>
     </div>
   </div>

   <div class="portlet" id="p-personal">
     <h5>Personal tools</h5>

     <div class="pBody">
       <ul>
         <li id="pt-userpage"><a
href="/wiki/index.php/User:WikiSysop" class="new">WikiSysop</a></li>
         <li id="pt-mytalk"><a
href="/wiki/index.php/User_talk:WikiSysop" class="new">My talk</a></li>
         <li id="pt-preferences"><a
href="/wiki/index.php/Special:Preferences">My preferences</a></li>
         <li id="pt-watchlist"><a
href="/wiki/index.php/Special:Watchlist">My watchlist</a></li>
         <li id="pt-mycontris"><a
href="/wiki/index.php/Special:Contributions/WikiSysop">
My contributions</a></li>
         <li id="pt-logout"><a
href="/wiki/index.php?title=Special:Userlogout&amp;returnto=Main_Page">
Log out</a></li>
       </ul>
     </div>
   </div>

   <div class="portlet" id="p-logo">
     <a style="background-image: url(/wiki/skins/common/images/wiki.png);"
```

```
href="/wiki/index.php/Main_Page" title="Main Page"></a>
    </div>

    <div class='portlet' id='p-navigation'>
      <h5>Navigation</h5>

    <div class='pBody'>
      <ul>
        <li id="n-mainpage"><a href="/wiki/index.php/Main_Page">
Main Page</a></li>
        <li id="n-portal"><a
href="/wiki/index.php/ProfWikis_-_MySQL:Community_Portal">
Community portal</a></li>
        <li id="n-currentevents"><a
href="/wiki/index.php/Current_events">Current events</a></li>
        <li id="n-recentchanges"><a
href="/wiki/index.php/Special:Recentchanges">Recent changes</a></li>
        <li id="n-randompage"><a
href="/wiki/index.php/Special:Random">Random page</a></li>
        <li id="n-help"><a
href="/wiki/index.php/Help:Contents">Help</a></li>
        <li id="n-sitesupport"><a
href="/wiki/index.php/ProfWikis_-_MySQL:Site_support">Donations</a></li>
      </ul>
    </div>
  </div>

  <div id="p-search" class="portlet">
    <h5><label for="searchInput">Search</label></h5>

    <div id="searchBody" class="pBody">
      <form action="/wiki/index.php/Special:Search" id="searchform"
name="searchform">
      <div>
       <input id="searchInput" name="search" type="text" accesskey="f" value="" />
<input type='submit' name="go" class="searchButton" id="searchGoButton"
value="Go" /> <input type='submit' name="fulltext" class="searchButton"
id="mw-searchButton" value="Search" />
      </div>
      </form>
    </div>
  </div>

  <div class="portlet" id="p-tb">
    <h5>Toolbox</h5>

    <div class="pBody">
      <ul>
        <li id="t-whatlinkshere"><a
href="/wiki/index.php/Special:Whatlinkshere/Main_Page">
What links here</a></li>
        <li id="t-recentchangeslinked"><a
href="/wiki/index.php/Special:Recentchangeslinked/Main_Page">
Related changes</a></li>
```

```
        <li id="t-upload"><a
href="/wiki/index.php/Special:Upload">Upload file</a></li>
        <li id="t-specialpages"><a
href="/wiki/index.php/Special:Specialpages">Special pages</a></li>
        <li id="t-print"><a
href="/wiki/index.php?title=Main_Page&amp;printable=yes">
Printable version</a></li>
        <li id="t-permalink"><a
href="/wiki/index.php?title=Main_Page&amp;oldid=150">Permanent link</a></li>
      </ul>
    </div>
  </div>
  </div><!-- end of the left (by default at least) column -->

  <div class="visualClear"></div>

  <div id="footer">
    <div id="f-poweredbyico">
      <a href="http://www.mediawiki.org/"><img src="/wiki/skins/common/
images/poweredby_mediawiki_88x31.png" alt="Powered by MediaWiki" /></a>
    </div>
    <div id="f-copyrightico"></div>
    <ul id="f-list">
      <li id="lastmod"></li>
      <li id="viewcount"></li>
      <li id="copyright"></li>
      <li id="privacy"></li>
      <li id="about"></li>
      <li id="disclaimer"></li>
    </ul>
  </div>
</div>
</body>
```

Creating a New Skin

You create a new skin by subclassing `SkinTemplate` and `QuickTemplate`, both of which are defined in `/includes/SkinTemplate.php`. The easiest way to create your new skin is to use an existing skin as the basis for your own. To create a new skin, follow these steps:

1. Copy the `/skins/monobook` directory to a new directory with a name based on your skin, such as `/skins/profwiki`. This directory contains `main.css`, plus a handful of graphics that are used in the skin.

2. Copy `/skins/Monobook.php` to `/skins/ProfWiki.php`.

3. Two classes are defined in `Monobook.php`. Change `class SkinMonoBook extends SkinTemplate` to `class SkinProfWiki extends SkinTemplate`. Then change `class MonoBookTemplate extends QuickTemplate` to `class ProfWikiTemplate extends QuickTemplate`.

4. The class now named `SkinProfWiki` contains the following three lines:

```
$this->skinname = 'monobook';
$this->stylename = 'monobook';
```

```
$this->template = 'MonoBookTemplate';
    These values should be changed to reflect the new skin name:
$this->skinname = 'profwiki';
$this->stylename = 'profwiki';
$this->template = 'ProfWikiTemplate';
```

5. Set `$wgDefaultSkin='profwiki'` in `LocalSettings.php`.

With these steps finished, the skin is ready to be customized.

Summary

In this chapter, you learned how magic words, templates, and skins provide advanced editing capability to users, and provide a means of standardizing the look and feel of your wiki. You learned how to use the most commonly used magic words, and how to create templates, as well as how to customize the skin currently used on your wiki. These customizations are just the start of what you can do with MediaWiki. In Chapter 9, you will learn how to install and use extensions and how to create your own magic words to extend the functionality of your wiki.

9

Extensions

By now, you are familiar with magic words and how to use them with wikitext. In this chapter, you will learn how to create your very own magic words and special pages. Of necessity, this means diving a little deeper into the inner workings of MediaWiki, and it requires familiarity with PHP. If you are completely unfamiliar with PHP and computer programming, you can find several good books that can help you.

> See especially *Beginning PHP, Apache, MySQL Web Development*, by Michael K. Glass et al. (Wrox, 2004).

Otherwise, read on and learn about MediaWiki's extension mechanism.

Extensions enable you to customize MediaWiki to your individual needs. The MediaWiki community has made a fairly large number of extensions available, which are a good starting place to learn how to write them. Extensions are surprisingly easy to write in MediaWiki. They are made possible by a rather large collection of *hooks* throughout the application that you can register callback functions with, which are then called at opportune times.

XML tag extensions and parser functions are callback functions that enable you to extend wikitext. There are a large number of other hooks, though, that give you the opportunity to modify MediaWiki behavior at all stages of the page delivery process.

In addition to learning how to use hooks in this chapter, you will also learn how to create your own special pages.

MediaWiki Hooks

A hook is an array of functions (if any functions have been registered) that are carried out every time a given section of code is executed. XML tag extensions and parser functions are two special cases of hooks that are used to extend wikitext. Many more, however, are available to you. The list of available hooks is long and growing, and not all of them are documented. You can find the latest documentation at www.mediawiki.org/wiki/Manual:MediaWiki_hooks. In addition, you can search for undocumented hooks by running the following scripts from the command line: maintenance/findhooks.php.

In order to understand how hooks work, and decide which hooks are good candidates to accomplish whatever it is you want to accomplish with your extension, it is necessary to have a basic understanding of the sequence of events that takes place when a page is requested in MediaWiki. The next section reviews that process in some detail, after which we will delve into the specifics of creating your own extensions. Examples are provided to get you started.

The Parsing Process

Every request begins with a call to index.php, the PHP script that serves as an entry point to the MediaWiki application. In most typical uses of PHP, PHP code is embedded into HTML pages. MediaWiki does things the other way around. The PHP files that comprise MediaWiki are all PHP code. If you are familiar with computer programming, but perhaps not familiar with PHP, you need to understand how code is executed in PHP because it will help you understand the following sections.

A PHP script executes either when it is requested by the HTTP server or when it is included in another PHP page. Whenever a PHP script is included in another script, the scope of the included script's execution is limited to the current insertion. The only exception to this is PHP scripts that define functions or classes. The code in a function isn't executed until the function is called by a statement in the script. Classes aren't executed, they are instantiated, so they must be instantiated in code.

Look at the first line of code in index.php, and you'll see the following line:

```
require_once( './includes/WebStart.php' );
```

require_once is one of the ways that PHP includes one PHP script in another script. The once refers to the fact that this script should only be included one time. The PHP parser will then avoid loading it again, even if it encounters the same line of code later in the script.

When a page is first requested, the WebStart.php script is executed, so in order to follow the logic of the application, you need to open WebStart.php and start at the top. It is this functionality that often makes PHP code so difficult to decipher — the code frequently jumps from page to page and it can be tedious to follow. Fortunately for us, the developers of MediaWiki have made it possible to extend and customize MediaWiki without needing to modify the base code. It is helpful, however, to understand the basic mechanics of how a request in MediaWiki is processed.

The WebStart.php script then makes some security checks and loads the Defines.php file, which initializes a list of constants used by the application, followed by the familiar LocalSettings.php (which in turn loads and thereby executes DefaultSettings.php). Finally, Setup.php is executed, which sets up a host of global variables and includes still more PHP scripts used by MediaWiki. Setup.php also instantiates some very important objects that you will need to know about when writing extensions: $wgUser, $wgOut, $wgParser, $wgTitle, and $wgArticle, which are discussed in more detail momentarily.

All of this happens when index.php includes WebStart.php at the very beginning of a page request. The next two lines of code in index.php are as follows:

```
require_once( "includes/Wiki.php" );
$mediaWiki = new MediaWiki();
```

The MediaWiki class is defined in `Wiki.php`, and a new `$mediaWiki` object is instantiated. The MediaWiki class is intended to be the base class for the MediaWiki application. It's *intended* because the developers are still migrating MediaWiki into a more object-oriented architecture. While good headway is being made, not all of the functionality is encapsulated in objects, and a lot of global variables and global functions are floating around. Nevertheless, the request is processed by the MediaWiki object. The following snippet of code from the `index.php` script shows the stages of the request cycle in MediaWiki. Additional comments in the code provide some explanation for each step:

```
# Generate a title object
$wgTitle = $mediaWiki->checkInitialQueries(
    $title,$action,$wgOut, $wgRequest, $wgContLang );

# Some debugging and error checking code has been deleted for clarity
# Set global variables in mediaWiki, based in some instances on values
# set in LocalSettings.php
$mediaWiki->setVal( 'Server', $wgServer );
$mediaWiki->setVal( 'DisableInternalSearch', $wgDisableInternalSearch );
$mediaWiki->setVal( 'action', $action );
$mediaWiki->setVal( 'SquidMaxage', $wgSquidMaxage );
$mediaWiki->setVal( 'EnableDublinCoreRdf', $wgEnableDublinCoreRdf );
$mediaWiki->setVal( 'EnableCreativeCommonsRdf', $wgEnableCreativeCommonsRdf );
$mediaWiki->setVal( 'CommandLineMode', $wgCommandLineMode );
$mediaWiki->setVal( 'UseExternalEditor', $wgUseExternalEditor );
$mediaWiki->setVal( 'DisabledActions', $wgDisabledActions );

# Initialize the Article object, which is responsible for building the page
# In the mediaWiki->initialize method, the article object is instantiated,
# and then mediaWiki->performAction is called, which will cause the appropriate
# page to be displayed, depending on the requested action.
$wgArticle = $mediaWiki->initialize ( $wgTitle, $wgOut, $wgUser, $wgRequest );

# The following methods perform some cleanup tasks, and are
# positioned here after the article has been created for performance
# reasons.
$mediaWiki->finalCleanup ( $wgDeferredUpdateList, $wgLoadBalancer, $wgOut );
    wfDebug("PROF: Do updates\n");
$mediaWiki->doUpdates( $wgPostCommitUpdateList );

$mediaWiki->restInPeace( $wgLoadBalancer );
```

That concludes the high-level overview of how a request is processed, but it leaves out a fair amount of detail. A lot is going on behind the scenes. Before a page is delivered, permissions need to be checked, wikitext needs to be converted into HTML, and the overall page needs to be displayed and configured appropriately for the user requesting the page. This brings us to the `$wgUser`, `$wgOut`, and `$wgParser` objects.

The user object represents the user making the request, whether it's an anonymous user or a sysop, and MediaWiki uses this object to determine whether the page can be delivered, and what options to display on the page according to the permissions granted to the user.

The `$wgOut` object is the output page, which results in the HTML that is sent back to the requesting browser. `$wgParser` is the parser object, responsible for parsing wikitext and turning it into HTML. The following sections walk through the parsing process. Mind you, this is not for your moral edification; there are very practical applications for this knowledge. When you are writing extensions for MediaWiki, such as XML-type wikitext extensions or parser functions, your code will be executed during the parsing process and you will need to be familiar with what happens.

Step 1: Start with Raw Wikitext

When a page is first requested, the page content, stored as wikitext, is retrieved and converted into HTML by the parser. This, of course, is a simplified view, ignoring things like caching, but that's basically what happens. The process of parsing the wikitext into HTML is handled by code in `includes/Parser.php`, which defines the `Parser`, `ParserOptions` and `ParserOutput` classes, all of which laboriously, with much Sturm und Drang and sound and fury, convert humble wikitext into magnificent HTML.

The parser doesn't just scan through the wikitext once and then spit out some HTML. That would be too easy. This parser isn't happy until it has chewed through the wikitext nine or ten times. Needless to say, the parser is not a model of efficiency and grace (which is why you learn all about caching in Chapter 11). In all fairness, it is a powerful parser that does a lot of cool tricks. The reason for so much of the code is partly because of the demands of parsing wikitext, but also because the developers have provided many hooks that enable others to extend MediaWiki so easily.

The simplest way to see what is happening is to follow wikitext through the process. The following wikitext is fresh from the database, waiting to be parsed:

```
==Sample Wikitext==

I want to use '''a few''' different wikitext features.

<nowiki>
===This won't be parsed===
</nowiki>

This links to the [[Main Page]] and this links to [[User:WikiSysop]].

<pre>
when does this return?
</pre>

===Sample tag hook===

<mytaghook arg1="Red" arg2="Blue">My content</mytaghook>

===Sample parser function===

{{example: Red | Blue}}
```

Step 2: Remove Text That Shouldn't Be Parsed

The first thing the parser does is strip out `<nowiki>`, `<pre>`, and `<gallery>` tags (and the content they contain) and replace them with a unique identifier (so they can be unstripped later). `<nowiki>` and `<pre>` are stripped out because, by definition, they aren't parsed. The reason why `<gallery>` is stripped out has to do with a bug in the parser, so it is handled separately. Most important, XML tag extensions are stripped out as well, which keeps them from being parsed as raw wikitext, which takes place in the step that follows this one.

The following code contains comments to make the code easier to read, but they are not produced during the conversion process. You can see the unique tokens that now reside in the place where the `<nowiki>` and `<pre>` tags once resided, as well as our customized XML extension `<mytaghook arg1="Red" arg2="Blue" >My content</mytaghook>`:

```
==Sample Wikitext==

I want to use '''a few''' different wikitext features.

 <!-- Former "nowiki" tag -->
 UNIQ767b803742958244-nowiki-00000001-QINU

This links to the [[Main Page]] and this links to [[User:WikiSysop]].

 <!-- Former "pre" tag -->
 UNIQ767b803742958244-pre-00000002-QINU

===Sample tag hook===

 <!-- Former "mytaghook" tag -->
 UNIQ767b803742958244-mytaghook-00000003-QINU

===Sample parser function===

{{example: Red | Blue}}
```

Step 3: Generate Some (But Not All) of the Wikitext

The next step occurs when the `$wgParser->internalParse()` method is called. It does two things. First, it converts some of the wikitext, such as headings and inline styles, to HTML, and adds the edit links where appropriate. It also strips out all the wikilinks and replaces them with tokens that identify them so that they, too, can be reinserted at a later time, using a format like the following:

```
<!--LINK 0-->
```

Now the example parser function has been executed and its output inserted into the text:

```
<p><a name="Sample_Wikitext" id="Sample_Wikitext"></a></p>

<h2><span class="editsection">[<a
    href="/mysql/index.php?title=MediaWiki_Extensions&amp;action=edit&amp;section=1"
    title="Edit section: Sample Wikitext">edit</a>]</span> <span
    class="mw-headline">Sample Wikitext</span></h2>

<p>I want to use <b>a few</b> different wikitext features.
    UNIQ767b803742958244-nowiki-00000001-QINU This links to the <!--LINK 0-->
    and this links to <!--LINK 1-->. UNIQ767b803742958244-pre-00000002-QINU <a
    name="Sample_tag_hook" id="Sample_tag_hook"></a></p>

<h3><span class="editsection">[<a
    href="/mysql/index.php?title=MediaWiki_Extensions&amp;action=edit&amp;section=2"
    title="Edit section: Sample tag hook">edit</a>]</span> <span
```

```
    class="mw-headline">Sample tag hook</span></h3>

<p>UNIQ767b803742958244-mytaghook-00000003-QINU <a
    name="Sample_parser_function" id="Sample_parser_function"></a></p>

<h3><span class="editsection">[<a
    href="/mysql/index.php?title=MediaWiki_Extensions&amp;action=edit&amp;section=3"
    title="Edit section: Sample parser function">edit</a>]</span> <span
    class="mw-headline">Sample parser function</span></h3>

<!-- Parser functions are executed -->
<p>Function: example<br>
param1 value is: Red<br>
param2 value is: Blue<br>
<a href="http://127.0.0.1//mysql/index.php?title=MediaWiki_Extensions&amp;
    action=edit" class="external free" title="http://127.0.0.1//mysql/index.php?
    title=MediaWiki_Extensions&amp;action=edit" rel="nofollow">http://127.0.0.1//
    mysql/index.php?title=MediaWiki_Extensions&amp;action=edit</a></p>
```

Step 4: Unstrip Everything That You Stripped (Except <nowiki> Text)

In this step, all the things you stripped in Step 2 should be reinserted into the wikitext, except for the content nested in <nowiki> tags and content for links:

```
<p><a name="Sample_Wikitext" id="Sample_Wikitext"></a></p>

<h2><span class="editsection">[<a
    href="/mysql/index.php?title=MediaWiki_Extensions&amp;action=edit&amp;section=1"
    title="Edit section: Sample Wikitext">edit</a>]</span> <span
    class="mw-headline">Sample Wikitext</span></h2>

<p>I want to use <b>a few</b> different wikitext features.
    UNIQ767b803742958244-nowiki-00000001-QINU This links to the <!--LINK 0-->
    and this links to <!--LINK 1-->.</p>

<!-- "pre" text returned -->
<pre>
when does this return?
</pre>

<p><a name="Sample_tag_hook" id="Sample_tag_hook"></a></p>

<h3><span class="editsection">[<a
    href="/mysql/index.php?title=MediaWiki_Extensions&amp;action=edit&amp;section=2"
    title="Edit section: Sample tag hook">edit</a>]</span> <span
    class="mw-headline">Sample tag hook</span></h3>

<!-- "mytaghook" results are inserted into the text -->
<p>Input: My content<br>
Arg1 value is: Red<br>
Arg2 value is: Blue<br>
<a name="Sample_parser_function" id="Sample_parser_function"></a></p>
```

```
<h3><span class="editsection">[<a
    href="/mysql/index.php?title=MediaWiki_Extensions&amp;action=edit&amp;section=3"
    title="Edit section: Sample parser function">edit</a>]</span> <span
    class="mw-headline">Sample parser function</span></h3>

<p>Function: example<br>
param1 value is: Red<br>
param2 value is: Blue<br>
<a href="http://127.0.0.1//mysql/index.php?title=MediaWiki_Extensions&amp;
    action=edit" class="external free" title="http://127.0.0.1//mysql/index.php?
    title=MediaWiki_Extensions&amp;action=edit" rel="nofollow">http://127.0.0.1//
    mysql/index.php?title=MediaWiki_Extensions&amp;action=edit</a></p>
```

Step 5: Fix Common Errors

Nothing changes in our sample wikitext because I didn't make any of the errors that are routinely fixed. Basically, the code looks for some common mistakes that are made when people type wikitext and tries to fix them before proceeding.

Step 6: Generate Block-level HTML

Next, the block-level HTML that didn't get produced in Step 3 is now generated. In most cases, the block-level elements are already in place, but in places where <nowiki> text has been temporarily removed, the HTML needs to be fixed. Here is the original paragraph before the block-level HTML is generated:

```
<p>I want to use <b>a few</b> different wikitext features.
    UNIQ767b803742958244-nowiki-00000001-QINU This links to the <!--LINK 0-->
    and this links to <!--LINK 1-->.</p>
```

The following output shows the same paragraph after the block-level HTML is generated. You will notice that <p> tags have been added around the placeholder for <wikitext> and what was one paragraph before is now three:

```
<p>I want to use <b>a few</b> different wikitext features.</p>

<p>UNIQ767b803742958244-nowiki-00000001-QINU</p>

<p>This links to the <!--LINK 0--> and this links to <!--LINK 1-->.</p>
```

Step 7: Put Links Back in

Finally, the wikilinks are put back into the page. The following code snippet shows the links before they are returned:

```
<p>This links to the <!--LINK 0--> and this links to <!--LINK 1-->.</p>
```

This code shows the content with the links back in the page:

```
<p>This links to the <a href="/mysql/index.php/Main_Page"
    title="Main Page"> Main Page</a> and this links to <a
    href="/mysql/index.php?title=User:WikiSysop&amp;action=edit" class="new"
    title="User:WikiSysop">User:WikiSysop</a>.</p>
```

Step 8: Do Something Obscure with Chinese Text

This step translates from one form of Chinese text to another. Needless to say, nothing happens to our example wikitext because it's not in Chinese.

Step 9: Unstrip <nowiki> Elements

The <nowiki> tags have not been forgotten. They are now added back into the text, which means that we're done converting wikitext.

The original <nowiki> tag looked like this:

```
I want to use '''a few''' different wikitext features.

<nowiki>
===This won't be parsed===
</nowiki>

This links to the [[Main Page]] and this links to [[User:WikiSysop]].
```

Then, the tag was stripped and replaced with a placeholder:

```
<p>I want to use <b>a few</b> different wikitext features.</p>

<p>UNIQ767b803742958244-nowiki-00000001-QINU</p>

<p>This links to the <a href="/mysql/index.php/Main_Page"
    title="Main Page"> Main Page</a> and this links to <a
    href="/mysql/index.php?title=User:WikiSysop&amp;action=edit" class="new"
    title="User:WikiSysop">User:WikiSysop</a>.</p>
```

Finally, the raw content nested by the <nowiki> tag is returned, wrapped in <p> tags:

```
<p>I want to use <b>a few</b> different wikitext features.</p>

<p>===This won't be parsed===</p>

<p>This links to the <a href="/mysql/index.php/Main_Page"
    title="Main Page"> Main Page</a> and this links to <a
    href="/mysql/index.php?title=User:WikiSysop&amp;action=edit" class="new"
    title="User:WikiSysop">User:WikiSysop</a>.</p>
```

Step 10: Tidy Up the HTML

That leaves one last step, which is to tidy up the HTML with Tidy, if you have opted for that configuration in LocalSettings.php. In this case, there wasn't much to tidy up, so the content remains the same.

XML Tag Extensions

XML wikitext extensions take the form of XML tags that can optionally include attributes. The previous examples used to illustrate the stages of the parsing process included an XML extension function called `mytaghook`. In this section, you will learn how to create that extension, so that the user can enter the following XML:

```
<mytaghook arg1="Red" arg2="Blue">My content</mytaghook>
```

The output of the preceding XML will be as follows:

```
<p>Input: My content<br>
Arg1 value is: Red<br>
Arg2 value is: Blue<br></p>
```

Creating an XML tag extension is a three-part process:

1. The first step is to create a `MyTagHook.php` file in the `extensions` directory.

2. Define two functions in the `MyTagHook.php` file: `wfMyTagHook_Setup` and `wfMyTagHook_Render`.

3. Insert the following at the end of `LocalSettings.php`: `include ("extensions/MyTagHook.php");`

The Setup Function

Two functions need to be written. The first function will be used to register the second function with the parser. In the following example, I have created a function `wfMyTagHook_Setup` that is added to the `$wgExtensionFunctions` array. All functions appended in this way will be executed when the parser is instantiated, in order to register the callback function to be used by the parser, which is called `wfMyTagHook_Render`:

```
$wgExtensionFunctions[] = "wfMyTagHook_Setup";


# This function is called in Setup.php and it registers the name of the
# tag with the parser, as well as the callback function that renders the
# actual HTML output.
function wfMyTagHook_Setup() {
    global $wgParser;
    # If this were a parser function instead of an extension tag,
    # the $wgParser->setFunctionHook method would be called.
    # The renderMyTagHook function will be called in Parser->strip.
    $wgParser->setHook( "mytaghook", "wfMyTagHook_Render" );
}
```

The Render Function

In this example, the `wfMyTagHook_Render` function does not do anything particularly useful. It just returns information about the arguments that were passed to the function. The function receives three arguments:

❑   `$input`: a string representing the text between the opening and closing XML tags

❑   `$argv`: an associative array containing any attributes used in the XML tag

❑   `&$parser`: a reference to the parser object

```
function wfMyTagHook_Render( $input, $argv, &$parser ) {
   # This keeps the parser from caching output, which is especially
# useful when debugging.
$parser->disableCache();

   # This tag extension simply returns information about the request,
 # such as the value for $input, and the arguments.
 # The $output variable is a string, not on OutputPage object.
   $output = "Input: " . $input . "<br/>";
$output .="Arg1 value is: " .$argv["arg1"] . "<br/>";
$output .="Arg2 value is: " .$argv["arg2"] . "<br/>";
```

The Complete Extension

The complete extension script follows. In addition to the functions already discussed, some additional code has been added that keeps the code from being run outside of MediaWiki, and that generates credits for the author of the extension, which is displayed on the special page Special:Version:

```
<?php
# This is an example extension to wikitext, that adds additional
# XML tags to MediaWiki to be parsed as wikitext. The tags are
# structured like normal XML elements, such as:
#    <example arg1="some value">My input text/example>
# The function registered by this extension gets passed to the text between the
# tags as $input as well as an arbitrary number of arguments passed
# in the $argv array. These tag extensions are expected to return HTML.
# If wikitext is returned instead, it will not be parsed.
# To activate the extension, include it from your LocalSettings.php
# with: include("extensions/MyTagHook.php");

# This code keeps this PHP file from being run on the commandline;
# It can only be called from within MediaWiki.
if(! defined( 'MEDIAWIKI' ) ) {
   echo( "This is an extension to the MediaWiki package and cannot be run
   standalone.\n" );
   die( -1 );
} else {

# Give yourself credit. This will appear in the Special:Version page.
$wgExtensionCredits['parser'][] = array(
       'name' => 'My Tag Hook',
       'author' =>'Mark Choate',
       'url' => 'http://choate.info/',
       'description' => 'A simple example.'
       );
}


# Register the extension function. During the setup phase in Setup.php,
# all the extensions that have been registered (or appended) to the
   $wgExtensionFunctions
# array are executed. This is not the function that
   generates the content, but it is the
```

```
# function that registers the extension with the parser.
$wgExtensionFunctions[] = "wfMyTagHook_Setup";


# This function is called in Setup.php and it registers the name of the
# tag with the parser, as well as the callback function that renders the
# actual HTML output.
function wfMyTagHook_Setup() {
    global $wgParser;
    # If this were a parser function instead of an extension tag,
 # the $wgParser->setFunctionHook method would be called.
 # The renderMyTagHook function will be called in Parser->strip.
    $wgParser->setHook( "mytaghook", "wfMyTagHook_Render" );
}

# This is the callback function for converting the input text to HTML output.
# $input is the text that is nested in the XML tag. For example,
# in <example>My Text</example>, the value held in the $input variable
# will be "My Text". $argv is an array that contains the values of
# the XML element's attributes, such as <example arg1="Some data" arg2="More data">.
function wfMyTagHook_Render( $input, $argv, &$parser ) {
    # This keeps the parser from caching output, which is especially
 # useful when debugging.
$parser->disableCache();

    # This tag extension simply returns information about the request,
    # such as the value for $input, and the arguments.
    # The $output variable is a string, not on OutputPage object.
    $output = "Input: " . $input . "<br/>";
    $output .="Arg1 value is: " .$argv["arg1"] . "<br/>";
    $output .="Arg2 value is: " .$argv["arg2"] . "<br/>";

    return $output;
}
?>
```

The extension should then be included in the LocalSettings.php file, so that MediaWiki is aware of it:

```
include("extensions/MyTagHook.php");
```

The renderTagHook function is called Step 2 of the parsing process, in the strip function. The results of the function are not inserted into the original text, however, until Step 4, skipping Step 3, where the main wikitext is converted into HTML. As a consequence, XML tag extensions skip the conversion process, so that any wikitext returned by the function will not be converted into HTML.

Following is the source tag:

```
<mytaghook arg1="Red" arg2="Blue">My content</mytaghook>
```

Here are the tag results:

```
<!-- "mytaghook" results are inserted into the text -->
<p>Input: My content<br>
```

```
Arg1 value is: Red<br>
Arg2 value is: Blue<br></p>
```

Parser Functions

The first parser function demonstrated is called (imaginatively) Example, and it can be referenced in wikitext in the following way:

```
{{example: Red | Blue}}
```

This parser function will generate the following HTML:

```
<p>Function: example<br>
param1 value is: Red<br>
param2 value is: Blue<br>
</p>
```

Parser functions are very similar to XML tag extensions, with the primary difference being that you have to register the function as a magic word. The steps to creating a function are as follows:

1. Create an ExampleParserFunction.php file in the extensions directory.

2. Define three functions in the ExampleParserFunction.php file: wfExampleParserFunction_Setup, wfExampleParserFunction_Render, and wfExampleParserFunction_Magic.

3. Insert the following at the end of LocalSettings.php: include ("extensions/ExampleParserFunction.php");

Unlike XML tag extensions, parser functions are processed earlier enough that their output can be wikitext, which is converted to HTML. The parser functions are called in Step 3, during the process in which wikitext is converted to HTML.

This example makes use of magic words. In this case, the magic words provide localization for the name of the parser function itself; you have to register a magic word for the parser function to work. In this example, only one word is mapped to the key, but it is followed by an example with far more extensive customization.

The Setup Function

The setup function is very similar to the XML tag extension setup function, except that it registers the parser function using the $wgParser->setFunctionHook function, rather than $wgParser->setHook:

```php
<?php

# Define a setup function
$wgExtensionFunctions[] = 'wfExampleParserFunction_Setup';
```

```
function wfExampleParserFunction_Setup() {
        global $wgParser;

        # Set a function hook associating the "example" magic word with our function
        # Setting the third argument to "1" will enable you to create parser functions
        # that do not need to be preceeded with a "#" character. The primary benefit of
        # using "#" is that it avoids namespace collisions and other confusion.
        $wgParser->setFunctionHook( 'example', 'wfExampleParserFunction_Render', 1);
}
```

The Render Function

The `render` function generates the output based on the values passed in the parameters:

```
function wfExampleParserFunction_Render( &$parser, $param1
    = 'default1', $param2 = 'default2' ) {
        # The parser function itself
        # The input parameters are wikitext with templates expanded
        # The output should be wikitext too.

        $output = "Function: example<br/>";
        $output .="param1 value is: " . $param1 . "<br/>";
        $output .="param2 value is: " . $param2 . "<br/>";

        return $output;
}

?>
```

The Magic Function

The magic function is used to add new messages to the `MessageCache`. In this example, not much happens, but later you will see a more detailed explanation of what is happening here, in the section "Parser Functions with Messages."

```
# Add a hook to initialise the magic word
$wgHooks['LanguageGetMagic'][]        = 'wfExampleParserFunction_Magic';

function wfExampleParserFunction_Magic( &$magicWords, $langCode ) {
        # Parser functions are "magic words", which means that you can configure or
        # localize the word used to refer to the function.
        # All remaining elements are synonyms for our parser function.
        # This is a simple case, and uses the same word regardless of language.
        # The "0" value in the first element of the array signifies that this word
        # is not case sensitive.
        # This function is called by the LanguageGetMagic hook.
        $magicWords['example'] = array( 0, 'example' );

        # Return true so that the other functions will be loaded.
        return true;
}
```

The Complete Extension

Altogether, the different elements combine to create the complete extension:

```php
<?php

# Define a setup function
$wgExtensionFunctions[] = 'wfExampleParserFunction_Setup';

# Add a hook to initialise the magic word
$wgHooks['LanguageGetMagic'][]        = 'wfExampleParserFunction_Magic';

function wfExampleParserFunction_Setup() {
        global $wgParser;

        # Set a function hook associating the "example" magic word with our function
        # Setting the third argument to "1" will enable you to create parser functions
        # that do not need to be preceeded with a "#" character. The primary benefit of
        # using "#" is that it avoids namespace collisions and other confusion.
        $wgParser->setFunctionHook( 'example', 'wfExampleParserFunction_Render', 1 );
}

function wfExampleParserFunction_Magic( &$magicWords, $langCode ) {
        # Parser functions are "magic words", which means that you can configure or
        # localize the word used to refer to the function.
        # All remaining elements are synonyms for our parser function.
        # This is a simple case, and uses the same word regardless of language.
        # The "0" value in the first element of the array signifies that this word
        # is not case sensitive.
        # This function is called by the LanguageGetMagic hook.
        $magicWords['example'] = array( 0, 'example' );

        # Return true so that the other functions will be loaded.
        return true;
}

function wfExampleParserFunction_Render( &$parser, $param1
  = 'default1', $param2 = 'default2' ) {
        # The parser function itself
        # The input parameters are wikitext with templates expanded
        # The output should be wikitext too.

        # Global variables must be declared locally in order to be accessed.
        global $wgServer;

        $output = "Function: example<br/>";
        $output .="param1 value is: " . $param1 . "<br/>";
        $output .="param2 value is: " . $param2 . "<br/>";

        return $output;
}
?>
```

Default Values

Parser functions also support default values, and this function was declared with default values set for both param1 and param2:

```
function wfExampleParserFunction_Render( &$parser, $param1
    = 'default1', $param2 = 'default2' )
```

This means that you can also call the function with only one parameter, as in the following:

```
{{example: Red}}
```

The result of this function would be as follows:

```
<p>Function: example<br>
param1 value is: Red<br>
param2 value is: default2<br>
</p>
```

Return Values

Parser functions can return a string with the resulting text, or an array of values. The first element of the array is the resulting text, and the rest are flags, which can be set to true or false.

The return values include the following:

- ❏ found: Stop processing the template.
- ❏ nowiki: Do not process the wikitext.
- ❏ noparse: Do not remove unsafe HTML tags.
- ❏ noargs: If this is used in a template, do not replace the triple-brace arguments ({{{) in the return value.
- ❏ isHTML: The text is HTML and should not be parsed as wikitext.

Using Global Objects

Several global objects can be accessed when writing parser functions. The following function is a rewritten version of the earlier function, this time making use of global objects. This function gets a reference to the Title object from the parser and uses it to construct a URL to itself:

```
function wfExampleParserFunction_Render( &$parser, $param1 =
    'default1', $param2 = 'default2' ) {

  # Global variables must be declared locally in order to be accessed.
        global $wgServer;

        # You can access global variables through the parser object:
        $title = $parser->getTitle();
```

```
                   $output = $wgServer ."/" . $title->getEditURL();


                   return $output;
     }
```

The output of this page is as follows:

```
<p><a
    href="http://127.0.0.1//mysql/index.php?title=MediaWiki_
    Extensions&amp;action=edit" class="external free"
    title="http://127.0.0.1//mysql/index.php?title=MediaWiki_
    Extensions&amp;action=edit"
    rel="nofollow">http://127.0.0.1//mysql/index.php?title=MediaWiki_
    Extensions&amp;action=edit</a> Function:
    example</p>
```

Parser Functions with Messages

The following example illustrates a more complete use of the MessageCache object to translate terms for the parser function. This example uses a real MediaWiki extension as the starting point, but it has been simplified to make it easy to follow the logic of the code. The original extension is called ParserFunctions (as opposed to the built-in parser functions reviewed in the previous chapter), and is very popular. It was written by Tim Starling, and can be found at http://meta.wikimedia.org/wiki/ParserFunctions.

This simplified version is called ParserFunctionsLite, and in order to implement it, you need to do the following:

1.   Create a ParserFunctionsLite.php file in the extensions/ParserFunctionsLite directory, which you will have to create, as well as a ParserFunctionsLite.i18n.php file.

2.   Define the ParserFunctionsLite class.

3.   Define two functions in the ParserFunctionsLite.php file: wfParserFunctionsLite_Setup and wfParserFunctionsLite_Magic.

4.   Insert the following at the end of LocalSettings.php: include("extensions/ParserFunctionsLite/ParserFunctionsLite.php");

The Extension Object

In this example, a class is defined instead of a function. The class has two member functions that will be registered as callback functions for two different parser functions: ifhook and ifeq:

```
# In this example, a class is used rather than simply a function.
class ExtParserFunctionsLite {


  function clearState() {
        return true;
  }
```

```
function ifHook( &$parser, $test = ", $then = ", $else = " ) {
        if ( $test !== " ) {
                return $then;
        } else {
                return $else;
        }
}

function ifeq( &$parser, $left = ", $right = ", $then = ", $else = " ) {
        if ( $left == $right ) {
                return $then;
        } else {
                return $else;
        }
    }
}
```

The Setup Function

Because this extension is based on a class, the setup function takes a slightly different structure than the previous example. Before setting the hooks, the ExtParserFunctionsLite class needs to be instantiated. Then, when the setFunctionHook method is called, a reference to the object, and the function, is passed:

```
$wgExtensionFunctions[] = 'wfParserFunctionsLite_Setup';

function wfParserFunctionsLite_Setup() {
  global $wgParser, $wgMessageCache, $wgExtParserFunctionsLite,
    $wgMessageCache, $wgHooks;

  # Instantiate the object
$wgExtParserFunctionsLite = new ExtParserFunctionsLite;

# Since a class is being used, the function to call needs to be passed to
# the setFunctionHook method uding the setup phase.
$wgParser->setFunctionHook( 'if', array( &$wgExtParserFunctionsLite, 'ifHook' ) );
$wgParser->setFunctionHook( 'ifeq', array( &$wgExtParserFunctionsLite, 'ifeq' ) );
$wgHooks['ParserClearState'][] = array( &$wgExtParserFunctionsLite, 'clearState' );
}
```

The Magic Function

In the previous example, the magic function didn't have messages in different languages, so the function call was simple. In this example, translations are available, so the magic function includes the ParserFunctionsLite.i18n.php file, which includes the translations, and then loops through the array of translations looking for the ones that are intended for the current language, as referenced in $langCode:

```
$wgHooks['LanguageGetMagic'][]        = 'wfParserFunctionsLite_Magic';

function wfParserFunctionsLite_Magic( &$magicWords, $langCode ) {
  require_once( dirname( __FILE__ ) . '/ParserFunctionsLite.i18n.php' );
```

```
foreach( efParserFunctionsLite_Words( $langCode ) as $word => $trans )
  $magicWords[$word] = $trans;
return true;
}
```

ParserFunctionsLite.i18.php

The translations are defined as follows:

```php
<?php

/**
 * Get translated magic words, if available
 *
 * @param string $lang Language code
 * @return array
 */
function efParserFunctionsLite_Words( $lang ) {
$words = array();

/**
 * English
 */
$words['en'] = array(

        'if'            => array( 0, 'if' ),
        'ifeq'          => array( 0, 'ifeq' ),
);

/**
 * Farsi-Persian
 */
$words['fa'] = array(
        'if'            => array( 0, 'اگر',              'if' ),
        'ifeq'          => array( 0, 'اگرمساوی',                  'ifeq' ),
);

/**
 * Hebrew
 */
$words['he'] = array(
        'if'            => array( 0, 'יאות',         'if' ),
        'ifeq'          => array( 0, 'הווש',         'ifeq' ),
);

/**
 * Indonesian
 */
$words['id'] = array(
        'if'            => array( 0, 'jika',         'if' ),
        'ifeq'          => array( 0, 'jikasama',     'ifeq' ),
);

# English is used as a fallback, and the English synonyms are
# used if a translation has not been provided for a given word
```

```
return ( $lang == 'en' || !isset( $words[$lang] ) )
        ? $words['en']
        : array_merge( $words['en'], $words[$lang] );
}
```

Messages

The translation process requires some explanation. System messages are strings that are localized for the language that is set as the default language of the site, or the selected language of the user. There is a global object, $wgMessageCache, that contains all the messages available for the current language. It is an instance of the MessageCache class, and when it is instantiated it loads the messages that are defined in the message files in the /languages/messages/ directory. The messages themselves are loaded into an associative array called $magicWords, which maps string keys to their translated value.

MediaWiki provides developers with a way to add messages to the $wgMessageCache object without having to modify the underlying message files, and this is what is happening in the previous function.

In this example, the words that are added to the $wgMessageCache object depend upon the value passed in $langCode. The ParserFunctionsLite.php file contains messages in four languages: English, Farsi-Persian, Hebrew, and Indonesian. If the current language is English, then the messages for English are added to the $magicWords array. Otherwise, if it is Farsi-Persian, then the Farsi-Persian words are added, and so on. If no word is defined, or if the language is not defined, then the default fallback is English.

The $magicWords Array

Once the words are in the array, they are accessed by referencing the key. The most common way to retrieve a value is with the wfMsg global function:

```
function wfMsg( $key )
```

To use this method, you pass it the string key for the message, which is usually a lowercase version of the English translation. To illustrate, suppose the following magic word has been added to the $magicWords array:

```
$magicWords['example'] = array( 0, 'example' );
```

In this case, the key is 'example', and it is associated with the array(0, 'example'). The first digit indicates whether the word is case sensitive or not (in this case, it isn't), and the next element in the array is the translated word. In this example, the translated word is "example" too. This means that calling the function wfMsg('example') will return the string 'example'. Even though with English words it seems redundant to jump through this hoop, it is important conceptually to remember that you are getting a translation of the word associated with the key.

The Complete Extension

The complete extension is as follows:

```
<?php

if ( !defined( 'MEDIAWIKI' ) ) {
  die( 'This file is a MediaWiki extension, it is not a valid entry point' );
}
```

```
$wgExtensionFunctions[] = 'wfParserFunctionsLite_Setup';

$wgExtensionCredits['parserhook'][] = array(
 'name' => 'ParserFunctionsLite',
 'url' => 'Original code http://meta.wikimedia.org/wiki/ParserFunctions',
 'author' => 'Based on ParserFunctions.php by Tim Starling',
 'description' => 'A scaled down version of ParserFunctions.php',
);

$wgHooks['LanguageGetMagic'][]        = 'wfParserFunctionsLite_Magic';

class ExtParserFunctions {
 var $mExprParser;
 var $mTimeCache = array();
 var $mTimeChars = 0;
 var $mMaxTimeChars = 6000; # ~10 seconds

 function clearState() {
        $this->mTimeChars = 0;
        return true;
 }


 function ifHook( &$parser, $test = ", $then = ", $else = " ) {
        if ( $test !== " ) {
                return $then;
        } else {
                return $else;
        }
 }

 function ifeq( &$parser, $left = ", $right = ", $then = ", $else = " ) {
        if ( $left == $right ) {
                return $then;
        } else {
                return $else;
        }
 }
}

function wfParserFunctions_Setup() {
 global $wgParser, $wgMessageCache, $wgExtParserFunctions,
 $wgMessageCache, $wgHooks;

 $wgExtParserFunctionsLite = new ExtParserFunctionsLite;

 $wgParser->setFunctionHook( 'if', array( &$wgExtParserFunctionsLite, 'ifHook' ) );
 $wgParser->setFunctionHook( 'ifeq', array( &$wgExtParserFunctionsLite, 'ifeq' ) );
 $wgHooks['ParserClearState'][] = array( &$wgExtParserFunctionsLite, 'clearState' );
}

function wfParserFunctionsLite_Magic( &$magicWords, $langCode ) {
 require_once( dirname( __FILE__ ) . '/ParserFunctionsLite.i18n.php' );
```

```
    foreach( efParserFunctionsWords( $langCode ) as $word => $trans )
        $magicWords[$word] = $trans;
return true;
}
```

Hook Extensions

All of the previous examples showed you how to use hooks to add functionality to wikitext, but that is not the only use of hooks when writing extensions. You can also use hooks to customize the user interface, change the way the site functions, and even write your own actions. There are too many possible hooks to demonstrate all of them, but this section shows you how to use two different hooks in order to give you an idea of all that you can do.

As with all the other extensions, you need to create a file in the extensions directory and define your functions there. In addition, you need to include a reference to the file in LocalSettings.php.

ParserBeforeStrip Hook

The ParserBeforeStrip hook is called by the parser object right before the first step of the parsing process that strips out <nowiki> tags, and so on. In other words, this function is called when the raw wikitext is available and has not been modified at all by the parsing process. The ParserBeforeStrip hook sends a reference to the parser object, the raw wiki text, and the strip_state object. Unlike the other examples, which are only executed when a page author includes the XML tag or parser function in their page, this function executes anytime wikitext is parsed (which includes parts of a page other than just the article content).

Setting up a simple hook like this is simpler than parser functions and XML tag extensions. All you need to do is define the function and then register it with the hook itself. The following hook will serve as a filter that replaces the abbreviations *afaik, btw,* and *imho* with the phrases they represent, regardless of whether the user wants it changed or not. The function does a simple string replace with the PHP function str_replace:

```
$wgHooks['ParserBeforeStrip'][] = 'myfilter' ;

function myfilter ( &$parser, &$text, &$strip_state ) {
# This hook performs a simple text replacement before any of
# the raw wikitext is parsed.
$from = array("afaik", "btw", "imho");
$to   = array("As far as I know", "By the way", "In my humble opinion");
$text = str_replace($from, $to, $text);
}
?>
```

With this hook installed, the text "afaik, everyone liked the movie. I thought it stunk, imho" is translated into "As far as I know, everyone liked the movie. I thought it stunk, In my humble opinion."

EditPage::showEditForm:initial Hook

This hook is a little more complete than the previous hook. It enables you to add additional content to the edit page when a user is editing a document. The hook passes a reference to the EditPage object, which has defined five variables for the express purpose of enabling developers to leverage this hook.

You will find a reference to them in the `EditPage.php` file:

```
# Placeholders for text injection by hooks (must be HTML)
# extensions should take care to _append_ to the present value
public $editFormPageTop; // Before even the preview
public $editFormTextTop;
public $editFormTextAfterWarn;
public $editFormTextAfterTools;
public $editFormTextBottom;
```

The hook simply takes a reference to the `form` object and uses that to assign values to the object's member variables:

```php
<?php
$wgHooks['EditPage::showEditForm:initial'][] = 'myformhook' ;

function myformhook( &$form ) {
        # EditForm.php specifies the following variables for use
        # in hooks such as this one.
        $form->editFormPageTop = "<h2>Form Page Top</h2>";
        $form->editFormTextTop ="<h3>Form Text Top</h3>";
        $form->editFormTextAfterWarn = "<h4>Form After Warn</h4>";
        $form->editFormTextAfterTools = "<h5>Form After Tools</h5>";
        $form->editFormTextBottom = "<h5>Form Text Bottom</h5>";
}
```

With this hook in place, you can edit any page and the new text will be presented on that page, as shown in Figure 9-1.

Figure 9-1: Text inserted into the edit page by myformhook

Special Pages

Special pages are dynamic pages, and as such are different animals than XML tag extensions or parser functions. They share a lot in common, however, and the steps required to create a special page will be familiar to those of you who are already familiar with parser functions and tag extensions.

While not strictly necessary, MediaWiki encourages the convention of using three distinct PHP files for the development of a special page. In this case, the files are as follows:

❑ `SpecialPageExample.php`: The functions that register the special page

❑ `SpecialPageExample_body.php`: The `SpecialPage` subclass is defined here, and the execute method is over-ridden.

❑ `SpecialPageExample.i18n.php`: The localization for the message cache

Because special pages are dynamic pages, their content is often (but not necessarily) the output of a query against the database. The following example shows a special page that displays information about how many times it has been displayed.

SpecialPageExample.php

This file sets up the special page, but the process is quite a bit different from what takes place in other extensions. There is a global variable, `$wgAutoLoadClasses`, that contains references to PHP files whose contents should be loaded into memory when a request is received. This file adds the `SpecialPageExample` class to the list of classes that should be autoloaded. It also adds a reference to this page to the `$wgSpecialPages` global variable, so that the special page will be listed with the others:

```php
<?php
# Not a valid entry point, skip unless MEDIAWIKI is defined
if (!defined('MEDIAWIKI')) {
        echo <<<EOT
To install my extension, put the following line in LocalSettings.php:
require_once( "$IP/extensions/SpecialPageExample/SpecialPageExample.php" );
EOT;
        exit( 1 );
}

$wgAutoloadClasses['SpecialPageExample'] =
    dirname(__FILE__) . '/SpecialPageExample_body.php';
$wgSpecialPages['SpecialPageExample'] = 'SpecialPageExample';
$wgHooks['LoadAllMessages'][] = 'SpecialPageExample::loadMessages';

?>
```

SpecialPageExample_body.php

The `SpecialPage` class is a subclass in this file, and the execute method is overridden. This is where the content for the special page is generated. Because special pages are dynamic pages, one common use for them is to publish updated information directly from a database. The following example does just that, making a database call to the `site_stats` table in order to find out how many times this page has been accessed (I suppose it is a somewhat narcissistic special page, as its only reason for being is to report on itself):

```php
<?php
class SpecialPageExample extends SpecialPage
{
        function SpecialPageExample() {
                SpecialPage::SpecialPage("SpecialPageExample");
                self::loadMessages();
}

        function execute( $par ) {
                global $wgRequest, $wgOut;

                $this->setHeaders();

                # If parameters were passed in the query string, they
                # can be accessed through the global $wgRequest object.
                $param = $wgRequest->getText('param');

                # MediaWiki uses the convention that references to the database
                # should be called $dbr if it is for read access and $dbw
                # for write access. In most cases, you would be reading
                # from the database in a special page.
                $dbr =& wfGetDB( DB_SLAVE );
                $fields = array(
                        'ss_row_id',
                        'ss_total_views',
                        ) ;
                $res = $dbr->select('site_stats',
                        $fields, ", 'SpecialPageExample', array('LIMIT'=> 1) );
                while ( $row = $dbr->fetchObject( $res ) ) {
                  $wgOut->addHTML( "<p>Total Views: " . $row->ss_total_views );
        }

                $dbr->freeResult( $res );

                # Output
                $wgOut->addWikiText( wfMsg( 'specialpageexample' ) );
}

        function loadMessages() {
                static $messagesLoaded = false;
                global $wgMessageCache;

                if ( $messagesLoaded ) return true;
                $messagesLoaded = true;
                require( dirname( __FILE__ ) . '/SpecialPageExample.i18n.php' );
                foreach ( $allMessages as $lang => $langMessages ) {
                        $wgMessageCache->addMessages( $langMessages, $lang );
        }

                return true;
}
}
}
?>
```

SpecialPageExample.i18n.php

The i18n page for special pages works exactly like the equivalent page in the previous parser function example:

```php
<?php
$allMessages = array(
        'en' => array(
                'specialpageexample' => 'Special Page Example'
        )
);
?>
```

Summary

In this chapter, you have learned how to create your own extensions, including how to extend wikitext by adding new XML tag extensions and parser functions. You have also learned how to create your own special pages.

In the next chapter, you will learn how to interact with MediaWiki programmatically through MediaWiki's API, as well as how to use the `pywikipedia.py` bot to automate some of MediaWiki's processes.

10

The MediaWiki API

The ability to interact with MediaWiki through an application programming interface is an evolving feature. In this chapter, you will learn about *bots*, programs used to automate certain administrative tasks on MediaWiki, as well as the MediaWiki API, which is currently in development and is intended to provide a programming interface to MediaWiki so that external applications can interact with it.

Both the section on bots and the section on the API make extensive use of examples written in the Python programming language. Even if you do not know Python, you will be able to learn a lot about how bots and the API work, which you can use to develop scripts in your language of choice. With respect to the API, all interaction is managed through URLs, so you don't even have to write any script to see samples of the API output; simply type the URL in your browser and see what is returned.

Bots: pywikipedia.py

In MediaWiki parlance, a bot is a script or program that is used to perform some administrative task in support of a wiki. There is a special group called bot, so any bot that is used with MediaWiki must have a username that is in the bot group. A person with bureaucrat privileges is required to set the appropriate permissions.

The reason for requiring a special username is twofold. One, you do not want people to be able to automate tasks willy-nilly with your wiki. That's just asking for trouble from spammers and trolls. At the same time, tedious or time-consuming tasks can benefit greatly from automation. Because the work that bots do is often *en masse*, meaning that they perform some task that might affect hundreds of documents, MediaWiki treats changes made by bots a little differently. For example, when viewing recent changes, changes made by bots can be excluded. By having a special bot group, both issues are addressed.

Bots interact with MediaWiki programmatically, but to date most bots do not use any formal MediaWiki API, because there hasn't been one. While a new API is being crafted (which you will learn about later in the chapter), necessity requires bot developers to create other methods of interacting with MediaWiki programmatically, something that often involves writing scripts that interact with the standard MediaWiki HTML interface.

One particularly well-developed bot is `pywikipedia.py`, which can be downloaded at `http://sourceforge.net/projects/pywikipediabot/`.

Python 2.3 or later must be installed (it may work on earlier versions of Python, but this hasn't been tested). It is written in Python, and it is designed to be used with Wikipedia. This means that often some customizations need to be made to the scripts in order to make them work properly on a homegrown MediaWiki wiki.

The first step is to configure the bot with your site's information, and a username and password in the bot group.

Configuring pywikipedia.py

Two files need to be created in order to use pywikipedia: `user-config.py` and another file named after your wiki. In the example, the file is called `profwiki_family.py`, which includes a subclass of the `Family` class. The name that is chosen is important because pywikipedia needs to know which `family` object to instantiate.

profwiki_family.py

In the main directory of the pywikipedia distribution is a file called `family.py`, and a directory called `families`. The `family.py` file includes the base `Family` class that needs to be subclassed. The "family" in question is the family of sites that make up Wikipedia. In Wikipedia's case, the family sites are versions of Wikipedia in different languages, so much of the `family.py` file concerns itself with languages and being able to navigate around the collection of sites that make up Wikipedia.

Inside the `families` directory are sample subclasses of `Family` that have been developed by other MediaWiki users. These sample subclasses can be used as examples for more complex configuration.

Typically, most organizations will not have such a large family as Wikipedia, so the following example shows you how to subclass the `Family` class for a single site:

```
# -*- coding: utf-8 -*-

import family

# Prof Wikis, by Mark Choate for Wrox

class Family(family.Family):
    def __init__(self):
        family.Family.__init__(self)
        # The name assigned needs to be the same as the
        # prefix used to name the file - in this case,
```

```
        # that is profwiki_family.py
        self.name = 'profwiki'
        # There's only one language to the site, so I
        # associate the domain of my site with "en".
        # In this instance, I'm accessing the domain
        # locally. If the site were on a different
        # server, I would use the actual domain name of
        # the site.
        self.langs = {'en': '127.0.0.1',}
        # The name of my test wiki is 'Profwikis - MySQL
        # so I assign that to the following namespaces.
        self.namespaces[4] = {'_default': [u'Profwikis -
MySQL', self.namespaces[4]['_default']],}
        self.namespaces[5] = {'_default': [u'Profwikis -
MySQL talk', self.namespaces[5]['_default']],}
    # The version of MediaWiki I am using
    def version(self, code):
        return "1.9.3"
    # The path to the wiki
    def path(self, code):
        return '/mysql/index.php'
```

Save this file in the `families` directory. After it is complete, the `user-config.py` file needs to be created.

user-config.py

The default configuration is in `config.py`. Much like the difference between `DefaultSettings.php` and `LocalSettings.php`, `config.py` contains the default configuration data for the bot. Place any custom configuration data specific to your wiki in a file called `user-config.py`:

```
#One line saying "mylang='language'"
#One line saying "usernames['wikipedia']['language']='yy'"
mylang='en'
family='profwiki'
# The following user name MUST be in the bot group.
usernames['profwiki']['en']= u'Mchoate'
```

In the `profwiki_family.py` file is the following line:

```
self.langs = {'en': '127.0.0.1',}
```

The value for `"mylang"` in the `user-config` file corresponds with the language specified in `profwiki_family.py`. The following line in `user-config`:

```
family='profwiki'
```

corresponds with `self.name = 'profwiki'` in `profwiki_family.py`.

What all of this means is that when you execute a script using pywikipedia, the default language is English, which defaults to the server located at 127.0.0.1, using the path `mysql/index.php`. The script will log in as user Mchoate, which, if it is in the bot group, will then be allowed to make changes to the site.

editarticle.py

The main file is `wikipedia.py`, which is where much of the core functionality is coded. In most cases, a script includes the `wikipedia` module when executing code. The first example is `editarticle.py`, which is a script that enables you to edit articles directly through an external editor, rather than edit them on the wiki website. I won't go into all the specific details of the implementation, but I do want to point out that the script imports the `wikipedia` module and the `config` module, which gives it all the information needed to log in and edit a file:

```
import wikipedia
import config
```

```
mchoate$ ./editarticle.py
Checked for running processes. 1 processes currently
    running, including the current process.
Page to edit:
```

Type in the page title you want to edit at the prompt, and a Tkinter window will be displayed with the wikitext to be edited (as shown in Figure 10-1).

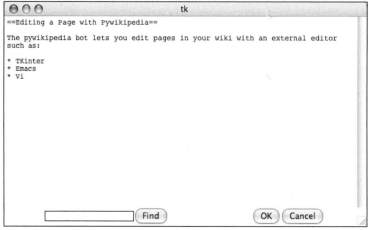

Figure 10-1: The Tkinter editing window

In order to edit in a different editor, the `user-config.py` file needs to be updated. The next example shows how to edit the pages using Emacs. The following line must be added to `user-config.py`:

```
editor = 'emacs'
```

Once this is done, you start the script just like before, but Emacs is launched instead of the Tkinter window, as shown in Figure 10-2.

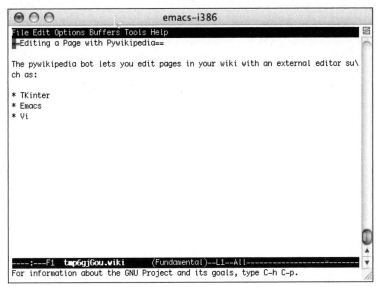

Figure 10-2: Editing wikitext using Emacs

The script works by getting a copy of the page from the wiki and then saving the data to a temporary file. In the following output sample, the temporary file that was created was /tmp/tmp8YFggr.wiki.

Then, the editor that is configured opens the temporary file. Once the edits are made and the file is saved, the script checks to see whether any changes have been made. If there were, it prompts the user to provide a short summary of what was changed (just like you do when editing a page through a Web interface). Once that's entered, the file is then uploaded to the server:

```
mchoate$ ./editarticle.py
Checked for running processes. 1 processes currently
    running, including the current process.
Page to edit: Main Page
Getting page [[Main Page]]
Running editor...
/tmp/tmp8YFggr.wiki
+
+ The file has been modified.

What did you change?  I added a new sentence.
Getting a page to check if we're logged in on profwiki:en
Changing page [[en:Main Page]]
```

spellcheck.py

One other useful script available in pywikipedia is spellcheck.py, which (not surprisingly) performs a spell-check on wiki pages. In order to use spellcheck.py you first have to download a dictionary

file from `http://pywikipediabot.cvs.sourceforge.net/pywikipediabot/pywikipedia/spelling/`.
Included are files for several languages. The file for English is `spelling-en.txt`, which should be downloaded into the spelling directory in the pywikipedia distribution (it weighs in at about 2.5 megabytes of data, which is why they don't include it in the main distribution).

Once the spelling dictionaries are in place, spell-checking a page is simply a matter of executing the `spellcheck.py` script and passing it the name of the page to spell-check. In the next example, the article titled "Main Page" is going to be spell-checked:

```
mchoate$ ./spellcheck.py "Main Page"
```

When the script finds a questionably spelled word, the user is prompted through the console with various options. Like most spell-checkers, you are given the option to add the word to the dictionary, to ignore the word, to replace the text, to replace the text while not saving the alternative in the database, to guess, to edit by hand, or to stop checking the page altogether. In the following example, the spell-checker questions the spelling of "pywikipedia," and, amusingly, the spelling of "wiki." Once finished, the changes are saved and then uploaded back to the wiki:

```
Checked for running processes. 3 processes currently running,
    including the current process.
Getting wordlist
Wordlist successfully loaded.
Getting page [[Main Page]]
===============================================================
Found unknown word 'Pywikipedia'
Context:
==Editing a Page with Pywikipedia==

The pywikipedia bot lets you edit
---------------------------------------------------------------
a: Add 'Pywikipedia' as correct
c: Add 'pywikipedia' as correct
i: Ignore once
r: Replace text
s: Replace text, but do not save as alternative
g: Guess (give me a list of similar words)
*: Edit by hand
x: Do not check the rest of this page
: c
===============================================================
Found unknown word 'wiki'
Context:
kipedia bot lets you edit pages in your wiki with an external editor such as:

*
---------------------------------------------------------------
a: Add 'wiki' as correct
i: Ignore once
r: Replace text
s: Replace text, but do not save as alternative
g: Guess (give me a list of similar words)
*: Edit by hand
```

```
x: Do not check the rest of this page
: a
=================================================================
Found unknown word 'TKinter'
Context:
 with an external editor such as:

* TKinter
* Emacs
* Vi

The file has been modified
-----------------------------------------------------------------
a: Add 'TKinter' as correct
c: Add 'tKinter' as correct
i: Ignore once
r: Replace text
s: Replace text, but do not save as alternative
g: Guess (give me a list of similar words)
*: Edit by hand
x: Do not check the rest of this page
: a
Which page to check now? (enter to stop)
```

These are only two examples of the scripts included in pywikipedia that can be used to assist in the maintenance of your wiki. Also included are scripts for harvesting images, uploading images, changing categories, and more. Many of them are tailored to Wikipedia, so you may find that they need to be edited to suit your needs. You will also notice that some of them require Python to run, because the script needs to access the X-Windows server.

API.php

The developers of MediaWiki know that an easier-to-use API for MediaWiki would be a great improvement. Page through the code in pywikipedia and you'll see that it's a fairly complicated bit of programming … and very long. A new API is being developed to streamline the developer's work, and while it is not completed, it already is very capable, and affords the developer a simple, efficient way of interacting directly with the wiki's data.

Because the API is in a state of change, be sure to check www.mediawiki.org/wiki/API for the latest information about supported features. The developer is Yuri Astrakhan (User:Yurik on MediaWiki.org).

Configuration

The first step to using the API is to configure MediaWiki to use it. Add the following to LocalSettings.php:

```
/**
 * Enable direct access to the data API
 * through api.php
```

```
*/
$wgEnableAPI = true;
$wgEnableWriteAPI = true;
```

The API scripts are found in the `/includes/api/` directory, and the entry point is `api.php`, which is in the top-level directory of MediaWiki, along with `index.php`. In order to access the API, all you need to do is replace `index.php` in the URL with `api.php`, like so (substituting your domain name, of course):

```
http://127.0.0.1/wiki/api.php
```

Accessing the API

Because of the simplicity of the API, you can use a variety of ways to access it. Command-line tools such as wget and curl work, as do JavaScript, ruby, PHP, and Python. Any language that can generate an HTTP request can be used to access the API.

Actions

The current API implements five basic actions (and an edit action should be available by the time this book is published):

- **Help:** The help action returns basic documentation about how to use the API.
- **Login:** Because some activities require a user to be logged in, a login action is included.
- **Opensearch:** This implements the OpenSearch protocol and enables the developer to search the contents of the wiki. You can learn more about the OpenSearch protocol at `http://opensearch.org/`.
- **Feedwatchlist:** This returns an RSS feed of a user's watchlist.
- **Query:** This action enables developers to query the MediaWiki database.

Using these actions is demonstrated later in the chapter.

Formats

The available formats are as follows: `json`, `jsonfm`, `php`, `phpfm`, `wddx`, `wddxfm`, `xml`, `xmlfm`, `yaml`, `yamlfm`, and `rawfm` (the default value is `xmlfm`). The formats that end with `fm` are HTML representations of the output so that it can be displayed on a webpage. All actions can use any output style, with one exception. The Feedwatchlist action's output can only be one of two flavors of XML: RSS or Atom.

The following examples are based on a simply query action that requests information about the wiki's Main Page article. The URL looks like this:

```
action=query&format=json&titles=Main+Page&meta=siteinfo&prop=info
```

In order to generate the different output formats, just change `format=json` to represent the desired output.

JSON Format

JSON is a format based on JavaScript. You can find specifications for it at `http://json.org/`. Following are the HTTP headers returned by this request. Notice that the `Content-Type` header value is `application/json`:

```
Date: Thu, 09 Aug 2007 02:58:44 GMT
Server: Apache/1.3.33 (Darwin) PHP/5.2.0
X-Powered-By: PHP/5.2.0
Set-Cookie: wikidb_profwiki__session=onggurki4gg6v56ik26s9feef1; path=/
Expires: Thu, 01 Jan 1970 00:00:01 GMT
Cache-Control: s-maxage=0, must-revalidate, max-age=0
Connection: close
Transfer-Encoding: chunked
Content-Type: application/json; charset=utf-8
```

The actual JSON output follows (it has been reformatted to make it more legible:

```
{"query":
    {"pages":
        {"1":
            {"pageid":1,"ns":0,"title":"Main
    Page","touched":"2007-07-21T18:34:55Z","lastrevid":166
            }
        },"general":
        {"mainpage":"Main
    Page","base":"http:\/\/127.0.0.1\/mysql\/index.php\/Main_Page",
    "sitename":"ProfWikis - MySQL","generator":"MediaWiki 1.9.3","case":"first-
    letter","rights":""
        }
    }
}
```

XML Format

The HTTP headers for the XML format are the same as for JSON, except that the `Content-Type` is now `text/xml`:

```
Content-Type: text/xml; charset=utf-8
```

The equivalent XML output follows:

```
<?xml version="1.0" encoding="utf-8"?>
<api>
    <query>
        <pages>
            <page pageid="1" ns="0" title="Main Page"
    touched="2007-07-21T18:34:55Z" lastrevid="166"/>
        </pages>
        <general mainpage="Main Page"
    base="http://127.0.0.1/mysql/index.php/Main_Page"
    sitename="ProfWikis - MySQL" generator="MediaWiki 1.9.3"
    case="first-letter" rights=""/>
    </query>
</api>
```

WDDX Format

WDDX (Web Distributed Data eXchange) is a standard originally developed by Macromedia for its Cold Fusion server product. The specification can be found at `www.openwddx.org`. While it has largely been surpassed by other data exchange specifications, it is still widely enough used that the developers felt it was important enough to include (the last news item on the OpenWDDX website was posted in 2001). The wordy WDDX output for the query follows (again formatted for clarity):

```
<?xml version="1.0"?>
<wddxPacket version="1.0">
    <header/>
    <data>
        <struct>
            <var name="query">
                <struct>
                    <var name="pages">
                        <struct>
                            <var name="1">
                                <struct>
                                    <var name="pageid">
                                        <number>1</number>
                                    </var>
                                    <var name="ns">
                                        <number>0</number>
                                    </var>
                                    <var name="title">
                                        <string>Main Page</string>
                                    </var>
                                    <var name="touched">
                                        <string>2007-07-21T18:34:55Z</string>
                                    </var>
                                    <var name="lastrevid">
                                        <number>166</number>
                                    </var>
                                </struct>
                            </var>
                        </struct>
                    </var>
                    <var name="general">
                        <struct>
                            <var name="mainpage">
                                <string>Main Page</string>
                            </var>
                            <var name="base">
                                <string>http://127.0.0.1/mysql/index.php/Main_Page
</string>
                            </var>
                            <var name="sitename">
                                <string>ProfWikis - MySQL</string>
                            </var>
                            <var name="generator">
                                <string>MediaWiki 1.9.3</string>
                            </var>
                            <var name="case">
```

```
                    <string>first-letter</string>
                  </var>
                  <var name="rights">
                      <string/>
                  </var>
              </struct>
            </var>
          </struct>
        </var>
      </struct>
    </data>
  </wddxPacket>
```

PHP Format

The PHP serialized format is useful for PHP-based clients (see www.php.net/serialize). The
Content-Type is application/vnd.php.serialized:

```
Content-Type: application/vnd.php.serialized; charset=utf-8
```

The icky output is as follows:

```
a:1:{s:5:"query";a:2:{s:5:"pages";a:1:{i:1;a:5:{s:6:"pageid
  ";i:1;s:2:"ns";i:0;s:5:"title";s:9:"Main
  Page";s:7:"touched";s:20:"2007-07-21T18:34:55Z";s:9:"lastrevid";
  i:166;}}s:7:"general";a:6:{s:8:"mainpage";
  s:9:"Main Page";s:4:"base";s:42:"http://127.0.0.1/mysql/
  index.php/Main_Page";s:8:"sitename";s:17:"ProfWikis - MySQL";
  s:9:"generator";s:15:"MediaWiki 1.9.3";s:4:"case";s:12:"first-letter";
  s:6:"rights";s:0:"";}}}
```

YAML Format

Read all about YAML (and find out the definitive answer to the question regarding what YAML actually
means) here: http://yaml.org/. The YAML Content-Type is as follows:

```
Content-Type: application/yaml; charset=utf-8
```

Here is the YAML output:

```
query:
  pages:
    -
      pageid: 1
      ns: 0
      title: Main Page
      touched: 2007-07-21T18:34:55Z
      lastrevid: 166
  general:
    mainpage: Main Page
    base: >
      http://127.0.0.1/mysql/index.php/Main_Page
    sitename: ProfWikis - MySQL
```

```
generator: MediaWiki 1.9.3
case: first-letter
rights:
```

The API provides a rich set of options in terms of how the data is transferred to your application. The final choice ultimately depends upon the developer's preference, or is contingent upon other environmental factors.

In the next section, the API is illustrated with a Python script. In these examples, the selected output is XML, but it could just as easily be JSON, YAML or WDDX, as Python libraries exist to parse these formats as well.

Python Script

The following examples all come from a Python script written to illustrate the actions and the output of the MediaWiki API. This script is loosely based on a sample script for the old MediaWiki "Query" API, posted on MediaWiki at `http://en.wikipedia.org/wiki/User:Yurik/Query_API/User_Manual#Python`, but it has been expanded considerably.

I provide examples of all of the major actions, but the script is by no means exhaustive, in part because the API is still in a state of flux, with new features being added regularly. It can best be used as a starting point for developing your own scripts. It was also written with an eye toward being clear and easy to understand, rather than being particularly efficient or clever. It requires the use of Python 2.5.

Obviously, this exercise will be more informative if you are familiar with Python, but even if you are not a Python expert, you should be able to follow along as long as you have a solid understanding of computer programming. In the code and in other places where it is appropriate, you will see some additional explanation about what the Python code is doing, for readers who are unfamiliar with the language.

The first block of code in the script does some preparatory work, such as import libraries and define global variables used by the script. The urllib2 library is particularly useful in this case because it offers a rich set of tools for accessing resources through URLs, including cookie management, which is needed to track the logged-in status of the script when performing tasks that require special permissions. All the functions return XML, which is parsed by Python's ElementTree class. The global variables need to be customized to your site. The QUERY_URL is simply the base URL of the request, and the COOKIEFILE variable identifies where the cookie file will be stored, which enables the script to log in and stay logged in over a series of requests.

```python
#!/usr/bin/env python
# encoding: utf-8
"""
api.py

Created by Mark on 2007-08-06.
Copyright (c) 2007 The Choate Group, LLC. All rights reserved.
"""

import sys
import os
```

```
import urllib
import urllib2
import cookielib
import xml.etree.ElementTree
import StringIO

# global variables for the query url, http headers and the location
# of the cookie file to be used by urllib2
QUERY_URL = u"http://127.0.0.1/mysql/api.php"
HEADERS = {"User-Agent"  : "API Test/1.0"}
COOKIEFILE = "/Users/mchoate/Documents/Code/MediaWiki/test.cookie"
```

The `ApiRequest` class is being defined in the next block of code. The class will be used like this:

```
api = ApiRequest()
f = api.doHelp()
```

In the first line, the `ApiRequest` is instantiated, and then the `api` object calls the `doHelp()` convenience method, which returns a file-like object that contains the XML data returned by MediaWiki:

```
class ApiRequest:
    """
    Encapsulates the HTTP request to MediaWiki, managing cookies and
    handling the creation of the necessary URLs.
    """
    def __init__(self):
        pass

    def _initCookieJar(self):
        """
        The LWPCookieJar class saves cookies in a format compatible with
        libwww-perl, which looks like this:

        #LWP-Cookies-2.0
        Set-Cookie3: wikidb_profwiki_Token=8ade58c0ee4b60180ab7214a93403554;
        path="/"; domain="127.0.0.1"; path_spec; expires="2007-09-08 22:36:14Z";
        version=0
        Set-Cookie3: wikidb_profwiki_UserID=3; path="/"; domain="127.0.0.1";
        path_spec; expires="2007-09-08 22:36:14Z"; version=0
        Set-Cookie3: wikidb_profwiki_UserName=Mchoate; path="/";
        domain="127.0.0.1"; path_spec; expires="2007-09-08 22:36:14Z"; version=0

        """
        cj = cookielib.LWPCookieJar()

        # If the cookie file exists, then load the cookie into the cookie jar.
        if os.path.exists(COOKIEFILE):
            cj.load(COOKIEFILE)

        # Create an opened for urllib2. This means that the cookie jar
        # will be used by urllib2 when making HTTP requests.
        opener = urllib2.build_opener(urllib2.HTTPCookieProcessor(cj))
        urllib2.install_opener(opener)
        return cj
```

```
    def _saveCookieJar(self,cj):
        """
        Save the cookies in the cookie file.
        """
        cj.save(COOKIEFILE)

    def execute(self, args):
        """
        This is a generate method called by the convenience methods.
        The request takes place in three stages. First, the cookie jar
        is initialized and the cookie file is loaded if it already exists. Then,
        the dictionary "args" is urlencoded and urllib2 generates the HTTP request.
        The result of the request is returned as a file-like object. Once it is
        received, the cookie data is saved so that it will be available for the
        next request, and the data is returned to the calling method.
        """
        cj = self._initCookieJar()
        req = urllib2.Request(QUERY_URL, urllib.urlencode(args), HEADERS)
        f = urllib2.urlopen(req)
        self._saveCookieJar(cj)
        return f
```

The remaining methods all call the `execute` method, using arguments appropriate for the kind of request being made. Not every option is explored in the remaining code, but the script is easily extended with new request types.

Help

In order to get the latest information, you can make a help call to the API, which is particularly helpful considering the fact that the API is in an evolving state. The URL looks like this:

```
api.php?action=help
```

Alternatively, because it is the default action, it can also look like this:

```
api.php
```

When this is executed, a fairly detailed list of actions and their associated parameters is returned.

ApiRequest.doHelp()

The `ApiRequest` Python class creates a Help action request with the following method. The values that will be passed to the `execute()` method are set in a dictionary object:

```
def doHelp(self, format="xml"):
    args={"action": "help",
            "format": format}
    f = self.execute(args)
    return f
```

When the `execute()` method is called, the Python dictionary object is converted to a URL (`?action=help&format=xml`), and then the HTTP request is made. The results are returned in a file-like object, which, in addition to the usual Python file object methods, such as read(), also has two additional methods that can be useful, geturl() and info(), whose functionalities are described in the sample code that follows:

```
api = ApiRequest()
    f = api.doHelp()

    # Print a string representation of the URL that was called.
    # Note that this doesn't include the arguments, so it would
    # look something like this: http://127.0.0.1/wiki/api.php
    print f.geturl()

    # Print the headers from the HTTP response.
    print f.info()

    # Print the contents of the file-like object, which can be
    # xml, wddx, yaml, json, etc., depending on the format requested.
    print f.read()
```

Login

The login action has two required parameters and one optional parameter. Required are lgname and lgpassword; optional is lgdomain. The URL required to execute this action is as follows:

```
api.php?lgname=Mchoate&lgpassword=XXX&format=xml
```

The XML output of the action includes information about whether the login attempt was successful, the user ID of the person logged in, as well as the username, and a token that signifies a successful login, which can be used in subsequent requests to identify the logged in user.

MediaWiki also sets a cookie on the browser if the login is successful. In the mediawikiapi.py script, the urllib2 object handles accepting the cookie and sending it back on subsequent requests, which supersedes the need to use the token. The cookie encodes the same data as the value for lgtoken.

```
<?xml version="1.0" encoding="utf-8"?>
<api>
    <login result="Success" lguserid="3" lgusername="Mchoate"
    lgtoken="8ade58c0ee4b60180ab7214a93403554"/>
</api>
```

The doLogin() method functions slightly differently than the other methods do in that it doesn't return data from the request. Instead, it returns a Boolean value indicating whether the login was successful or not. This method can be called like so:

```
api = ApiRequest()
if api.doLogin("Mchoate", "connor"):
    print "Login was successful.\n\n"
else:
    print "Login failed.\n\n"
```

ApiRequest.doLogin()

The `doLogin()` method implementation follows. Notice in the code that the XML returned is parsed by `ElementTree`, and the content of the XML is tested in order to determine whether the login was successful or not:

```python
def doLogin(self, name, password, domain="", format="xml"):
    """
    The login action is used to login. If successful, a cookie
    is set, and an authentication token is returned.

    Example:
        api.php?action=login&lgname=user&lgpassword=password
    """
    args={
        "action"    : "login",
        "format"    : format,
        "lgname"    : name,
        "lgpassword": password,
    }
    # The domain is optional
    if domain:
        args.update({"lgdomain":domain})

    # MediaWiki returns an XML document with a blank line at
    # the top, which causes an error while parsing. The
    # following code strips whitespace at the front and
    # back of the XML document and returns a string.
    s = self.execute(args).read().strip()

    # ElementTree expects a file-like object,
    # so one is created for it.
    f = StringIO.StringIO(s)
    root = xml.etree.ElementTree.parse(f).getroot()

    # The root element is the <api> element.
    login = root.find("login")

    # The <login> element has an attribute 'result'
    # that returns 'Success' is the login was successful
    test = login.attrib["result"]
    if test == "Success":
        return True
    else:
        return False
```

Opensearch

This action enables you to search your wiki. The method is very similar to the `doHelp()` method and should be self-explanatory.

ApiRequest.doOpensearch()

```python
def doOpenSearch(self, search="", format="xml"):
    args={
        "action"    : "search",
```

```
        "format"    : format
      }
    f = self.execute(args)
    return f
```

Feedwatchlist

The Feedwatchlist action returns either an Atom or an RSS feed containing a list of pages that are being watched by the user. In this respect, it differs from the other actions in that it returns a special XML document. Unlike the others, it does not have a format parameter. Instead, it has a `feedformat` parameter than can be either `"rss"` or `"atom"`.

ApiRequest.doFeedWatchlist()

```
def doFeedWatchList(self, feedformat="rss"):
    args={
        "action"    : "feedwatchlist",
        "feedformat": feedformat
    }
    f = self.execute(args)
    return f
```

RSS Feed

If an RSS feed is requested, then the following XML will be returned:

```
<?xml version="1.0" encoding="utf-8"?>
<?xml-stylesheet type="text/css"
   href="http://127.0.0.1/mysql/skins/common/feed.css?42b"?>
<rss version="2.0" xmlns:dc="http://purl.org/dc/elements/1.1/">
    <channel>
            <title>ProfWikis - MySQL - My watchlist [en]</title>
            <link>http://127.0.0.1/mysql/index.php/Special:Watchlist</link>
            <description>My watchlist</description>
            <language>en</language>
            <generator>MediaWiki 1.9.3</generator>
            <lastBuildDate>Thu, 09 Aug 2007 22:33:30 GMT</lastBuildDate>
            <item>
                <title>Main Page</title>
                <link>http://127.0.0.1/mysql/index.php/Main_Page</link>
                <description> (WikiSysop)</description>
                <pubDate>Sat, 21 Jul 2007 18:31:51 GMT</pubDate>
            <dc:creator>WikiSysop</dc:creator>   </item>
    </channel>
</rss>
```

Atom Feed

If an `"atom"` feed is requested, then the data is reformatted to this specification:

```
<?xml version="1.0" encoding="utf-8"?>
<?xml-stylesheet type="text/css"
```

```
      href="http://127.0.0.1/mysql/skins/common/feed.css?42b"?>
<feed xmlns="http://www.w3.org/2005/Atom" xml:lang="en">
               <id>http://127.0.0.1/mysql/api.php</id>
               <title>ProfWikis - MySQL - My watchlist [en]</title>
               <link rel="self" type="application/atom+xml"
      href="http://127.0.0.1/mysql/api.php"/>
               <link rel="alternate" type="text/html"
      href="http://127.0.0.1/mysql/index.php/Special:Watchlist"/>
               <updated>2007-08-09T22:33:31Z</updated>
               <subtitle>My watchlist</subtitle>
               <generator>MediaWiki 1.9.3</generator>

        <entry>
               <id>http://127.0.0.1/mysql/index.php/Main_Page</id>
               <title>Main Page</title>
               <link rel="alternate" type="text/html"
      href="http://127.0.0.1/mysql/index.php/Main_Page"/>
                           <updated>2007-07-21T18:31:51Z</updated>

               <summary type="html"> (WikiSysop)</summary>
               <author><name>WikiSysop</name></author> </entry>
        </feed>
```

Query

The query action is the workhorse of the MediaWiki API. It takes a complex set of parameters whose composition varies depending on the various kinds of queries that are available. The base query URL starts like this:

```
api.php?action=query
```

This doesn't get you very far because all queries need to have some kind of parameters that narrow down the selection of what is returned (otherwise, what's the point of querying?). The group of queries uses one of the following parameters: titles, pageids, or revids. These are described in the section "Searching by Title, Page ID, or Revision ID" that follows. The next query type is a list, which is described in the "Lists" section, followed by the last basic type, generators, discussed in the "Generators" section.

Searching by Title, Page ID, or Revision ID

There are three parameters, titles, pageids, and revids, that enable you to query MediaWiki by title, page ID, or revision ID, respectively. All three work similarly, so the following examples use only titles; just bear in mind that you can do the same thing with the other parameters as well.

In all three cases, you can search for more than one value. To do so, you only need to separate the values by the pipe (|) character (a pattern used throughout the API), as is shown in the following example:

```
api.php?action=query&titles=Main+Page|Some+Other+Page&format=xml
```

Because the output of query actions are more varied than those of the others reviewed, the following sections use a slightly different format to describe them. First, you will see examples showing how the URLs can be formed to get the particular information you are looking for. Once you've reviewed the important variations, then you will learn the `mediawikiapi.py` script method that can be used to generate the different requests.

Simple Titles Query

A basic query that requests pages based upon their titles is illustrated in the following example:

```
api.php?action=query&titles=Main+Page&format=xml
```

The XML-formatted output of this request includes information about the page ID, plus the namespace of the page (which in this case is the default namespace):

```
<?xml version="1.0" encoding="utf-8"?>
<api>
    <query>
        <pages>
            <page pageid="1" ns="0" title="Main Page"/>
        </pages>
    </query>
</api>
```

This, of course, is of little value unless you simply wanted to know the page ID for this particular page. Chances are good you will want more information, and this information is requested by the `prop` parameter, which can be one of two values, both of which are illustrated next.

Property: info

The following URL requests general information about the page titled "Main Page" by assigning the `info` value to the `prop` parameter:

```
api.php?action=query&format=xml&titles=Main+Page&prop=info
```

The output of this request now includes more information: the date the page was last "touched," and the last revision id (or current revision id, depending on whether you are a glass half-empty or glass half-full kind of person):

```
<?xml version="1.0" encoding="utf-8"?>
<api>
    <query>
        <pages>
            <page pageid="1" ns="0" title="Main Page"
   touched="2007-07-21T18:34:55Z" lastrevid="166"/>
        </pages>
    </query>
</api>
```

Property: revisions

The second value available to `prop` is the `revisions` value:

```
api.php?action=query&format=xml&titles=Main+Page&prop=revisions
```

When this value is used, additional information is returned about the last (or current) revision id. Actually, the only new data it adds by default is the `oldid` number:

```
<?xml version="1.0" encoding="utf-8"?>
<api>
    <query>
        <pages>
            <page pageid="1" ns="0" title="Main Page">
                <revisions>
                    <rev revid="166" pageid="1" oldid="157"/>
                </revisions>
            </page>
        </pages>
    </query>
</api>
```

There are times when you want more data about previous revisions, so the MediaWiki API provides a handful of parameters that can be used alongside the `prop` parameter when its value is set to `revisions`. These parameters are outlined in the following table.

Parameter	Value
Rvprop	Determines which revision properties to return. Values can be: `timestamp`, `user`, or `comment`. More than one value can be included by separating them with a | character, like so: `rvprop=timestamp|user|comment`.
rvlimit	Determines the maximum number of revision pages to return. The default is 10.
rvstartid	The value is the revision id, which indicates the starting point of the list of revisions that will be returned. Note that the `rvstartid` value can be higher or lower than the `rvendid` value, depending on the direction of the sort, as specified in `rvdir` (see below).
rvendid	The ending point of the range of revision IDs whose starting point is specified by `rvstartid`.
rvstart	The timestamp of the starting point of the revisions to return.
rvend	The timestamp of the ending point of the revisions to return.
rvdir	Determines the sort direction of the returned list of revisions, either from older to newer or newer to older. The possible values are either `older` or `newer`. The default is `older`, which lists the revisions in descending order, with the newest revision first.

Using these parameters can be somewhat tricky at first if you do not understand the impact that `rvdir` has on the output. It is best illustrated with a few examples. The following URL illustrates a basic request that includes a request for information about when each revision was created, who created it, and any user comments that may have been added. It also limits results to 10 revisions and returns the list of revisions in reverse order of the creation date, so that the most recent revision is listed first, followed by the rest in descending order:

```
api.php?format=xml&rvprop=timestamp%7Cuser%7Ccomment&
  prop=revisions&rvdir=older&titles=Main+Page&rvlimit=
  10&action=query
```

The XML output is as follows:

```
<?xml version="1.0" encoding="utf-8"?>
<api>
    <query>
        <pages>
            <page pageid="1" ns="0" title="Main Page">
                <revisions>
                    <rev revid="166" pageid="1" oldid="157"
user="WikiSysop" timestamp="2007-07-21T18:31:51Z"/>
                    <rev revid="165" pageid="1" oldid="156"
user="WikiSysop" timestamp="2007-07-17T23:47:46Z"/>
                    <rev revid="150" pageid="1" oldid="141"
user="WikiSysop" timestamp="2007-06-21T19:02:09Z"/>
                    <rev revid="149" pageid="1" oldid="140"
user="WikiSysop" timestamp="2007-06-21T19:00:21Z"/>
                    <rev revid="146" pageid="1" oldid="137"
user="WikiSysop" timestamp="2007-06-21T16:19:19Z"/>
                    <rev revid="134" pageid="1" oldid="125"
user="WikiSysop" timestamp="2007-06-21T14:58:39Z"/>
                    <rev revid="93" pageid="1" oldid="87"
user="WikiSysop" timestamp="2007-06-04T20:05:07Z"/>
                    <rev revid="91" pageid="1" oldid="85"
user="WikiSysop" timestamp="2007-06-01T19:48:49Z"/>
                    <rev revid="77" pageid="1" oldid="74"
user="WikiSysop" timestamp="2007-05-31T18:12:51Z"/>
                    <rev revid="76" pageid="1" oldid="73"
user="WikiSysop" timestamp="2007-05-31T17:43:53Z"/>
                </revisions>
            </page>
        </pages>
    </query>
    <query-continue>
        <revisions rvstartid="64"/>
    </query-continue>
</api>
```

At the end of the XML data is a `<query-continue>` XML tag. This is here because the request limited the returned values to no more than 10. Because there are more than 10 revisions for this page, the id of the next revision in sequence is returned so that it can be used on subsequent requests.

Revision Direction: older The next query is just like the previous query except that two parameters are added: `rvstartid` and `rvendid`. The query says to start with revision ID 77 and to end with revision ID 150:

```
api.php?format=xml&rvprop=timestamp%7Cuser%7Ccomment&prop=
    revisions&rvdir=older&rvstartid=77&titles=Main+Page&rvlimit
    =10&rvendid=150&action=query
```

When this query is executed, the following data is returned:

```
<?xml version="1.0" encoding="utf-8"?>
<api>
    <query>
        <pages>
            <page pageid="1" ns="0" title="Main Page"/>
        </pages>
    </query>
</api>
```

You may have noticed that something is missing. Where are the revisions between 77 and 150? The answer is that the request is asking for a set of information that cannot exist. The order of the results is the same as the previous query, which means that the most recent revision is first, followed by the other revisions in descending order. This request tells MediaWiki to start at the 77th revision and to end at the 150th revision.

Because it is ordered in descending order, and the most recent revision is 166, MediaWiki returns nothing. One solution is to tell MediaWiki to start with the 150th revision and to end with the 77th revision. The other solution is to request the list in the reverse direction, from oldest to newest.

Revision Direction: newer The modified request now looks like the following — the only change is setting the `rvdir` parameter to the value `newer`:

```
format=xml&rvprop=timestamp%7Cuser%7Ccomment&prop=revisions
    &rvdir=newer&rvstartid=77&titles=Main+Page&rvlimit=10&
    rvendid=150&action=query
```

The results of this query are markedly different from the first. The first revision listed has a revision ID of 77, and the last revision has an ID of 150, so it has constrained the list according to the start and end properties set in the query.

```
<?xml version="1.0" encoding="utf-8"?>
<api>
    <query>
        <pages>
            <page pageid="1" ns="0" title="Main Page">
                <revisions>
                    <rev revid="77" pageid="1" oldid="74"
    user="WikiSysop" timestamp="2007-05-31T18:12:51Z"/>
                    <rev revid="91" pageid="1" oldid="85"
    user="WikiSysop" timestamp="2007-06-01T19:48:49Z"/>
                    <rev revid="93" pageid="1" oldid="87"
    user="WikiSysop" timestamp="2007-06-04T20:05:07Z"/>
                    <rev revid="134" pageid="1" oldid="125"
```

```
   user="WikiSysop" timestamp="2007-06-21T14:58:39Z"/>
                    <rev revid="146" pageid="1" oldid="137"
   user="WikiSysop" timestamp="2007-06-21T16:19:19Z"/>
                    <rev revid="149" pageid="1" oldid="140"
   user="WikiSysop" timestamp="2007-06-21T19:00:21Z"/>
                    <rev revid="150" pageid="1" oldid="141"
   user="WikiSysop" timestamp="2007-06-21T19:02:09Z"/>
                  </revisions>
              </page>
          </pages>
      </query>
</api>
```

ApiRequest.doTitlesQuery()

Because there are so many variations to the parameters that can be used when making these kinds of queries, the query code in the example uses a Python idiom that enables you to pass a varying number of parameters to the method. Note that the same basic method can be used for pageids and revids queries with only the slight modification of swapping pageids wherever titles appears, or revids wherever titles appears:

```
def doTitlesQuery(self, titles, format, **args):
        args.update({
        "action": "query",
        "titles": titles,
        "format": format}
        )
        f = self.execute(args)
        return f
```

The **args argument is a dictionary of key value pairs that is generated by adding named parameters to the method call. This method requires a value for titles and format, but will accept any number of named parameters, as illustrated in the following example, which shows three different but perfectly acceptable ways of calling the method:

```
api = ApiRequest()
f = api.doTitlesQuery("Main Page", "xml")
f = api.doTitlesQuery("Main Page", "xml", rvprop="info")
f = api.doTitlesQuery("Main Page", "xml", rvprop="revisions", rvlimit="10")
```

Lists

Queries that return lists work a little differently than the queries seen thus far. There are a few important things to understand:

1. You can request eight pre-defined lists: allpages, logevents, watchlist, recentchanges, backlinks, embeddedin, imagelinks, and usercontribs. These are described in detail below.

2. Lists are used instead of titles, pageids and revids. All four of these query types are mutually exclusive.

3. Lists cannot be used with any of the prop and revision parameters.

4. There is an exception to rule number 3. Lists can be used as what is called a *generator* in the API, which means that the list can be used in place of `titles`, `pageids`, and `revids`, in which case all of the `prop` and `revision` parameters are available to the request. This means that instead of typing in a long list of page titles to search for, you can use a `list` as the source. This concept is best illustrated with examples, which can be found in the section "Generators" later in this chapter.

A basic list query is constructed like the following URL:

```
api.php?action=query&format=xml&list=allpages
```

The output of such a query follows:

```
<?xml version="1.0" encoding="utf-8"?>
<api>
    <query-continue>
        <allpages apfrom="Image galleries"/>
    </query-continue>
    <query>
        <allpages>
            <p pageid="49" ns="0" title="ASamplePage"/>
            <p pageid="28" ns="0" title="A new page"/>
            <p pageid="33" ns="0" title="Basic Image Links"/>
            <p pageid="34" ns="0" title="Basic Media Namespace Links"/>
            <p pageid="41" ns="0" title="College Basketball"/>
            <p pageid="42" ns="0" title="College Football"/>
            <p pageid="39" ns="0" title="College Sports"/>
            <p pageid="20" ns="0" title="Core parser functions"/>
            <p pageid="19" ns="0" title="Headings"/>
            <p pageid="35" ns="0" title="Image Alignment"/>
        </allpages>
    </query>
</api>
```

An important item to note is that by default, all requests are limited to 10 items. This can be overridden by the correct parameter, which varies according to which list type is being requested. Each list type has its own collection of parameters that it can use, and these are documented in the following pages, along with sample output.

List: allpages

Parameter	Value
apfrom	Returns a list of pages ordered alphabetically, starting with titles equal to or higher than the letter or letters used. If `apfrom="bamboozled"`, then the list will return only those pages that come after `bamboozled` when sorted alphabetically.
apprefix	Returns a list of pages whose title starts with the string passed as the value. If `apprefix="Ma"`, then all pages whose title starts with `Ma` will be returned. If you leave the parameter empty, like `apprefix='"'`, then no pages will be returned. Leave it out of the query entirely if you do not want to use it.

Parameter	Value
apnamespace	The number of the namespace from which the list should be derived. It should be a value from 0 to 15 (unless you've added custom namespaces).
apfilterredir	Determines which pages to list based upon one of three values: all, redirects and nonredirects. The default is all.
aplimit	Determines the maximum number of pages to return. The default is 10.

In the previous section, an example of a simple request was already illustrated. The following request is a little more complicated, and uses the parameters available to the allpages request:

```
api.php?apfilterredir=all&apprefix=M&format=xml&list=allpages
    &apfrom=A&apnamespace=0&action=query&prop=revisions&
    aplimit=10
```

The preceding request asks for all pages that start with the letter A or higher in the alphabet and all pages that have the prefix of M. Of course, because M comes after A in the alphabet, all pages with titles that start with M are included in the results:

```
<?xml version="1.0" encoding="utf-8"?>
<api>
    <query>
        <allpages>
            <p pageid="24" ns="0" title="Magic Words"/>
            <p pageid="10" ns="0" title="Magic Words that
show information about the page"/>
            <p pageid="9" ns="0" title="Magic Words that use underscores"/>
            <p pageid="11" ns="0" title="Magic word tests"/>
            <p pageid="1" ns="0" title="Main Page"/>
            <p pageid="22" ns="0" title="Math"/>
            <p pageid="51" ns="0" title="MediaWiki Extensions"/>
        </allpages>
    </query>
</api>
```

The remaining list types all have unique parameters, but there is a lot of overlap with the parameters used in the previous example. Therefore, the next sections document the parameters each list type uses, but do not provide specific output examples.

List: logevents

Parameter	Value
letype	Filters log events based on the type of log event. Legal values are block, protect, rights, delete, upload, move, import, renameuser, newusers, and makebot. Separate each value with a pipe (|) if you are filtering on more than one value.
lestart	The timestamp of the starting point of the list of log events that will be returned.

Parameter	Value
leend	The timestamp of the ending point of the list of log entries that will be returned.
ledir	The sort order of the list of log entries that is returned. The value can be `newer` or `older`. The default value is `older`.
leuser	Filters entries by username.
letitle	Returns log entries for a given page.
lelimit	Determines the maximum number of log entries to return. The default is 10.

List: watchlist

Parameter	Value
wlallrev	Includes all revisions of the pages in the watchlist that will be returned. This parameter doesn't take a value; if it is present in the query, all revisions are returned. If it is absent, only the current page is returned. `action=query&list=watchlist&wlallrev`
wlstart	The timestamp of the starting point of the watchlist that will be returned.
wlend	The timestamp of the ending point of the watchlist that will be returned.
wlnamespace	The number of the namespace from which the list should be derived. It should be a value from 0 to 15 (unless you've added custom namespaces).
wldir	Determines the sort direction of the returned list of pages, either from older to newer or newer to older. The value is either `older` or `newer`, and the default value is `older`.
wllimit	Determines the maximum number of pages to return. The default is 10.
wlprop	Specifies which additional items to get (nongenerator mode only). The value can be one or more of the following: `user`, `comment`, `timestamp`, and `patrol`. When using multiple values, separate them with a pipe (`|`).

List: recentchanges

Parameter	Value
rcstart	The timestamp of the starting point of the list of recent changes that will be returned.
rcend	The timestamp of the ending point of the list of recent changes that will be returned.

Parameter	Value
rcdir	Determines the sort direction of the returned list of recent changes, either from older to newer or newer to older. The value is either older or newer.
rcnamespace	The number of the namespace from which the list should be derived. It should be a value from 0 to 15 (unless you've added custom namespaces).
rcprop	Includes additional properties in the return values. The value can be one or more of the following: user, comment, and flags. When using multiple values, separate them with a pipe (|).
rcshow	Filters returned items based on the criteria specified in the value. Possible values are minor, !minor, bot, !bot, anon, and !anon. Values that start with ! are negations. In other words, minor means include minor changes in the results, whereas !minor means do not include minor changes in the results. Likewise, you can specify whether to include changes made by bots and changes made by anonymous users.
rclimit	Determines the maximum number of pages to return. The default is 10.

List: backlinks

Parameter	Value
blcontinue	When more results are available, use this to continue.
blnamespace	The number of the namespace from which the list should be derived. It should be a value from 0 to 15 (unless you've added custom namespaces).
bllimit	Determines the maximum number of pages to return. The default is 10.

List: emeddedin

Parameter	Value
einamespace	The number of the namespace from which the list should be derived. It should be a value from 0 to 15 (unless you've added custom namespaces).
eiredirect	If the linking page is a redirect, this finds all pages that link to that redirect (not implemented).
eilimit	Determines the maximum number of pages to return. The default is 10.

List: imagelinks

Parameter	Value
ilnamespace	The number of the namespace from which the list should be derived. It should be a value from 0 to 15 (unless you've added custom namespaces).
illimit	Determines the maximum number of pages to return. The default is 10.

List: usercontribs

Parameter	Value
uclimit	Determines the maximum number of contributions to return. The default is 10.
ucstart	The timestamp of the starting point of the list of user contributions that will be returned.
ucend	The timestamp of the ending point of the list of user contributions that will be returned.
ucuser	The username whose contributions will be returned
ucdir	Determines the sort direction of the returned list of user contributions, either from older to newer or newer to older. The value is either older or newer.

ApiRequest.doListQuery(list=allpages, **listargs)

The Python method used to generate list queries is similar to the one used to generate titles queries. This generic query can be used for any kind of list type:

```
def doListQuery(self, list, format, **args):
        args.update({
        "action": "query",
        "list": list,
        "format": format}
        )
        f = self.execute(args)
        return f
```

No programmer likes to type any more than they have to, so slightly more convenient methods have been included for each specific kind of list to be queried:

```
def doListAllpagesQuery(self, **args):
        args.update({
        "action":"query",
        "list": "allpages",
        })
        f = self.execute(args)
        return f
```

```python
    def doListLogeventsQuery(self, **args):
        args.update({
        "action":"query",
        "list": "logevents",
        })
        f = self.execute(args)
        return f

    def doListWatchlistQuery(self, **args):
        args.update({
        "action":"query",
        "list": "watchlist",
        })
        f = self.execute(args)
        return f

    def doListRecentchangesQuery(self, **args):
        args.update({
        "action":"query",
        "list": "recentchanges",
        })
        f = self.execute(args)
        return f

    def doListBacklinksQuery(self, **args):
        args.update({
        "action":"query",
        "list": "backlinks",
        })
        f = self.execute(args)
        return f

    def doListEmbeddedinQuery(self, **args):
        args.update({
        "action":"query",
        "list": "embeddedin",
        })
        f = self.execute(args)
        return f


    def doListImagelinksQuery(self, **args):
        args.update({
        "action":"query",
        "list": "imagelinks",
        })
        f = self.execute(args)
        return f

    def doListUsercontribsQuery(self, **args):
        args.update({
        "action":"query",
        "list": "usercontribs",
        })
        f = self.execute(args)
        return f
```

Generators

Earlier in this chapter, you learned that lists could be used as generators in place of `titles`, `pageids`, and `revids` queries. You also saw that this concept is most easily understood by looking at sample output, which is what you will see here.

In order to use a list as a generator, all you need to do is refer to it as a generator in the query. Instead of `list=allpages`, use `generator=allpages`, as illustrated in the following example:

```
api.php?generator=allpages&format=xml&action=query
```

That's all there is to it. The advantage to using a generator is that you then have access to the `prop` and `revision` parameters and can thus query a much richer set of information than you can with lists alone.

The following two API requests will return the same data, even though one is a generator and the other is a list:

```
api.php?action=query&format=xml&generator=allpages
api.php?action=query&format=xml&list=allpages
```

Both of these requests return the following data:

```xml
<?xml version="1.0" encoding="utf-8"?>
<api>
    <query-continue>
        <allpages gapfrom="Image galleries"/>
    </query-continue>
    <query>
        <pages>
            <page pageid="49" ns="0" title="ASamplePage"/>
            <page pageid="28" ns="0" title="A new page"/>
            <page pageid="33" ns="0" title="Basic Image Links"/>
            <page pageid="34" ns="0" title="Basic Media Namespace Links"/>
            <page pageid="41" ns="0" title="College Basketball"/>
            <page pageid="42" ns="0" title="College Football"/>
            <page pageid="39" ns="0" title="College Sports"/>
            <page pageid="20" ns="0" title="Core parser functions"/>
            <page pageid="19" ns="0" title="Headings"/>
            <page pageid="35" ns="0" title="Image Alignment"/>
        </pages>
    </query>
</api>
```

The difference becomes apparent when you use both the generator and the `prop` parameter:

```
api.php?action=query&format=xml&generator=allpages&prop=revisions
```

This request returns the following data:

```xml
<?xml version="1.0" encoding="utf-8"?>
<api>
    <query-continue>
        <allpages gapfrom="Image galleries"/>
    </query-continue>
```

```
    <query>
        <pages>
            <page pageid="49" ns="0" title="ASamplePage">
                <revisions>
                    <rev revid="164" pageid="49" oldid="155"/>
                </revisions>
            </page>
            <page pageid="28" ns="0" title="A new page">
                <revisions>
                    <rev revid="111" pageid="28" oldid="102" minor=""/>
                </revisions>
            </page>
            <page pageid="33" ns="0" title="Basic Image Links">
                <revisions>
                    <rev revid="121" pageid="33" oldid="112"/>
                </revisions>
            </page>
            <page pageid="34" ns="0" title="Basic Media Namespace Links">
                <revisions>
                    <rev revid="123" pageid="34" oldid="114"/>
                </revisions>
            </page>
            <page pageid="41" ns="0" title="College Basketball">
                <revisions>
                    <rev revid="138" pageid="41" oldid="129"/>
                </revisions>
            </page>
            <page pageid="42" ns="0" title="College Football">
                <revisions>
                    <rev revid="139" pageid="42" oldid="130"/>
                </revisions>
            </page>
            <page pageid="39" ns="0" title="College Sports">
                <revisions>
                    <rev revid="143" pageid="39" oldid="134"/>
                </revisions>
            </page>
            <page pageid="20" ns="0" title="Core parser functions">
                <revisions>
                    <rev revid="160" pageid="20" oldid="151"/>
                </revisions>
            </page>
            <page pageid="19" ns="0" title="Headings">
                <revisions>
                    <rev revid="59" pageid="19" oldid="56"/>
                </revisions>
            </page>
            <page pageid="35" ns="0" title="Image Alignment">
                <revisions>
                    <rev revid="127" pageid="35" oldid="118"/>
                </revisions>
            </page>
        </pages>
    </query>
</api>
```

There are, of course, a large number of variations to the kind of requests that can be made this way, and all of the `revision` properties can be used as well to construct complex queries.

ApiRequest.doGeneratorQuery()

The Python method to request a generator is almost identical to the list request, except that the `generator` parameter is used instead of the `list` parameter:

```
def doGeneratorQuery(self, list, format, **args):
        args.update({
        "action": "query",
        "generator": list,
        "format": format}
        )
        f = self.execute(args)
        return f
```

This method can be used to replicate the queries used to illustrate generator output by using them in the following way:

```
api = ApiQuery()
f = api.doGeneratorQuery("allpages", "xml")
    print f.read()

f = api.doGeneratorQuery("allpages", "xml", prop="revisions")
    print f.read()
```

In Development

One feature missing from the API is the capability to edit pages programmatically. This feature is currently under active development and will be available in future versions of MediaWiki.

api.py

The complete code of the `api.py` script follows:

```
#!/usr/bin/env python
# encoding: utf-8
"""
api.py

Created by Mark on 2007-08-06.
Copyright (c) 2007 The Choate Group, LLC. All rights reserved.
"""

import sys
import os
import urllib
import urllib2
import cookielib
import xml.etree.ElementTree
import StringIO
```

```
# Customize the following values for your wiki installation
QUERY_URL = u"http://127.0.0.1/mysql/api.php"
HEADERS = {"User-Agent"  : "API Test/1.0"}
COOKIEFILE = "/Users/mchoate/Documents/Code/Metaserve/MediaWiki/test.cookie"


class ApiRequest:
    """
    Encapsulates the HTTP request to MediaWiki, managing cookies and
    handling the creation of the necessary URLs.
    """

    def _initCookieJar(self):
        """
        The LWPCookieJar class saves cookies in a format compatible with
        libwww-perl, which looks like this:

        #LWP-Cookies-2.0
        Set-Cookie3: wikidb_profwiki_Token=8ade58c0ee4b60180ab7214a93403554;
path="/"; domain="127.0.0.1"; path_spec; expires="2007-09-08 22:36:14Z";
version=0
        Set-Cookie3: wikidb_profwiki_UserID=3;
path="/"; domain="127.0.0.1"; path_spec; expires="2007-09-08 22:36:14Z";
version=0
        Set-Cookie3: wikidb_profwiki_UserName=Mchoate;
path="/"; domain="127.0.0.1"; path_spec; expires="2007-09-08 22:36:14Z";
version=0

        """
        cj = cookielib.LWPCookieJar()
        # If the cookie file exists, then load the cookie into the cookie jar.
        if os.path.exists(COOKIEFILE):
            cj.load(COOKIEFILE)
        # Create an opened for urllib2. This means that the cookie jar
        # will be used by urllib2 when making HTTP requests.
        opener = urllib2.build_opener(urllib2.HTTPCookieProcessor(cj))
        urllib2.install_opener(opener)
        return cj

    def _saveCookieJar(self,cj):
        cj.save(COOKIEFILE)


    def doHelp(self, format="xml"):
        args={"action": "help",
            "format": format}
        f = self.execute(args)
        return f

    def doLogin(self, name, password, domain="", format="xml"):
        """
        The login action is used to login. If successful, a cookie
        is set, and an authentication token is returned.
```

```
    Example:

      api.php?action=login&lgname=user&lgpassword=password
    """
    args={
        "action"    : "login",
        "format"    : format,
        "lgname"    : name,
        "lgpassword": password,
    }
    # The domain is optional
    if domain:
        args.update({"lgdomain":domain})

    # MediaWiki returns an XML document with a blank line at
    # the top, which causes an error while parsing. The
    # following code strips whitespace at the front and
    # back of the XML document and returns a string.
    s = self.execute(args).read().strip()

    # ElementTree expects a file-like object,
    # so one is created for it.
    f = StringIO.StringIO(s)
    root = xml.etree.ElementTree.parse(f).getroot()

    # The root element is the <api> element.
    login = root.find("login")

    # The <login> element has an attribute 'result'
    # that returns 'Success' is the login was successful
    test = login.attrib["result"]
    if test == "Success":
        return True
    else:
        return False


def doOpenSearch(self, search="", format="xml"):
    args={
        "action"    : "search",
        "format"    : format
    }
    f = self.execute(args)

def doFeedWatchList(self, feedformat="rss"):
    args={
        "action"    : "feedwatchlist",
        "feedformat": feedformat,
    }
    f = self.execute(args)
    return f
```

```
    def doQuery(self, **args):
        return self.execute(args)

    def doTitlesQuery(self, titles="Main Page", prop="info", meta="siteinfo", for-
mat="xml"):
        args={
        "action": "query",
        "titles": titles,
        "prop": prop,
        "meta": meta,
        "format": format
        }
        f = self.execute(args)
        return f


    def doTitlesQueryNoMeta(self, titles="Main Page", prop="info", format="xml"):
        args={
        "action": "query",
        "titles": titles,
        "prop": prop,
        "format": format
        }
        f = self.execute(args)
        return f


    def doSimpleTitlesQuery(self, titles="Main Page", format="xml"):
        args={
        "action": "query",
        "titles": titles,
        "format": format
        }
        f = self.execute(args)
        return f

    def doTitlesQuery2(self, titles="Main Page",
rvprop="timestamp|user|comment", rvlimit="50", rvdir="forward", format="xml"):
        args={
        "action": "query",
        "titles": titles,
        "prop": "revisions",
        "rvprop": rvprop, #timestamp|user|comment|content
        "rvlimit": rvlimit,
        #"rvstartid": "77",
        #"rvendid": "200",
        #"rvstart": rvstart, #timestamp
        #"rvend": rvend, #timestamp
        "rvdir": rvdir, #newer|older
        "format": format
        }
        f = self.execute(args)
        return f
```

```python
    def doTitlesQuery3(self, titles="Main Page",
rvprop="timestamp|user|comment", rvlimit="50", rvdir="older", format="xml"):
        args={
        "action": "query",
        "titles": titles,
        "prop": "revisions",
        "rvprop": rvprop, #timestamp|user|comment|content
        "rvlimit": rvlimit,
        "rvstartid": "77",
        "rvendid": "150",
        #"rvstart": rvstart, #timestamp
        #"rvend": rvend, #timestamp
        "rvdir": rvdir, #newer|older
        "format": format
        }
        f = self.execute(args)
        return f

    def doGeneratorQuery2(self, list_="allpages",
apfrom="aardvark", apnamespace="0", apfilterredir="all", aplimit="10",
apprefix="",rvprop="timestamp|user|comment", format="xml"):
        args={
            "action": "query",
            "generator": list_,
            "prop": "revisions",
            "rvprop": rvprop, #timestamp|user|comment|content
            "apfrom":apfrom,
            "apnamespace":apnamespace,
            "apfilterredir": apfilterredir,
            "aplimit": aplimit,
            "apprefix": apprefix,
            "format": format
        }
        f = self.execute(args)
        return f

    def doGeneratorQuery(self, list, format, **args):
        args.update({
        "action": "query",
        "generator": list,
        "format": format}
        )
        f = self.execute(args)
        return f

    def doListQuery(self, list, format, **args):
        args.update({
        "action": "query",
        "list": list,
        "format": format}
        )
        f = self.execute(args)
        return f
```

```python
    def doListAllpagesQuery(self, apfrom="aardvark", apnamespace="0",
apfilterredir="all", aplimit="10", apprefix="", format="xml"):
        args={
        "action":"query",
        "list": "allpages",
        "apfrom":apfrom,
        "apnamespace":apnamespace,
        "apfilterredir": apfilterredir,
        "aplimit": aplimit,
        "apprefix": apprefix,
        "prop":"revisions",
        "rvprop":"timestamp|user|comment",
        "format":format
        }
        f = self.execute(args)
        return f

    def doSimpleListAllpagesQuery(self, apfrom="A", apnamespace="0",
apfilterredir="all", aplimit="10", apprefix="M", format="xml"):
        args={
        "action":"query",
        "list": "allpages",
        "apfrom":apfrom,
        "apnamespace":apnamespace,
        "apfilterredir": apfilterredir,
        "aplimit": aplimit,
        "apprefix": apprefix,
        #"prop":"revisions",# doesn't do anything for the list
        #"rvprop":"timestamp|user|comment",
        "format":format
        }
        f = self.execute(args)
        return f

    def doListLogeventsQuery(self, **args):
        args.update({
        "action":"query",
        "list": "logevents",
        })
        f = self.execute(args)
        return f

    def doListWatchlistQuery(self, **args):
        args.update({
        "action":"query",
        "list": "watchlist",
        })
        f = self.execute(args)
        return f

    def doListRecentchangesQuery(self, **args):
        args.update({
        "action":"query",
        "list": "recentchanges",
```

```
        })
        f = self.execute(args)
        return f

    def doListBacklinksQuery(self, **args):
        args.update({
        "action":"query",
        "list": "backlinks",
        })
        f = self.execute(args)
        return f

    def doListEmbeddedinQuery(self, **args):
        args.update({
        "action":"query",
        "list": "embeddedin",
        })
        f = self.execute(args)
        return f

    def doListImagelinksQuery(self, **args):
        args.update({
        "action":"query",
        "list": "imagelinks",
        })
        f = self.execute(args)
        return f

    def doListUsercontribsQuery(self, **args):
        args.update({
        "action":"query",
        "list": "usercontribs",
        })
        f = self.execute(args)
        return f

    def execute(self, args):
        """
        This is a generate method called by the convenience methods.
        The request takes place in three stages. First, the cookie jar
        is initialized and the cookie file is loaded if it already exists. Then,
        the dictionary "args" is urlencoded and urllib2 generates the HTTP request.
        The result of the request is returned as a file-like object. Once it is
        received, the cookie data is saved so that it will be available for the
        next request, and the data is returned to the calling method.
        """
        cj = self._initCookieJar()
        req = urllib2.Request(QUERY_URL, urllib.urlencode(args), HEADERS)
        f = urllib2.urlopen(req)
        self._saveCookieJar(cj)
        return f


if __name__ == '__main__':
```

```
# Test methods
api = ApiRequest()
f = api.doHelp()

if api.doLogin("Mchoate", "connor"):
    print "Login was successful.\n\n"
else:
    print "Login failed.\n\n"
print "--------------------------------------\n"

  f = api.doTitlesQuery(titles="Main Page", prop="info", meta="siteinfo", for-
mat="xml")

  f = api.doTitlesQueryNoMeta(titles="Main Page", prop="info", format="xml")

  f = api.doTitlesQueryNoMeta(titles="Main Page", prop="revisions", format="xml")

  f = api.doSimpleTitlesQuery(titles="Main Page", format="xml")

  f = api.doTitlesQuery2(titles="Main Page", rvprop="timestamp|user|comment",
rvlimit="10",rvdir="older", format="xml")

  f = api.doTitlesQuery3(titles="Main Page", rvprop="timestamp|user|comment",
rvlimit="10",rvdir="older", format="xml")

  f = api.doTitlesQuery3(titles="Main Page", rvprop="timestamp|user|comment",
rvlimit="10",rvdir="newer", format="xml")

  f = api.doGeneratorQuery2(list_="allpages", rvprop="timestamp|user|comment",
format="xml")

  f = api.doListAllpagesQuery()

  f = api.doSimpleListAllpagesQuery()

  f = api.doListQuery("allpages", "xml")

  f = api.doGeneratorQuery("allpages", "xml")

  f = api.doGeneratorQuery("allpages", "xml", prop="revisions")
```

Summary

In this chapter, you learned how to configure and run sample scripts from the pywikipedia bot, as well as how to interact with the new MediaWiki API using Python. These tools can be used to automate certain administrative tasks and can save administrators a significant amount of time. Eventually, the full MediaWiki API will make it possible to create robust client applications for MediaWiki.

In the next chapter, you will learn about site maintenance and administration of your wiki, including performance management through caching.

11

Wiki Performance

This chapter takes a look at how to performance-tune MediaWiki sites. Because of Wikipedia's success, you could consider it to be a worst-case scenario in terms of performance management. It is fairly safe to say that most other installations will have much less traffic and be much less complex than the one in place for Wikipedia, but it's nice to know that there's no doubt that MediaWiki can scale.

When MediaWiki receives a request for a page, it performs a number of tasks — from ensuring that the user requesting the page is allowed to see it to converting wikitext to HTML, and then generating the page itself, delivering the appropriate layout based upon the preferences of the user. As programmers are wont to say: this is not a trivial task. Consider the fact that Wikipedia is reportedly the eighth most visited website in the world and one can see that for the developers of MediaWiki, performance is an important issue.

A website lives in a complex environment and numerous factors influence a site's performance characteristics. From a user's perspective, performance is simply a measure of how long it takes for a page to load after the user has clicked a link to that page. When a user clicks on a link, a request is sent to the host server in the form of an HTTP header, a simple string of text that looks like this:

```
GET /mysql/index.php/Main_Page HTTP/1.1
Host: 127.0.0.1
User-Agent: Mozilla/5.0 (Macintosh; U; Intel Mac OS X; en-US; rv:1.8.1.6)
    Gecko/200707250 Firefox/2.0.0.6
Accept: text/xml,application/xml,application/xhtml+xml,text/html;q=0.9,text/
    plain;q=0.8,image/png,*/*;q=0.5
Accept-Language: en-us,en;q=0.5
Accept-Encoding: gzip,deflate
Accept-Charset: ISO-8859-1,utf-8;q=0.7,*;q=0.7
Keep-Alive: 300
Connection: keep-alive
```

This request has to find the host server and then travel through a series of networks to get there, where the server gets the request and returns a new header, followed by the content of the page. This round-trip is made in a matter of seconds and appears almost instantaneous to the user when everything goes well. Of course, things never go well all the time, and many factors can influence the time it takes for the request/response cycle to complete.

Factors that affect a site's performance include the amount of bandwidth available to the user whose computer is making the request; how far away the server is from the computer making the request; general network congestion, which can slow down the trip to and from the host server; and the bandwidth available to the server.

On the server itself, performance factors include the size of the webpages, the speed of the microprocessor and the amount of RAM available to it, how long it takes to read data from hard drives or to query the database, as well as internal network traffic. Finally, the software used to run the site, obviously, is a factor in a site's performance. Because of all the factors that contribute to a site's perceived performance, optimizing performance can be a complex activity.

Wikipedia Architecture

Fortunately, the developers of MediaWiki have been very open about the kind of hardware they have in place, as well as how they have configured it. Information about Wikipedia's installation can be found at `http://meta.wikimedia.org/wiki/Wikimedia_servers`.

MediaWiki uses a variety of strategies to manage the load on their servers and to optimize their performance. The following list outlines their basic architecture:

- ❑ **Load balancing:** Round-robin DNS routes requests to multiple Squid servers.

- ❑ **Squid:** Squid is a caching proxy server based on the Harvest Cache Daemon developed in the early 1990s. Originally funded by an NFS grant, Squid is now developed by volunteers. It sits between the user making the request and the Apache Web server, and performs two tasks. First, it caches frequently requested content so that when it is requested, the Squid server handles the request instead of passing the request on to Apache. This reduces the load on the Apache servers.
  Second, Squid can be used to intelligently map incoming requests to Apache servers in a way that distributes the request loads to different machines. Running a proxy server is a complex task that if not done correctly can leave a site open to security vulnerabilities. MediaWiki supports Squid, but you won't learn about it in any detail here, as that is a subject beyond the scope of this book. In fact, only the most active wikis would need something like Squid. The vast majority will find Memcached and other caching strategies more than adequate. To learn more about Squid, visit `www.squid-cache.org`.

- ❑ **Memcached:** Memcached was developed by Danga Interactive for `LiveJournal.com`, and it is known as a distributed memory object caching system. In other words, it keeps webpages cached in memory so that when they are requested, they can be sent back directly to the client and not read off a hard drive or regenerated by a PHP script.

- ❑ **Apache/PHP:** The PHP scripts are compiled into bytecode and then executed. In the default PHP installation, the scripts are compiled every time they are requested. One way to improve performance is to cache the bytecode that is produced by the scripts so that it isn't regenerated every time. MediaWiki supports three different products that do this: Alternative PHP Cache (APC), eAccelerate, and Turck MMCache.

❑ **Relational Databases:** These are database clusters in a master/slave configuration. In a typical configuration, the "master" database is the only database that can be written to, and one or more "slaves" are used for all "read" requests. The master then synchronizes the new data with the data in the slaves. (Database load balancer: LoadBalancer.php)

❑ **Full-text search (Lucene):** In a default installation, MediaWiki uses the full-text indexing capabilities of either MySQL or Postgres relational databases, but because these are relational databases and are not designed from the ground up for full-text searches, their performance degrades as the size of the full-text database grows, as well as when the number of searches increases. As a consequence, Wikipedia uses Lucene, which is a full-text search engine that's part of the Apache Foundation family of open-source projects.

The Wikipedia installation uses all of these features to one degree or another to deliver Wikipedia content to the world. Unfortunately, a detailed discussion of proxy servers, database architecture, and the Lucene search engine are beyond the scope of this book (and are worthy of entire books themselves, of which there are many).

This chapter focuses on the most commonly used performance-enhancing techniques and describes how to configure MediaWiki's cache. The chapter concludes with information about how to backup and restore your wiki.

Caching

MediaWiki provides a flexible caching mechanism and can implement caching in a number of ways.

The PHP Memcached client script is included in the MediaWiki distribution, and this forms the basic approach used by MediaWiki. Wikipedia and related sites use Memcached, and this is what they recommend. However, for single-server installations, Memcached can be overkill because it runs in a separate process and needs to be monitored. In those instances, MediaWiki can use one of several other caching mechanisms, including APC, eAccelerator, or Turck MMCache.

These other methods are subclasses of the `BagOStuff` class, which is defined in `BagOStuff.php`. These subclasses adopt the same interface as the Memcached PHP client, so the MediaWiki code is the same regardless of which caching mechanism you decide to use — the only difference is whether the `memcached` object is used, or one of the `BagOStuff` variants.

MediaWiki can cache HTML files on the file system, or it can cache serialized PHP objects in a database (or dbm file).

Purging the Cache

One of the most common sources of problems for new MediaWiki developers is the cache. Typically, a developer makes a change to some code and then goes to view it in the browser and doesn't see the changes just made. Whenever something is not doing what it is supposed to do, it's a good idea to suspect a cache problem. Developers have two caches to worry about: the browser cache and the MediaWiki cache.

To purge the browser cache, do the following:

❑ **IE:** Press Ctrl+F5, or press Control and then click the Reload button.

❑ **Mozilla:** Press Ctrl+F5 (Command+F5 on a Macintosh), or press the Ctrl key and click the Reload button.

❑ **Safari:** Press Command+Shift+R, or press the Command key and click the Reload button.

To purge the MediaWiki cache, add the purge action to the end of the URL of a file:

```
/wiki/index.php/Main_Page?action=purge
```

You can also purge all caches, both browser caches and server-side caches, by setting the value of $wgCacheEpoch in LocalSettings.php to the current date, as illustrated in the following example:

```
/**
 * Set this to current time to invalidate all prior cached pages. Affects both
 * client- and server-side caching.
 * You can get the current date on your server by using the command:
 *    date +%Y%m%d%H%M%S
 */
$wgCacheEpoch = '20070822000000';
```

Cache Types

You just learned there are two caches, a browser cache and the MediaWiki cache. That is only partly true. MediaWiki has an aggressive and far-reaching caching strategy embedded in the application and actually has several different kinds of caches caching different things.

In addition to the browser cache, there is a file cache and a collection of object caches.

Browser Cache

The HTTP specification defines HTTP headers that are to be used by clients (browsers) to manage their cache. In order to enable client-side caching, the $wgCachePages variable must be set to true (the default):

```
# Client-side caching:

/** Allow client-side caching of pages */
$wgCachePages        = true;
```

In order to understand how this changes MediaWiki's behavior, it's helpful to understand how HTTP 1.1 handles caching. What follows is a brief, and not complete, description of the caching process used by browsers so that you will understand how MediaWiki changes response headers when this value is set.

When a browser requests a page, the server's response includes HTTP headers, as well as the page that was requested. The HTTP headers that are sent back to the browser, called the *response headers*, can contain information that the browser uses to cache the page.

The Expires header is optional; it tells the browser explicitly when to stop caching a page. When a browser makes a request, it first checks to see whether the page is in the cache and if it has an expiration date. If it has expired, then it will check to see whether the page has been modified since the last download. If it has been modified, then it will download a new copy; otherwise, it displays the page in the cache. The following example shows the Expires header:

```
Expires: Thu, 23 Aug 2007 14:19:41 GMT
```

The next two response headers are called *validators* because they are used to determine whether a page has changed and needs to be retrieved from the server, rather than the cache. These response headers are Last-Modified and Etag (shown here):

```
Last-Modified: Wed, 30 May 2007 01:01:53 GMT
Etag: "655194-9f2f-465ccd01"
```

When a browser caches a page, it stores this information along with it. The next time it requests the same page, it includes the following request headers, which are used to validate the cache based on the Last-Modified time or the Etag:

```
If-Modified-Since: Wed, 30 May 2007 01:01:53 GMT
If-None-Match: "655194-9f2f-465ccd01"
```

In the preceding example, these headers tell the server that if the page has been modified since May 30, 2007 at 1:01:53 GMT, or if the Etag as generated by the server does not match the Etag sent in the If-None-Match header, then a new instance of the page should be sent. Otherwise, it returns a header with the following message:

```
HTTP/1.x 304 Not Modified
```

ETags (or *entity tags*) were introduced in the HTTP 1.1, and they are used in cache management. They are a unique value (or hash) normally created using a file's inode, size, and last modified time. They can be customized using the FileEtag directive (see the Apache HTTPD documentation for more information); and in MediaWiki, the MediaWiki application creates the Etag, using its own formula.

When $wgCachePages is set to True, ETags are used in non-dynamically generated pages, which allows the client to cache those files. If the $wgUseETag variable is set to True in LocalSettings.php, then an ETag is used on dynamically generated pages, too.

In the following request/response example, MediaWiki has been configured to cache files, but has not been configured to use ETags. This is a request for a static file, called SampleImageUpload.png:

```
GET /mysql/images/b/b5/SampleImageUpload.png HTTP/1.1
Host: 127.0.0.1
User-Agent: Mozilla/5.0 (Macintosh; U; Intel Mac OS X; en-US; rv:1.8.1.6)
    Gecko/20070725 Firefox/2.0.0.6
Accept: image/png,*/*;q=0.5
Accept-Language: en-us,en;q=0.5
Accept-Encoding: gzip,deflate
Accept-Charset: ISO-8859-1,utf-8;q=0.7,*;q=0.7
Keep-Alive: 300
Connection: keep-alive
Referer: http://127.0.0.1/mysql/index.php/Image_links
```

Despite the fact that MediaWiki has not been configured to use ETags, the response returns an ETag. That's because ETags are generated and sent automatically for static pages. At the most basic level, a file is cached by a browser as long as the Last-Modified value does not change. When this page is requested again, the browser will send an `If-Modified-Since` request header to the server. If the file has been modified since the modification in the cache, then a new file will be sent:

```
HTTP/1.x 200 OK
Date: Wed, 22 Aug 2007 23:10:01 GMT
Server: Apache/1.3.33 (Darwin) PHP/5.2.0
Last-Modified: Wed, 30 May 2007 01:01:53 GMT
Etag: "655194-9f2f-465ccd01"
Accept-Ranges: bytes
Content-Length: 40751
Keep-Alive: timeout=15, max=98
Connection: Keep-Alive
Content-Type: image/png
```

In this example, MediaWiki has been configured to cache pages, as well as to use ETags. Because ETags are automatic on static files, our expectation is that ETags will not be used on dynamic pages, such as articles, as well. This is a new page that the browser has not visited before, so the request headers are standard:

```
http://127.0.0.1/mysql/index.php/A_new_page

GET /mysql/index.php/A_new_page HTTP/1.1
Host: 127.0.0.1
User-Agent: Mozilla/5.0 (Macintosh; U; Intel Mac OS X; en-US; rv:1.8.1.6)
    Gecko/20070725 Firefox/2.0.0.6
Accept: text/xml,application/xml,application/xhtml+xml,text/html;q=0.9,text/
    plain;q=0.8,image/png,*/*;q=0.5
Accept-Language: en-us,en;q=0.5
Accept-Encoding: gzip,deflate
Accept-Charset: ISO-8859-1,utf-8;q=0.7,*;q=0.7
Keep-Alive: 300
Connection: keep-alive
Referer: http://127.0.0.1/mysql/index.php/Main_Page
```

When the response headers are returned, however, you see several new header tags, including `Etag`, `Expires`, `Cache-Control`, in addition to the familiar `Last-Modified`:

```
HTTP/1.x 200 OK
Date: Wed, 22 Aug 2007 23:11:44 GMT
Server: Apache/1.3.33 (Darwin) PHP/5.2.0
X-Powered-By: PHP/5.2.0
Content-Language: en
Etag: W/"wikidb-profwiki_:pcache:idhash:28-0!1!0!!en!2--20070604224328"
Vary: Accept-Encoding,Cookie
Expires: Thu, 01 Jan 1970 00:00:00 GMT
Cache-Control: private, must-revalidate, max-age=0
Last-Modified: Wed, 22 Aug 2007 23:11:18 GMT
Keep-Alive: timeout=15, max=98
Connection: Keep-Alive
Transfer-Encoding: chunked
Content-Type: text/html; charset=UTF-8
```

The two items we are most concerned with now are the `Etag` and `Cache-Control` response headers. Earlier, this section mentioned the `Last-Modified` and `If-Modified-Since` headers. These are examples of validators. When HTTP 1.1 was released, it contained a specification for a new kind of validator called an ETag, which is what we see in this example:

```
Etag: W/"wikidb-profwiki_:pcache:idhash:28-0!1!0!!en!2--20070604224328"
Cache-Control: private, must-revalidate, max-age=0
```

It works like this: When the browser requests a file, it is sent back with an ETag, which is stored in the cache along with the file. The `Cache-Control` header says `must-revalidate`, which means that it must check the ETag stored in the cache with the new ETag that is sent. If they are the same, then the file hasn't changed and the complete file is transferred. If it has not changed, then HTTP returns with a "304 Not Modified" response.

In the following example, the same page is requested again. The page has already been requested once, so it is in the browser cache. Because caching has been enabled, the `If-Modified-Since` header, plus a new one, `If-None-Match`, which you can see in the following example, references the ETag of the file that was just received:

```
GET /mysql/index.php/A_new_page HTTP/1.1
Host: 127.0.0.1
User-Agent: Mozilla/5.0 (Macintosh; U; Intel Mac OS X; en-US; rv:1.8.1.6)
    Gecko/20070725 Firefox/2.0.0.6
Accept: text/xml,application/xml,application/xhtml+xml,text/html;q=0.9,text/
    plain;q=0.8,image/png,*/*;q=0.5
Accept-Language: en-us,en;q=0.5
Accept-Encoding: gzip,deflate
Accept-Charset: ISO-8859-1,utf-8;q=0.7,*;q=0.7
Keep-Alive: 300
Connection: keep-alive
Referer: http://127.0.0.1/mysql/index.php/Main_Page
If-Modified-Since: Wed, 22 Aug 2007 23:11:18 GMT
If-None-Match: W/"wikidb-profwiki_:pcache:idhash:28-0!1!0!!en!2--20070604224328"
Cache-Control: max-age=0
```

Compare the `If-None-Match` value in the request header with the `Etag` value in the previous response header — they are both the same. This means the file hasn't changed, so the HTTP server dutifully sends back the appropriate HTTP response:

```
HTTP/1.x 304 Not Modified
Date: Wed, 22 Aug 2007 23:12:52 GMT
Server: Apache/1.3.33 (Darwin) PHP/5.2.0
Connection: Keep-Alive
Keep-Alive: timeout=15, max=93
Etag: W/"wikidb-profwiki_:pcache:idhash:28-0!1!0!!en!2--20070604224328"
Expires: Thu, 01 Jan 1970 00:00:00 GMT
Cache-Control: private, must-revalidate, max-age=0
Vary: Accept-Encoding, Cookie
```

File Cache

The file cache is used only for non-logged in users. It works by caching the contents of the HTML file that MediaWiki produces in response to a request. In order for it to work, you must set the $wgUseFileCache variable to `true` in `LocalSettings.php`, and set the $wgShowIPinHeader variable to `false`. Setting the

$wgFileCacheDirectory setting is optional; if it is not set, then MediaWiki will use the default value of {$wgUploadDirectory}/cache. When you do configure the cache directory yourself, you must include a full path to the directory, and you must ensure that the directory is writeable by the Web server:

```
$wgUseFileCache = true;
$wgFileCacheDirectory = "/tmp/yourcache";
// Setting $wgShowIPinHeader to false removes the
// personal tool links at the top of the page for
// anonymous users, who are identified by their
// IP address. This improves caching by showing
// all anonymous users the same page.
$wgShowIPinHeader = false;
```

You can also configure MediaWiki to compress the cached files in order to save bandwidth when they are requested. If you do this, you need to disable the ob_gzhandler in LocalSettings.php, like so:

```
if ( $wgCommandLineMode ) {
 if ( isset( $_SERVER ) && array_key_exists( 'REQUEST_METHOD', $_SERVER ) ) {
        die( "This script must be run from the command line\n" );
 }
} elseif ( empty( $wgNoOutputBuffer ) ) {
 ## I have commented out the following line to disable it
 #if( !ini_get( 'zlib.output_compression' ) ) @ob_start( 'ob_gzhandler' );
}
$wgUseGzip = false;
```

More information about the file cache can be found at http://meta.wikimedia.org/wiki/Help:File_cache.

Memcached

Memcached is a distributed object store that you can run on any number of servers. The primary benefit of being distributed is that it is highly scalable. If you need more caching, just add another memcached server. You do incur some additional overhead because the cached data is retrieved through a TCP/IP connection, but the benefit of having multiple servers, and the ability to share things such as session data across servers, more than makes up for this deficit.

MediaWiki comes with a Memcached client. It is the Memcached client that saves objects into the store and retrieves them using a unique key. Internally, the client knows which of the available memcached servers a given object is stored in, so it can request it directly.

Benefits

Memcached allows you to run multiple servers. Because the Memcached client manages the delegation of keys, it knows on which of the available Memcached servers a given object is stored. This makes it possible to cache session data across multiple Web servers, something that is not possible with APC and similar tools.

Installing

You can install Memcached by going to www.danga.com/memcached/download.bml, or through fink (Macintosh) or yum (Linux). A Windows port of Memcached is available at http://jehiah.cz/

projects/memcached-win32/, which is linked to from the danga.com website. I have not used this port, however, and cannot speak to how well it works with MediaWiki.

If you are going to compile Memcached, you need to make sure that PHP is compiled with --enable-sockets, and that you have a current copy of the libevent library (www.monkey.org/provos/libevent/). Linux users may also want the epoll-rt patch for the Linux kernel, available from www.xmailserver .org/linux-patches/nio-improve.html.

Configuring MediaWiki

You must tell MediaWiki what to cache, as well as how to cache it. All of this is configured in LocalSettings.php:

```
/**
 * Object cache settings
 * See Defines.php for types
 */
$wgMainCacheType    = CACHE_NONE;
$wgMessageCacheType = CACHE_ANYTHING;
$wgParserCacheType  = CACHE_ANYTHING;
```

The cache types, defined in Defines.php, are as follows:

```
/**#@+
 * Cache type
 */
define( 'CACHE_ANYTHING', -1 );   // Use anything, as long as it works
define( 'CACHE_NONE', 0 );        // Do not cache
define( 'CACHE_DB', 1 );          // Store cache objects in the DB
define( 'CACHE_MEMCACHED', 2 );   // MemCached, must specify servers in
                                  // $wgMemCacheServers
define( 'CACHE_ACCEL', 3 );       // APC, eAccelerator or Turck, whichever is
                                  //available
define( 'CACHE_DBA', 4 );         // Use PHP's DBA extension to store in a DBM-style
                                  //database
/**#@-*/
```

You will see a reference to $wgUseMemCached in DefaultSettings.php, but this has been deprecated, and you should use $wgMainCacheType instead:

```
$wgMainCacheType = CACHE_MEMCACHED;
```

The following are additional configuration items for Memcached:

```
$wgParserCacheExpireTime = 86400;
$wgSessionsInMemcached = false;
$wgLinkCacheMemcached = false; # Not fully tested

/**
 * Memcached-specific settings
 * See docs/memcached.txt
 */
$wgMemCachedDebug    = false; # Will be set to false in Setup.php,
  if the server isn't working
```

```
$wgMemCachedServers = array( '127.0.0.1:11000' );
$wgMemCachedPersistent = false;
```

Configuring and Running Memcached

Because memcached runs as a different process from your Web server, it's possible for the Memcached server to go down while your Apache/PHP server is still running. You wiki will not crash if this happens, but it will slow down considerably, even slower than it was before caching any data.

There are two ways to identify servers. The first simply lists the IP address and the port on which Memcached will be listening:

```
$wgMemCachedServers = array( "127.0.0.1:11000" );
```

The second way passes an array with two items, the IP/port plus a number identifying how much memory to allocate for the server. These two different formats can be combined when configuring memcached in LocalSettings.php, as in the following example (from memcached.txt in the MediaWiki distribution):

```
$wgMemCachedServers = array(
    "127.0.0.1:11000", # one gig on this box
    array("192.168.0.1:11000", 2 ) # two gigs on the other box
  );
```

Memcached is launched from the command line. In the following example, Memcached is launched in daemon mode, using the IP 127.0.0.1, with the port 11000 and 64 MB of memory allocated to the cache:

```
memcached -d -l 127.0.0.1 -p 11000 -m 64
```

The most commonly used options are listed in the following table.

-l	Specifies the IP address from which the Memcached server can be accessed. If it is running on the same server as the Web server, then it should be 127.0.0.1, the loopback address.
-d	Runs Memcached in daemon mode.
-m	Sets the maximum amount of memory to be used for object caching. The default value is 64 megabytes.
-c	max simultaneous connections
-p	Specifies the default port on which the server will listen for connections. The default is 11211.
-M	Memcached keeps as many objects in memory as it has available. When a new object is added to it that would take up more memory than is available, it drops the oldest item. This disables the automatic removal of items in the cache when no more memory is available. Generally speaking, you should rely on the automatic removal of old items and not set this option.
-h	Shows the version of Memcached.
-v	Tells Memcached to be verbose in its output.

-vv	Tells Memcached to be extremely verbose.
-D	Sets the delimiter between prefixes and ids. The default is ":", which is what MediaWiki uses, so don't change it.

In addition to these, there are other, more obscure optimizations that can be made. For details, check the man page for Memcached.

Memcached stores objects in hash tables, so each object is assigned a unique key. The Memcached client generates the keys and uses the keys to determine the server on which the object is stored. It is helpful to know how the client generates the key in case you want to look it up in Memcached. MediaWiki creates the following caches when using Memcached:

❑ **User Cache:** The user cache stores an instance of the class User, which includes session data.

    ❑ key: $wgDBname:user:id:$sId

❑ **Newtalk:** This caches data that identifies a talk page as "new."

    ❑ key: $wgDBname:newtalk:ip:$ip

❑ **LinkCache:** Recall that articles are created in MediaWiki by creating a link to the article. If the article does not yet exist, when you follow the link you are taken to the edit page so that you can create it. A link to a page that does not exist looks different than a link to a page that does exist. Depending on the configuration, purple links link to existing pages and red links link to pages that have not been created. The LinkCache class keeps track of article titles, and whether the articles exist yet, which is used to create the right kind of link when wikitext is being parsed.

    ❑ key: $wgDBname:lc:title:$title

❑ **MediaWiki namespace:** The MediaWiki namespace is used for storing system messages so that they can be appropriately localized. If Memcached is configured to cache messages, then this key is used.

    ❑ key: $wgDBname:messages

❑ **Watchlist:** Caches the user's watchlist

    ❑ key: $wgDBname:watchlist:id:$userID

❑ **IP blocks:** IP blocks are lists of IP addresses that have been blocked from accessing the wiki. Looking up IP addresses individually would use too many resources, so they can be cached.

    ❑ key: $wgDBname:ipblocks

Alternative PHP Cache (APC)

Like Memcached, Alternative PHP Cache (APC) caches PHP objects in memory. The primary distinction is that Memcached is a distributed object store, whereas APC is local to the machine. This means that if you are running a single-server wiki, then APC is probably your best choice. In that context, APC outperforms Memcached because you make Memcached requests through TCP/IP, which is naturally slower than accessing the APC cache.

MediaWiki also supports eAccelerator and Turck MMCache, but this chapter does not cover them in detail. While Turck MMCache is still in use, the open-source project itself is no longer actively maintained. eAccelerator is based on Turck MMCache and is still an actively maintained project, but recent versions have had problems working with PHP. eAccelerator version 0.9.4 doesn't work with PHP 5.1. Version 0.9.5 does work with 5.1, but requires a patch to work with PHP 5.2 in order to avoid a segmentation fault. By all reports, version 0.9.5.1 appears to work fine. Because eAccelerator is finicky about which versions of PHP it runs on, this discussion focuses on Alternative PHP Cache. Not only is it actively maintained, but it works with a variety of versions of PHP so there does not seem to be a compelling reason not to use APC.

More information on the other alternatives can be found here:

- ❑ http://eaccelerator.net/
- ❑ http://turck-mmcache.sourceforge.net/index_old.html

Installing APC

APC is most easily installed using PECL:

```
$ pecl install AP
```

Windows users can download PECL binaries at www.php.net/downloads.php.

APC is a PHP extension, so the PHP.ini file needs to be configured properly before MediaWiki can use it. First, you should ensure that the extension path in PHP.ini is correct, and that APC has been installed in the extension directory, which is determined by PHP.ini:

```
;;;;;;;;;;;;;;;;;;;;;;;;;;
; Paths and Directories ;
;;;;;;;;;;;;;;;;;;;;;;;;;;


; Directory in which the loadable extensions (modules) reside.
extension_dir = "/usr/local/php5/lib/php/extensions/no-debug-non-zts-20060613/"
```

Once the extensions directory is verified, you need to add the apc.so extension (or apc.dl if you are a Windows user) to PHP.ini, as shown in the following example:

```
;;;;;;;;;;;;;;;;;;;;;;;;
; Dynamic Extensions ;
;;;;;;;;;;;;;;;;;;;;;;;;
;
; If you wish to have an extension loaded automatically, use the following
; syntax:
;
;    extension=modulename.extension
;
; For example, on Windows:
;
;    extension=msql.dll
;
```

```
;  ... or under UNIX:
;
;    extension=msql.so
;
; Note that it should be the name of the module only; no directory information
; needs to go here.  Specify the location of the extension with the
; extension_dir directive above.

extension=apc.so
```

Configuring MediaWiki

The following items need to be configured in LocalSettings.php. The CACHE_ACCEL global tells MediaWiki to use either APC, eAccelerator, or MMTurck Cache, depending on which cache is installed in PHP:

```
$wgMainCacheType = CACHE_ACCEL;
$wgMessageCacheType = CACHE_ ACCEL;
$wgParserCacheType = CACHE_ACCEL G;
```

The following value is set in terms of seconds, and determines how long the parsed output should be cached:

```
$wgParserCacheExpireTime = 86400;
```

Monitoring APC

When you downloaded APC, the distribution should have included a file called apc.php. Copy this file into the main directory of your MediaWiki installation and configure it. At the very least, you need to assign a new admin password — as long as it is "password," the apc.php script will not return any information. The other configuration options are, as they should be, optional:

```
////////// BEGIN OF DEFAULT CONFIG AREA ///////////////////////////////////////
      ////////////////////////

defaults('USE_AUTHENTICATION',1);// Use (internal) authentication - best choice if
                                 // no other authentication is available
                                 // If set to 0:
                                 //   There will be no further authentication. You
                                 //   will have to handle this by yourself!
                                 // If set to 1:
                                 //   You need to change ADMIN_PASSWORD to make
                                 //   this work!
defaults('ADMIN_USERNAME','apc'); // Admin Username
defaults('ADMIN_PASSWORD','password'); // Admin Password - CHANGE THIS TO ENABLE!!!
//defaults('DATE_FORMAT', "d.m.Y H:i:s");     // German
defaults('DATE_FORMAT', 'Y/m/d H:i:s');     // US

defaults('GRAPH_SIZE',200);     // Image size
```

Save the changes you made, and then you can use apc.php to monitor caching (see Figure 11-1). This particular configuration is fine for testing, but you should probably not have this file exposed on a production server.

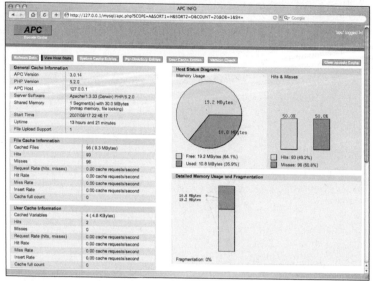

Figure 11-1: View the apc.php script to monitor APC's caching

Improving Performance

In addition to caching, there are several things wiki administrators can do to improve the overall performance of their wikis.

Serializing Messages

Message files are located in the Languages folder of your MediaWiki distribution. According to the MediaWiki developers, they decided that it is faster to load serialized message files from the file system than it is to load it from APC or Memcached. Therefore, they've provided a way to serialize all the message files in the serialized folder.

In order to do this, you need to have GNU `make` installed. Simply change directories into the serialized folder and type the following at the command line:

```
make
```

After running this on OS X, the serialized directory took up 19.8 MB of space.

Miser Mode

If true, `$wgMiserMode` disables database-intensive features. This includes reading special pages marked as expensive from the cache instead of regenerating them every time they are requested:

```
/** Disable database-intensive features */
$wgMiserMode = false;
$wgAllowSlowParserFunctions = false;
```

Figures 11-2 and 11-3 show the Special:Statistics page when marked as false and true, respectively.

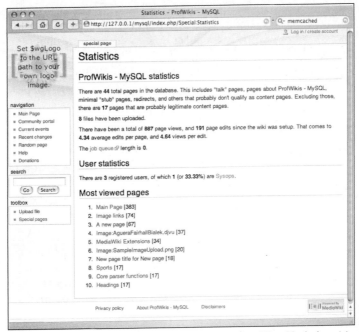

Figure 11-2: The Special:Statistics page when $wgMiserMode is set to false

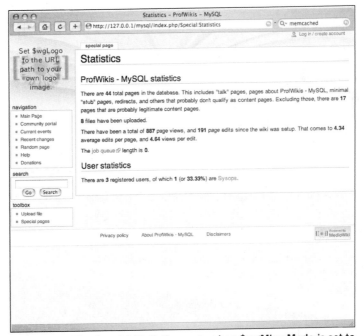

Figure 11-3: The Special:Statistics page when $wgMiserMode is set to true

Managing Spiders

One source of strain on any Web server is spiders. Spiders are software applications that crawl a site in order to make copies of the content on the site, or to index it for a search engine. In many cases you will be more than happy to have your site crawled, but there are also many spiders that you want to block as well.

Robots Exclusion Standard

The Robots Exclusion Standard (usually just referred to as robots.txt, in reference to the file that contains the exclusion rules) is supposed to provide Web servers a way to communicate with spiders and indicate to them what you want indexed. For a site run by MediaWiki, it is likely that you do want article pages indexed, but you may not want special pages indexed, or talk pages, and so on.

A good place to look for ideas and suggestions about what you want to do is http://meta.wikimedia .org/robots.txt.

The following excerpt of Wikimedia's robots.txt file shows you how to configure your server appropriately. Spiders are identified by their user-agent, which is information that is passed to the server from the HTTP request. The value for the user-agent is easily spoofed, so you cannot rely on it entirely. However, although there are some well-known spiders that you may not want indexing your site, you can generally rely on the user-agent identity reported.

The robots.txt file used by MediaWiki excludes some spiders because they are related to advertising, or because they otherwise misbehave and put too much a strain on the servers. In the next example, you will see how the robots.txt file excludes all spiders from user-agents that start with "Mediapartners-Google*":

```
# robots.txt for http://www.wikipedia.org/ and friends
#
# Please note: There are a lot of pages on this site, and there are
# some misbehaved spiders out there that go _way_ too fast. If you're
# irresponsible, your access to the site may be blocked.
#
# advertising-related bots:
User-agent: Mediapartners-Google*
Disallow: /


#
# Sorry, wget in its recursive mode is a frequent problem.
# Please read the man page and use it properly; there is a
# --wait option you can use to set the delay between hits,
# for instance.
#
User-agent: wget
Disallow: /


# Don't allow the wayback-maschine to index user-pages
#User-agent: ia_archiver
#Disallow: /wiki/User
#Disallow: /wiki/Benutzer
```

Wikipedia administrators have also decided to keep all spiders from indexing dynamically generated pages. While this isn't necessarily always the best thing to do, the logic is that because they are dynamically generated, the spiders' results will not always be accurate. Add to that the fact that dynamically generated pages are more expensive to produce in terms of server performance. Therefore, they concluded they would keep them from being indexed.

```
# Friendly, low-speed bots are welcome viewing article pages, but not
# dynamically-generated pages please.
#
# Inktomi's "Slurp" can read a minimum delay between hits; if your
# bot supports such a thing using the 'Crawl-delay' or another
# instruction, please let us know.
#
User-agent: *
Disallow: /w/
Disallow: /trap/
Disallow: /wiki/Special:Random
Disallow: /wiki/Special%3ARandom
Disallow: /wiki/Special:Search
Disallow: /wiki/Special%3ASearch
Disallow: /wiki/Spesial:Search
#ar
Disallow: /wiki/%D8%AE%D8%A7%D8%B5:Search
Disallow: /wiki/%D8%AE%D8%A7%D8%B5%3ASearch
## <snip>
## *at least* 1 second please. preferably more :D
## we're disabling this experimentally 11-09-2006
#Crawl-delay: 1
```

In addition to the `robots.txt` file, instructions for spiders can also be embedded in the metadata of a file. The following `meta` tag tells the spider not to index the file:

```
<meta name="robots" content="noindex">
```

If you want the file to be indexed, then use the following:

```
<meta name="robots" content="index">
```

In addition to indexing, you can tell the spider whether to follow links on the page, and attempt to spider those pages as well. (This is what crawling a site is: starting with one page, gathering all the links on that page, and then retrieving all the links on each of the pages linked to, and so on.) The `content` attribute in that case would be set to either follow or not follow. The index and follow values can also be combined, as shown here:

```
<meta name="robots" content="index,follow">
<meta name="robots" content="noindex,follow">
<meta name="robots" content="index,nofollow">
<meta name="robots" content="noindex,nofollow">
```

Finally, you can use two shortcuts that enable you to either both index and follow all links, or not index and follow links:

```
<meta name="robots" content="all">
<meta name="robots" content="none">
```

In order to generate these meta tags on MediaWiki pages, you need to configure MediaWiki to do so. You can tell MediaWiki which articles to index or not index by setting the $wgArticleRobotPolicies with an array of article titles, as shown in the following example:

```
$wgArticleRobotPolicies = array( 'Main Page' => 'noindex' );
```

You can also configure the indexing policy based on namespace. The following example causes a 'noindex' meta tag to be placed on all pages in the NS_TALK namespace:

```
$wgNamespaceRobotPolicies = array( NS_TALK => 'noindex' );
```

Setting the following variable in LocalSettings.php causes all external links in wikitext to be given the rel = "nofollow" attribute, which serves the same purpose as the metatags just described:

```
/**
 * If true, external URL links in wiki text will be given the
 * rel="nofollow" attribute as a hint to search engines that
 * they should not be followed for ranking purposes as they
 * are user-supplied and thus subject to spamming.
 */
$wgNoFollowLinks = true;
```

Setting this variable defines the namespaces that do not apply to the $wgNoFollowLinks variable:

```
/**
 * Namespaces in which $wgNoFollowLinks doesn't apply.
 * See Language.php for a list of namespaces.
 */
$wgNoFollowNsExceptions = array();
```

Google Sitemaps

Google sitemaps also provide information to the spider, telling it which pages to index. However, rather than being an exclusionary approach like robots.txt, it is an inclusionary approach. This means that the default answer is no; and unless a page is on the sitemap, it won't be spidered. Since Google first started using sitemaps, Yahoo! and Microsoft have signed on, and it is becoming something of a standard. You can read details about it at http://sitemaps.org/.

The maintenance script is called generateSitemap.php and when executed, produces the following output:

```
0 ()
        sitemap-wikidb-profwiki_-NS_0-0.xml.gz
1 (Talk)
        sitemap-wikidb-profwiki_-NS_1-0.xml.gz
6 (Image)
        sitemap-wikidb-profwiki_-NS_6-0.xml.gz
10 (Template)
        sitemap-wikidb-profwiki_-NS_10-0.xml.gz
14 (Category)
        sitemap-wikidb-profwiki_-NS_14-0.xml.gz
```

The output of `generateSitemap.php` is six files. One of the files is a sitemap index file that lists all the other files. It's named sitemap-index-{*database-name*}.xml, where *database-name* is the name of your wiki's database:

```
<?xml version="1.0" encoding="UTF-8"?>
<sitemapindex xmlns="http://www.google.com/schemas/sitemap/0.84">
 <sitemap>
        <loc>sitemap-wikidb-profwiki_-NS_0-0.xml.gz</loc>
        <lastmod>2007-08-22T20:10:21Z</lastmod>
 </sitemap>
 <sitemap>
        <loc>sitemap-wikidb-profwiki_-NS_1-0.xml.gz</loc>
        <lastmod>2007-08-22T20:10:21Z</lastmod>
 </sitemap>
 <sitemap>
        <loc>sitemap-wikidb-profwiki_-NS_6-0.xml.gz</loc>
        <lastmod>2007-08-22T20:10:21Z</lastmod>
 </sitemap>
 <sitemap>
        <loc>sitemap-wikidb-profwiki_-NS_10-0.xml.gz</loc>
        <lastmod>2007-08-22T20:10:21Z</lastmod>
 </sitemap>
 <sitemap>
        <loc>sitemap-wikidb-profwiki_-NS_14-0.xml.gz</loc>
        <lastmod>2007-08-22T20:10:21Z</lastmod>
 </sitemap>
</sitemapindex>
```

The remaining files are gzipped by default. The following is an excerpt from one of the files that shows the basic format of the output. One thing you should notice is that it uses `localhost` for the host, which is not what we want:

```
<?xml version="1.0" encoding="UTF-8"?>
<urlset xmlns="http://www.google.com/schemas/sitemap/0.84">
 <url>
        <loc>http://localhost/mysql/index.php/ASamplePage</loc>
        <lastmod>2007-07-12T19:30:33Z</lastmod>
        <priority>1.0</priority>
 </url>
 <url>
        <loc>http://localhost/mysql/index.php/A_new_page</loc>
        <lastmod>2007-06-04T22:43:28Z</lastmod>
        <priority>1.0</priority>
 </url>
</urlset>
```

Because this script is run on the command line, it has no way of knowing what the proper host name will be for spiders trying to access the wiki from elsewhere. To correct this, specify the host on the command line like so:

```
php generateSitemap.php choate.info
```

This will generate the following output:

```
?xml version="1.0" encoding="UTF-8"?>
<urlset xmlns="http://www.google.com/schemas/sitemap/0.84">
 <url>
        <loc>http://choate.info/mysql/index.php/ASamplePage</loc>
        <lastmod>2007-07-12T19:30:33Z</lastmod>
        <priority>1.0</priority>
 </url>
 <url>
        <loc>http://choate.info/mysql/index.php/A_new_page</loc>
        <lastmod>2007-06-04T22:43:28Z</lastmod>
        <priority>1.0</priority>
 </url>
</urlset>
```

For information about what options are available, enter the following command:

```
php generateSitemap.php --help
```

The output is as follows:

```
Usage: php generateSitemap.php [host] [options]
        host = hostname
        options:
                --help   show this message
                --fspath        The file system path to save to, e.g /tmp/sitemap/
                --path  The http path to use, e.g. /wiki
                --compress=[yes|no]     compress the sitemap files, default yes
```

The `--fspath` option specifies the directory in which the output should be saved. If it is not specified, then it defaults to the current directory.

The `--path` option specifies that path portion of the URL (the part after the domain, such as `/wiki`). In most cases, it can figure this out itself.

If `--compress=yes`, then the output will be compressed in gzip format (which also happens to be the default).

The sitemap files should be placed in the root directory of MediaWiki in order to be indexed. You can tell spiders where to find the sitemap by including it in `robots.txt`:

```
Sitemap: sitemap.xml
```

You can also submit the sitemap file directly to the individual search engines.

Maintenance Scripts

MediaWiki comes with a long list of maintenance scripts in the maintenance directory of the MediaWiki installation. Most of them are PHP scripts that are run from the command line. There are far too many to review all of them here, but there is one set of scripts that is important to cover: `dumpBackup.php` and `importDump.php`, both of which can be used to make backups of your wiki.

Configuration

You should first configure `AdminSettings.php` before running any maintenance scripts. It can be found in the base directory of your MediaWiki installation.

```php
<?php
/**
 * This file should be copied to AdminSettings.php, and modified
 * to reflect local settings. It is required for the maintenance
 * scripts which run on the command line, as an extra security
 * measure to allow using a separate user account with higher
 * privileges to do maintenance work.
 *
 * Developers: Do not check AdminSettings.php into Subversion
 *
 * @package MediaWiki
 */


/*
 * This data is used by all database maintenance scripts
 * (see directory maintenance/). The SQL user MUST BE
 * MANUALLY CREATED or set to an existing user with
 * necessary permissions.
 *
 * This is not to be confused with sysop accounts for the
 * wiki.
 */
$wgDBadminuser      = 'wikiadmin';
$wgDBadminpassword  = 'adminpass';
/*
 * Whether to enable the profileinfo.php script.
 */
$wgEnableProfileInfo = false;

?>
```

Backup

While you can perform backups of data in MySQL or Postgres, just as you would any other database, MediaWiki also provides an XML dump of the data in the database, which has the advantage of not containing any kind of user passwords or other sensitive data that a database dump would have. It also can be used to import into future versions of MediaWiki. While the database tables may change, the MediaWiki developers intend to support the XML format into the future.

The schema for the XML format can be found at www.mediawiki.org/xml/export-0.3.xsd, and this is the same format used by the Special:Export and Special:Import pages.

The `dumpBackup.php` script takes the following options:

```
This script dumps the wiki page database into an XML interchange wrapper
format for export or backup.

XML output is sent to stdout; progress reports are sent to stderr.
```

```
Usage: php dumpBackup.php <action> [<options>]
Actions:
  --full      Dump complete history of every page.
  --current   Includes only the latest revision of each page.
Options:
  --quiet     Don't dump status reports to stderr.
  --report=n  Report position and speed after every n pages processed.
              (Default: 100)
  --server=h  Force reading from MySQL server h
  --start=n   Start from page_id n
  --end=n     Stop before page_id n (exclusive)
  --skip-header Don't output the <mediawiki> header
  --skip-footer Don't output the </mediawiki> footer
  --stub      Don't perform old_text lookups; for 2-pass dump

Fancy stuff:
  --plugin=<class>[:<file>]   Load a dump plugin class
  --output=<type>:<file>      Begin a filtered output stream;
                              <type>s: file, gzip, bzip2, 7zip
  --filter=<type>[:<options>] Add a filter on an output branch
```

To get a full dump of the data, enter the following command (on Unix-like systems). The data is sent to standard output, so you can redirect standard output into a file `test-xml-dump.xml`:

```
php ./dumpBackup.php --full > test-xml-dump.xml
```

The root element in the XML document is `<mediawiki>`:

```
<mediawiki xmlns="http://www.mediawiki.org/xml/export-0.3/"
    xmlns:xsi="http://www.w3.org/2001/XMLSchema-instance"
    xsi:schemaLocation="http://www.mediawiki.org/xml/export-0.3/
    http://www.mediawiki.org/xml/export-0.3.xsd" version="0.3" xml:lang="en">
<!-- Body goes here-->
</mediawiki>
```

The rest of the XML output is divided into two sections. The first section, which is wrapped in the `<siteinfo>` tag, contains basic information about the site, including the list of namespaces:

```
<siteinfo>
  <sitename>ProfWikis - MySQL</sitename>
  <base>http://localhost/mysql/index.php/Main_Page</base>
  <generator>MediaWiki 1.9.3</generator>
  <case>first-letter</case>
    <namespaces>
    <namespace key="-2">Media</namespace>
    <namespace key="-1">Special</namespace>
    <namespace key="0" />
    <namespace key="1">Talk</namespace>
    <namespace key="2">User</namespace>
    <namespace key="3">User talk</namespace>
    <namespace key="4">ProfWikis - MySQL</namespace>
```

```
            <namespace key="5">ProfWikis - MySQL talk</namespace>
            <namespace key="6">Image</namespace>
            <namespace key="7">Image talk</namespace>
            <namespace key="8">MediaWiki</namespace>
            <namespace key="9">MediaWiki talk</namespace>
            <namespace key="10">Template</namespace>
            <namespace key="11">Template talk</namespace>
            <namespace key="12">Help</namespace>
            <namespace key="13">Help talk</namespace>
            <namespace key="14">Category</namespace>
            <namespace key="15">Category talk</namespace>
        </namespaces>
    </siteinfo>
```

The rest of the document is a series of `<page>` tags. Each `<page>` tag contains all the revisions of that page if the --full option was used, or only the most recent revision if --current was used. The following sample shows output for a page with two revisions:

```
<page>
    <title>Main Page</title>
    <id>1</id>
    <restrictions>edit=autoconfirmed:move=autoconfirmed</restrictions>
    <revision>
      <id>1</id>
      <timestamp>2007-04-10T14:37:02Z</timestamp>
      <contributor>
        <ip>MediaWiki default</ip>
      </contributor>
      <text xml:space="preserve">&lt;big&gt;'''MediaWiki has been
    successfully installed.'''&lt;/big&gt;

Consult the [http://meta.wikimedia.org/wiki/Help:Contents User's Guide] for
    information on using the wiki software.

      </text>
    </revision>
    <revision>
      <id>2</id>
      <timestamp>2007-04-10T14:39:17Z</timestamp>
      <contributor>
        <ip>192.168.1.10</ip>
      </contributor>
      <comment>/* Getting started */</comment>
      <text xml:space="preserve">&lt;big&gt;'''MediaWiki has been
    successfully installed.'''&lt;/big&gt;

Consult the [http://meta.wikimedia.org/wiki/Help:Contents User's Guide] for
    information on using the wiki software.

Welcome to my new wiki, for my book [[Professional Wikis]].</text>
    </revision>
</page>
```

Import Files

Files in this XML format can be imported using the `importDump.php` script in the maintenance directory. The best way to run it is to test it with the `--dry-run` option, as shown in the following example:

```
./importDump.php --dry-run test-xml-dump.xml
```

This will tell you whether there are any problems importing the data, but it won't actually import the data. Once you are sure you want to import it, you execute the script without the `--dry-run` option:

```
./importDump.php test-xml-dump.xml
```

Summary

In this chapter, you learned how to manage MediaWiki's caching features, as well as a few other techniques for optimizing your wiki's performance. In addition, you learned how to back up and restore your wiki. You have now learned how to install MediaWiki, edit pages in wikitext, and create your own MediaWiki extensions.

MediaWiki is a thriving, open-source project and, as a consequence, it is always evolving. What is most exciting about open-source software development is that the developers who use the project also have a say in the future of the project. If this book has whetted your appetite enough, then you can use your new skills to participate in the ongoing evolution of MediaWiki. If so, you can read about how to participate as a developer at www.mediawiki.org/wiki/How_to_become_a_MediaWiki_hacker.

Index